Bunion Derby

Bunion Derby

THE 1928 FOOTRACE ACROSS AMERICA

Charles B. Kastner

University of New Mexico Press
Albuquerque

Library of Congress Cataloging-in-Publication Data

Kastner, Charles B., 1955–

Bunion derby : the 1928 footrace across America / Charles B. Kastner.

p. cm.

Includes bibliographical references and index.

ISBN 978-0-8263-4301-7 (cloth : alk. paper)

1. Running races—United States—History. I. Title.

GV1061.2.K37 2007

796.42'50973—dc22

2007018749

To Mary,
who shows every inch as much courage
as the toughest of the bunioneers.

Contents

Acknowledgments

The string leading to *Bunion Derby* started at the foot of my late father-in-law's hospital bed in 1998. As he lay dying, he told me about a long-forgotten, fifty-two-mile footrace, run when he was just a boy in his hometown. After his death, I dug through the archives and discovered its history. Held in 1929, the race featured twenty-two local men with everyday jobs—milkmen, loggers, farm hands—who decided to run this extraordinarily long distance with little training, in hopes of winning a small cash prize. Only half reached the finish, and many of them hobbled across the line with bloody blisters the size of half dollars. The race organizers dubbed this tortuous event a "bunion derby."

I wondered where this funny-sounding name came from, and what motivated these seemingly sane men to do such a crazy thing. I learned the fifty-two-mile race was part of a brief explosion of ultramarathoning events by nonelite runners. It was set off by the first "bunion derby," the nickname for the first footrace across the United States—Los Angeles to New York City—in 1928. Common men with common jobs won the race. The international superstars, pegged as shoo-ins to win the event, dropped by the wayside along the brutal 3,400-mile course.

My fascination with the bunion derby resulted in a 2001 article for *Marathon and Beyond* magazine about Ed "the Sheik" Gardner's participation in the race. I want to thank the magazine's editor, Rich Benyo, for encouraging me to begin my five-year quest to expand the story into a book-length history.

I want to express a special thank you to Alison Stewart for her invaluable editorial help in drafting *Bunion Derby*, and, of course, to my family, Mary, Katie, Brian, and Andrew. They never lost faith in me, and didn't complain about the long hours I spent squirreled away writing the history of this great race.

Introduction

MARCH 9, 1928: WEEK 1 OF THE RACE. A LINE OF ABOUT 150 MEN stretches for miles along a thin, barren, rock-strewn road heading east across the blast furnace known as the Mojave Desert. They stagger—sunburned, wind-blasted, blistered—with muscles screaming in the ninety-five-degree heat. Passing cars kick up clouds of dust, choking the men and coating them with grit.[1] Already, about fifty men have dropped out.

Leading this caravan through hell is an unlikely black man of thirty, with cord-like muscles that pull his legs with the fluidity of a concert violinist. He moves with a God-given gift that comes partly from genetics but mostly from heart bred by the burden of being black, orphaned, and penniless in early twentieth-century America. In this heat, he wears his trademark outfit: white shorts, sleeveless white shirt, and a white turban-like towel that protects his neck from the burning sun. He adopted this uniform in Seattle where he's lived and raced since 1921. To his admirers, he looks like the dashing desert sheik portrayed on the silent screen by the matinee idol Rudolph Valentino. People would call out, "Oh, you Sheik!" as he trained—the name stuck, and Eddie Gardner became the Sheik of Seattle.[2]

This day, the Sheik has come to try something new. He is running across the United States. It is the first of its kind: a footrace from Los Angeles to New York in eighty-four days. The winner will receive twenty-five thousand dollars—a small fortune in 1928. The race is nicknamed the "Bunion Derby," after the aching bunions the participants are bound to get after pounding their feet for 3,400 miles. Race founder Charles C. Pyle, arguably the greatest sports promoter of his age, crowned himself Director General of the "First Annual International Trans-continental Foot Race." Accompanying him is his business partner and deputy director, Harold "Red" Grange, the greatest football player of the 1920s and heartthrob and hero to legions of fans.[3]

There are other stories to tell—199 in all—a patchwork quilt of the American dream. In a wild grab for glory, a cast of nobodies saw hope in the dust: blacks trying to escape the poverty and terror of the Old South; first-generation immigrants with their mother tongue still thick on their lips; Midwest farm boys with leather-brown tans. These men were the "shadow runners," men without fame, wealth, or sponsors, who came to Los Angeles to face the world's greatest runners and race walkers. This was a formidable field of past Olympic champions and professional racers that should have discouraged sane men from thinking they could win a transcontinental race to New York. Yet they came, flouting the odds. Charley Pyle's offer of free food and lodging to anyone who would take up the challenge opened the race to men of limited means.[4] For some, it was a cry from the psyche of no-longer-young men, seeking a last grasp at greatness or a summons to do the impossible. This pulled men on the wrong side of thirty from blue-collar jobs and families.

For footloose young men with a heavy dose of chutzpa and guts, it was an adventure before they entered the world of work and marriage. They left disapproving parents and hitchhiked, walked, or, like the Richman brothers of New York City, piled into a creaky jalopy they bought for twenty-five dollars, and headed for the land of sunshine.[5]

Some had more to prove. Fifteen-year-old Toby Cotton, a dirt-poor black and the eldest of six children, saw the race as a way to pull his family from poverty.[6] Others hoped to revive dying acting careers with the publicity. Then there were men who ran for civic pride—representing a town, fire department, Boy Scout troop, or American Legion chapter—hoping to get their organization a few lines of good press in a national newspaper. And some simply wanted to test themselves, to be part of something big by putting one foot in front of the other for eighty-four days on a ribbon of road that would become the heart of America's love affair with the open road—United States Highway Route 66.[7]

The 2,400-mile Route 66 runs between Los Angeles and Chicago, the toughest portion of the 3,400-mile transcontinental crossing. In 1928, it snaked through mountains, deserts, mud, sandstorms, and blizzards. The word "highway" was generous. Route 66 was a cobbled mix of old pioneer trails and byways designated as a national highway in 1926.[8] It was the infancy of motorized America, and standards were low. Little of the road was paved west of Oklahoma. Rain turned it to mud with the consistency of flypaper, and the sun baked the flypaper into dust.[9]

Route 66 would take the runners through Texas and the border states of Oklahoma and Missouri, where black men doffed their hats and stepped off sidewalks when a white man passed their way, and summary justice lay at the end of a rope for any black threatening the status quo of Jim-Crow America.[10] Farther east, the racers would head through the smoke-belching industrial heart of America—places like Chicago, Gary, and Cleveland—where men shaped steel into a million cheap cars that, within the decade, had put the middle class on wheels, clogged once-quiet streets, set off a siren call for better roads, and turned the air blue with smoke.[11]

When it was over, only fifty-five men reached New York City. The rest slowly disappeared along the way, along with their dreams. But 199 men began in California, cocky or desperate enough to risk the journey. This is their story.

PART I
A GRAND VISION

CHAPTER 1

America, Route 66, and Charley Pyle

America in 1928

THE UNITED STATES STOOD IN THE TWILIGHT, A LAST PAUSE BEFORE the tumbling stock market spiraled into the Great Depression. This was the decade of Wall Street speculation, prohibition, jazz, speakeasies, and machine-gun-toting gangsters who made millions supplying the country with illegal booze. Charles Lindbergh, in something akin to Neil Armstrong's walk on the moon, flew the Atlantic in his single-engine *Spirit of St. Louis* airplane. Most Americans hoped the ocean was broad enough to protect them from the problems of the old world, which had claimed the lives of millions of young men in the trenches of France during World War I and left the continent disillusioned and seething.[1] The United States had its own problems—rural poverty, racism, income inequality—but all were left to simmer beneath the surface of a society trying to forget the sorrows of the planet.[2]

And perhaps because all else seemed so somber, this was also the decade of sports mania, when fans followed the careers of men like baseball's "king of swat" Babe Ruth, and football's "galloping ghost" Harold "Red" Grange, with a fervor bordering on religious.[3]

Technology was driving America, breaking barriers everywhere and drawing the nation into a homogenous whole.[4] From an isolated farmhouse in Nebraska to a Manhattan brownstone, the explosive growth of radio receivers and stations flooded America with news of the nation and the world.[5]

And then came the cars.[6]

In 1900, Vermont required a driver to have someone walk in front of his car with a red flag, the United States produced 4,000 cars each year, and no filling stations existed in the entire country. By 1928, America was a country on wheels. The country produced 4.8 million cars a year with 26 million cars on the road. That year, there was one car per five people in the United States, compared to one car per 43 people in Great Britain, 325 in Italy, and 7,000 in Russia.[7] This widespread ownership was made possible by the mass-production techniques pioneered by Henry Ford. In 1920, he produced one car every 60 seconds, priced from $335 to $440, which was affordable to the American middle class.[8]

And so came the demand for better roads.

In 1914, there were almost no good roads outside the East Coast, and crossing the continent was an adventure. The Federal Road Act of 1916 offered money in matching grants to states that formed highway departments, thus prompting the launch of ambitious road-building programs.[9] The first highways were local ventures without federal coordination, but in 1925 the country adopted a plan for a national highway system.[10]

One author wrote, "The miracle was not the automobile. The miracle of the early twentieth century was the construction of a vast network of highways that gave the automobiles some place to go."[11] In the 1920s, the construction of highways and buildings employed more people and spent more money than any private industry.[12]

Cyrus Avery and Route 66

Cyrus Sterns Avery, a prominent Tulsa businessman, became a leader in the effort to develop national highways, and almost single-handedly created United States Highway Route 66. In 1923, he was appointed the first chairman of Oklahoma's three-man highway commission, and became a member of the American Association of Highway Officials. In 1924, this group petitioned the federal government to develop a comprehensive and uniform scheme of interstate routes and a common highway numbering system. The secretary of agriculture responded by appointing a board of state and federal highway officials to designate a national highway system from existing routes. And in 1925, the secretary approved approximately seventy-six thousand miles of the original eighty-one thousand submitted by state highway departments.[13]

As a delegate, Cyrus set about creating a road of his own—Route 66—a 2,400-mile road that started in Grant Park in Chicago, sliced through the Midwest and his hometown of Tulsa, and stopped in southern California near the Pacific Ocean in Santa Monica. In all, the road spanned two-thirds of the United States and three time zones, and passed through eight states: Illinois, Missouri, Kansas, Oklahoma, Texas, New Mexico, Arizona, and California.[14]

Though this new road had a title, it had little more than that. When Route 66 opened in 1926, only 800 miles were paved with the remaining 1,600 miles covered in dirt, gravel, or bricks. During the bunion derby, only Illinois and Kansas were entirely paved. From California to the Texas border, just 64 miles were paved, leaving 1,221 miles of dirt and gravel. Texas had yet to "see a cement mixer" with a road surface that in some places turned from dust to black goop during a rainstorm. Oklahoma had about a fourth paved, and Missouri two-thirds.[15] Barely fifteen feet wide and in many places with no shoulder at all, Route 66 was "fragile and puny."[16] It took until 1937 to pave the entirety of it.[17]

Despite its humble beginning, Route 66 would, during the 1930s and 1940s, become the "symbolic river of the American West in the auto age of the twentieth century."[18] But that was its future. In 1928, it was new and raw, waiting for greatness.

The Grand, Fertile Mind of Charley Pyle

Charles C. Pyle—better known as "C. C." for "Cash and Carry," "Cold Cash," or "Cross Country," as the mood fit—was forty-eight years old in 1928. He had cold blue eyes that could be "very hard boiled," a mustache, and a receding hairline with close-cropped, peppery gray-blond hair.[19] He was six feet, one inch tall and paunchy at 190 pounds, belying his years as a fair amateur boxer. A bit of a dandy, Charley wore spats, carried a cane, and was the most flawless dresser his business partner, Red Grange, had ever seen.[20]

His roots were Midwest, Scotch-Irish, and conservative. Charley was born in Delaware, Ohio, the son of a Methodist minister. His mother wanted him to follow his father, but Charley chose dollars instead of worshipers and dropped out of Ohio State University to pursue his business career. He launched into an astonishing variety of money-making schemes like selling Western Union clocks, running theater companies in the West, and boxing "all-comers" in California mining camps. He also managed to be married several times. By 1925, he returned to the Midwest and ran five movie theaters in Champaign, Illinois.[21]

One of his theaters, the Virginia, was located near the University of Illinois campus and frequented by the school's football players, including Harold "Red" Grange, a phenomenal all-American running back. At five feet, eleven inches, Red was a "swivel hipped halfback with great speed, swiftness and peripheral vision" and blessed with the common touch.[22] As one reporter said, "Like Smitty in the comic strip, Red's a regular guy. No stage stuff with him. Just big, his chest fairly bulging out of his shirt, his deep set brown eyes snapping, his auburn-tinted locks slicked down in the accepted collegiate style."[23] One admiring female said, "He doesn't act conceited in the least. His hair is just red enough to be right."[24]

Red first caught the attention of the national press in 1924 in a game against Michigan, where he ran for four touchdowns in the first quarter, scoring each time he touched the ball. After that, he became the most watched and photographed player in football—college or professional.[25]

In his senior year in 1925, Grange almost single-handedly destroyed the University of Pennsylvania football team, carrying the football thirty-six times for 363 yards and scoring three touchdowns. Two weeks later, there was serious talk of placing his name on the Republican ticket for the congressional primary, until someone realized that at twenty-two, he did not meet the age qualification to run for national office.[26]

In October 1925, he was in Pyle's theatre, watching the silent movie *The Freshman*, when an usher asked him to come up to Pyle's office. When Red walked in, C. C. Pyle said, "Grange, how would you like to make a hundred thousand dollars?" He proposed that Red join the

Chicago Bears after the last game, play out the professional season, then go on a nationwide tour so fans could see the "galloping ghost" in person. Grange agreed.[27]

The next morning, Red signed a two-year contract with Pyle, appeared in a Chicago Bears uniform on Thanksgiving Day, and drew a crowd of thirty-nine thousand—the largest crowd in professional football history. The pair then toured the East and West Coasts, likely earning $200,000, plus $125,000 in commercial endorsements including Red Grange sweaters, dolls, shoes, ginger ale, ball caps, cigarettes, and a starring role in a movie.[28] C. C. Pyle had struck gold, and it was Red Grange. In the late 1920s, when two-thirds of American families survived on $2,500 or less a year, he had made a fortune.[29] But Charley Pyle was not satisfied with a huge income. He wanted power—to see if he could bend the world of professional football to his will.

Figure 1. Left to right, Harold "Red" Grange and C. C. Pyle in dining car, circa 1926. Credit: Red Grange Collection, Special Collections, Wheaton College (IL).

For the 1926 football season, Charley told the owners of the Chicago Bears they could have Red for a one-third share in the franchise. When they refused, he leased Yankee Stadium in New York City and petitioned the National Football League for his own franchise. The league refused, so he formed the rival American Football League with nine teams and established his own, the New York Yankees. The country, however, was not ready for two leagues. Attendance was dismal and all but the Yankees folded by the end of the season. However, he got what he wanted: In 1927, the NFL brought Pyle and his Yankees into the fold.[30]

By the end of the 1927 season, Charley and Red had shaken professional football to the rafters, made a fortune, and owned their own NFL team. They were looking for a new mountain to climb, and Cyrus Avery and the Route 66 Association had just the thing.

CHAPTER 2

The Idea is Hatched

ONCE ROUTE 66 RECEIVED ITS FEDERAL HIGHWAY STATUS, CYRUS
Avery organized a Route 66 Highway Association with businessmen
from cities along the 2,400-mile route.[1] Its members wanted the millions
of new drivers flooding America's roads to know a route beckoned from
Chicago to Los Angeles—a new gateway to the golden West that, they
hoped, would bring paying customers through the association's once-
sleepy towns and cities. They wanted drivers to know about the road,
and they needed a way to tell them.

Whose Idea Was It, Anyway?

The origin of a footrace-to-advertise-the-route idea is open to debate.
One version is that the idea emerged from the association dinner in
Oklahoma City in early 1927. A member suggested holding a footrace
along the entire length of highway from Los Angeles to Chicago, then
continuing eastward to New York City. Lou Scott, public relations director for the association, liked the idea. It was new and quirky in a way that
might grab the attention of the national press if the right leader could be

found. Scott thought of Charley Pyle.[2] In another version, Pyle himself had the idea and asked to address the gathering.[3] Whatever happened, Charley attended an association meeting in the spring of 1927 and, with evangelic fervor, told the businessmen his race "would promote the sale of everything from mousetraps to [the] grand piano," and "turn the [association's] patchwork of gravel, dirt, and paved roads into gold."[4]

The members liked what he had to say. They returned to their respective chambers of commerce and received pledges of support including $5,000 each from Tulsa and Oklahoma City, and $2,500 each from Joplin, Springfield, Amarillo, and East St. Louis. The chambers promised to present these contributions to Pyle when he brought his race through their towns.[5] This footrace across America had all the trappings of a C. C. Pyle undertaking: It was big, no one had done it before, and most everyone outside of the association thought it couldn't be done.

Charley Pyle's Traveling City

With the association's backing, Pyle left for Los Angeles and began organizing the great race across America. He gave himself the grand title of director general, called his race the First Annual International Trans-continental (Los Angeles to New York) Foot Race, and appointed Red Grange his deputy director general.[6] The press soon gave the race a shorter and catchier nickname—the bunion derby—for the battered bunions participants were bound to get after negotiating 3,400 miles of some of the most extreme and varied terrain on earth.

In the summer of 1927, Charley began filling newspapers and billboards with word of wondrous prizes for the winners of his derby: $25,000 for first place; $10,000 for second; $5,000 for third; $2,500 for fourth; and $1,000 each for fifth through tenth places.[7] Each man who wanted to compete for these prizes had to sign a contract, though it would only apply to the top ten finishers. After the derby, the winners would let Pyle look after their interests for two years. He would have the authority to order them to appear in any sporting event of his choosing, and take 50 percent of any income they might earn from future sporting events, exhibitions, or movies, not including derby prize money.[8]

Each day's race would be a "stage race," a distinct distance run from one designated town to another. The men would start as a group, then

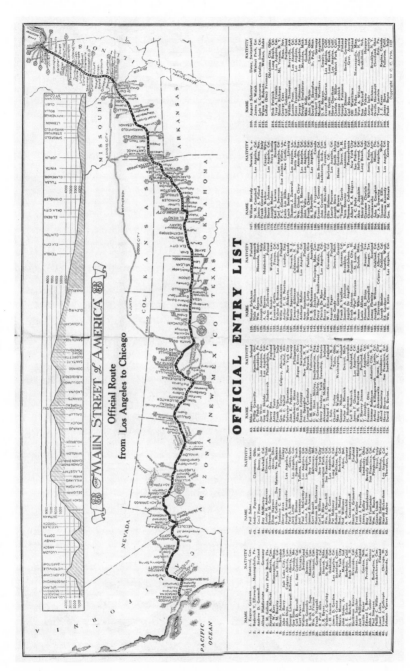

Figure 2. "Official Route from Los Angeles to Chicago." Credit: 1928 official
program, personal copy, author.

run or walk to the official finish line, where each man would have his time recorded and added to his total cumulative time. Participants had until midnight to complete the course or they were disqualified, with the proviso that a man could elect to stop before the deadline and make up the remaining distance the next morning, then complete the next day's distance as well. The man with the lowest elapsed time in New York City would win the race.[9]

Pyle did not develop training rules. He maintained, "If they want to stay up half the night attending a Saturday night dance, that's their business."[10]

The man Charley charged with enforcing the rules was forty-eight-year-old Arthur Duffy, who took a leave of absence from his job as a sports writer with the *Boston Globe*. The derby's new referee was tough and to the point—in 1902, he'd set the world record in the 100-yard dash while at Boston College, and then revealed that he had "received more than generous expense money from race promoters and insisted that most top runners had done the same." Unimpressed by his frankness, the Amateur Athletic Union revoked his world record.[11]

Pyle gave Duffy some off-season Yankee football players to serve in his race patrol, which involved driving the course in high-power cars to deter contestants from accepting rides or taking shortcuts. As part of his duties, Duffy maintained an official log of the men's times, using industrial time clocks and time cards. As a man approached the finish line, a spotter would call out his number, and his card would be put into a time clock as he crossed the line.[12]

Under the derby system, each contestant received a locker, cot, and space in the huge communal sleeping tent, complete with collapsible metal beds, mattresses, and portable hot showers. The men would eat breakfast and dinner from a commissary tent while supervised by dietitians. Lunch would be served on the road from the doors of a traveling truck.[13] Charley also had a medical tent staffed by a physician, a podiatrist, nurses, and massage therapists. He even brought along an expert shoe repairman, who repaired footwear from the back of his "Shoe Hospital truck."[14]

To move this traveling city, Charley needed a fleet of twenty-five trucks and a work gang of about fifty men. For eighty-four days, his crew would collapse and reassemble his tent city, and often in adverse conditions—the desert heat of the Mojave, the howling icy winds of the high country in Arizona and New Mexico, and ankle-deep mud in Texas.[15] The director general would face a logistic nightmare that would tax every ounce of his legendary charm and leadership skills.

International Trans-Continental Foot Race

Organized and Directed by C. C. PYLE

Open to Any Physically Fit Male Athlete in the World!

GENERAL INFORMATION

DATE OF START from Los Angeles, California, March 4, 1928.

FINISH in New York City.

ROUTE OF THE RACE will be over U. S. 66 Highway between Los Angeles and Chicago. Route between Chicago and New York will be announced later.

PRIZES:

To the winner	$25,000
Second	10,000
Third	5,000
Fourth	2,500
Fifth	1,000
Sixth	1,000
Seventh	1,000
Eighth	1,000
Ninth	1,000
Tenth	1,000

IN ORDER to win one of the above capital prizes contestant must finish the race in New York City.

ADDITIONAL MONEY PRIZES, which may be donated by counties, cities and towns along the route, will be awarded the first five contestants to arrive at night control point, where offered, without regard to positions these five contestants occupy in the race.

THE MANAGEMENT WILL PROVIDE, following the start of the race, lodging and food, medical supervision, transportation of a limited amount of personal effects, the same quality of pure drinking water along the route, but cannot assume any other expenses of the contestants. There will be no bonuses, guarantees or other financial assistance given any entrant by the management.

THE RACE WILL BE CONDUCTED in the following manner: The contestants will be started from Los Angeles. Night control points, ranging in distance of approximately forty to seventy-five miles apart, according to the condition of the road, climate, etc., will be specified in advance of start. Contestants may run or walk, as they please, the actual time consumed by each between their start from, and finish at, control points being credited daily. Each morning all contestants will start in the same manner as at Los Angeles, and will run daily on the same system. For example, should contestant Number 77 gain 30 minutes on the second contestant each day, he will be started each morning with the field, and although he may be leading the race by thirty hours on the day before the finish of the race in New York, he will be started with the field from the previous night control on the morning of the finish at the same time all other contestants start. This is the only manner in which the race can be supervised successfully by officials.

AT EACH NIGHT CONTROL STOP a commissary

and diet kitchen will be established for serving evening and morning meals under the supervision of expert dieticians. Medical and training headquarters will be established also in conjunction with the commissary, where doctors, nurses, trainers, rubbers, and handlers may administer care to contestants. Lunch, drink, shoe repair and medical aid stations will be established at points along the highway daily.

STATE, COUNTY AND CITY OFFICIALS will cooperate with officials of the race to insure athletes against undue hazards and possible injuries resulting from congestion, traffic and lack of proper police control.

A CARAVAN of trucks, busses, private and official cars to provide transportation for officials, doctors, directors, shoe-repairmen, equipment, newspaper and press correspondents, photographers, motion picture news weekly cameramen, personal effects, equipment, entertainment, etc., will accompany contestants over the entire route from Los Angeles to New York City.

EACH CONTESTANT will be required tod eposit in a Los Angeles bank one hundred dollars not later than twenty-four hours before the start of the race, which amount the bank will hold as trustee until the contestant either finishes the race in New York City or officially is declared out of the race. This is for the purpose of guaranteeing the management the contestant will not be without funds to reach home should he drop out of the race. The bank will wire the amount deposited to a contestant upon certification of race officials that contestant officially is out of the race.

THE PRINCIPAL OFFICIALS of the race will accompany the contestants from Los Angeles to New York City and will give close attention to providing comfort for the contestants and will strictly supervise the duties of local officials who will be recruited in advance from among representative citizens in different control cities. Unmarked cars containing officials will continuously patrol the course over which that day's run is being made, and will immediately report any contestant observed accepting rides or assistance or any infraction of the rules.

THE MANAGEMENT DESIRES to emphasize the point that all contestants will be so thoroughly supervised between control points that accepting rides or other unfair assistance cannot escape detection with immediate disqualification resulting.

EACH ENTRANT MUST REPORT in Los Angeles, California, at the official training grounds, for final conditioning for the race, not later than February 12, 1928, and must be willing at all times to submit to a physical examination by official physicians. All entrants must assume their own expenses until the actual start of the race on March 4th.

Figure 3. "General Information." Credit: 1928 official program, personal copy, author.

Figure 4. One of Pyle's specially designed buses in El Reno, Oklahoma.
Credit: El Reno Carnegie Library.

Charley would lead his crew eastward in *America*, one of two specially designed buses he had built for the race. *America* contained sleeping, bathing, and eating accommodations for fourteen, with an open
observation deck and a rear sleeping compartment lined with mahog-
any and blue mohair. Charley planned to use it as a place to entertain
and carry a corps of sports reporters who would accompany the derby
across the country. Pyle wanted his corps of reporters comfortable and
rested, ready to write stories that would keep millions scanning the
sports pages for news of his great race. A sister bus would house Charley,
Red, and other race officials. These palatial buses weighed about twenty-
four thousand pounds and cost twenty-five thousand dollars apiece.[16]

Paying the Bill
PLEDGES, ENDORSEMENTS, AND THE CARNIVAL
Pyle had used about $100,000 of his own money to put his tent city in
place, and would spend roughly $2,500 a day during the transcontinental

crossing, plus $48,000 in prize money in New York City. Taken together, he would pay upwards of $350,000 to hold his race—$3 to $4 million in today's dollars. But he wasn't worried. He believed he could finish in the black with the pledges he would collect from Route 66 cities and towns, payments from companies looking to advertise in the derby, and receipts from the traveling carnival he had attached to his race.[17]

And he did have endorsements. For example, the Sunkist Company agreed to supply his men with fresh oranges in exchange for advertising; a meat company sent hams and bacon and paid $5,000 for the privilege; a food company paid $6,000 to serve his men its breakfast cereal; a drug company paid $5,000 to provide rubbing liniment; another paid $7,500 to supply foot powder; and even the Mobil Oil Company contributed free oil for the fleet of cars and trucks.[18]

The most prominent endorsement of all, however, came from a national coffee distributor, the Cheek Neil Coffee Company. For the derby, it built the world's largest coffeepot at eleven feet high, bolted it to the chassis of a truck, and sent it to Los Angeles. Two company employees would travel across the country with the derby, roasting and blending Maxwell House coffee and serving ninety gallons a day to Charley's men. The duo prepared the coffee inside the gigantic pot using two gas-heated coffee urns. The company paid $5,000 for the honor of providing coffee and placing its advertising on derby vehicles.[19]

And then there was the traveling road show, with star attraction Red Grange. Charley thought droves of people would pay twenty-five cents to catch a glimpse of the Michael Jordan of his era, as he introduced the derby stars at an 8 p.m. show after the conclusion of each day's stage race. There were also food concessions; vaudeville acts; and sideshows like the Turtle Boy, the chicken that mooed like a cow, and a fearsome array of deadly Asian snakes charmed by the poison girl.[20] The bunion derby would be part footrace and part Hollywood production.

Charley Pyle also had the only portable radio station in the country—KGGM. When conditions were favorable, its 100 watts of power would be heard for 1,500 miles. It broadcasted race results, interviews with the race leaders, and musical pieces from Charley's twelve-piece jazz band he brought along as part of the entertainment.[21] Pyle thought he had his financial bases covered, and now all he needed were the contestants.

CHAPTER 3

The Stars

IN THE MONTHS LEADING UP TO THE RACE, PYLE SENT EMISSARIES to Europe and advertised in newspapers and national magazines, inviting able-bodied men to come to Los Angeles and test their mettle in the greatest footrace the world had known.[1] In the end, 199 answered the call and toed the line for the first footrace across America. And among these mostly unknown contestants, Charley sprinkled a small galaxy of stars with international reputations.

The Greatest Runner of His Generation

The first was the forty-four-year-old South African Arthur C. Newton, who held world record times for most distances between thirty and one hundred miles. Lanky, with close-cropped mustache and hair, he looked more the part of a tanned, middle-aged English banker than "the most phenomenal distance runner the world had ever known." Born in England in 1883 to the Reverend Henry Newton, he received a private school education before leaving for South Africa to take a teaching position at a preparatory school. He remained there for eight years before embarking on a scheme to grow cotton and coffee on a 1,350-acre grant of land from the South African government. His life as a farmer was cut short when he was called to military service in World War I. When he returned, he found the government had resettled black South Africans on his land and offered him no compensation for his loss.[2]

Angered and frustrated, the thirty-eight-year-old veteran decided to try drawing national attention to his grievance by winning his country's fifty-four-mile Comrades Marathon in 1922. After only five months of training, he won the grueling event. A year later, he shattered the course record by two hours, winning in six hours and fifty-two minutes.[3]

In the 1920s, Newton was a groundbreaking force in the sport of distance running. He changed perceptions about what the human body was capable of sustaining during training. Most distance runners limited their weekly workouts to no more than thirty miles, believing that higher mileage training strained the heart. Newton ignored the warning and often ran thirty miles a day, heralding the beginnings of modern high-mileage distance training. He brought a scientist's eye to running, having developed what he thought was a perfect stride length (three feet, seven inches) and height (just above the surface) to conserve energy. Arthur also developing an early sport drink by mixing lemonade and salt.[4]

By 1927, he had set world records for the thirty-, thirty-five-, forty-, forty-five-, fifty-, and one-hundred-mile distances. In January 1928, he bettered his own one-hundred-mile record, and reportedly averaged eight hundred miles a month in training. When he entered the derby, most observers thought the twenty-five-thousand-dollar first prize was his for the taking.[5] Pyle had the father of modern long-distance running in his galaxy of stars.

The Mighty Europeans

Pyle's next star was forty-year-old "Wee Willie" Kolehmainen, part of a famous Finnish running dynasty. He received his nickname from his short stature, being just five feet tall. In 1912, Willie and his brother Hannes arrived in the United States to study the methods of American professional runners. Willie remained and turned professional that same year, while Hannes retained his amateur status and returned to Finland. That year, Willie beat the 1910 Boston marathon winner and set an unmatched professional record of two hours, twenty-four minutes and thirty-two seconds. Later, he married an American and lived in New York City where he worked as a bricklayer. His brother Hannes developed a formidable international reputation, having won the 1920 Olympic gold medal in the marathon and two gold medals at shorter distances in the 1912 Stockholm Games. But in 1928, many observers considered Willie a better runner than Hannes, who accompanied him to Los Angeles as his trainer.[6]

A host of other Finns arrived in Los Angeles in the winter of 1928, including tiny, four-foot-nine-inch Olli Wanttinen, who would become a lead runner in the derby, despite his size, and August Fager, a Finnish-born member of the 1924 United States Olympic team.

The Estonian government sent Juri Lossman, the 1920 Olympic silver medalist in the marathon. Its leaders hoped Lossman's performance would bring much-needed publicity to the small, isolated country on the Russian side of the Baltic Sea. Another European standout was Guisto Umek, a temperamental, middle-aged race walker from Trieste, Italy, who reportedly had the favor of the Italian dictator, Benito Mussolini.[7]

The Hope of the New World

Few thought an American had a chance against this European assault. Sports writer Braven Dyer of the *Los Angeles Times* believed the consensus, claiming that the Europeans would win first prize in the derby, due to "a lack of capable distance runners in this country" and a long tradition of distance running in Europe.[8]

The great hope for the new world lay with champion race walker Phillip Granville, a thirty-two-year-old Jamaican-born tailor from Hamilton, Ontario. At about 185 pounds and over six feet tall, Granville was handsome, blessed with endurance, and spoke the King's English with the clipped vowels of an Oxford don. Phillip was a crowd pleaser with a winning smile and a complexion the color of cinnamon. He described his ethnicity as Jamaican Indian, but the black press considered him a "race man" and carefully followed his progress across the country.[9] After watching him race in Los Angeles, Braven Dyer said, "We are willing to go on record as selecting the big South Jamaica Indian as the man most likely to win the race."[10]

Granville had an amazing career. In 1923, he won the national walk-ing championship of Canada. In 1924, he went to Paris as part of the Canadian Olympic team but illness forced him out of the competition. In 1925, he raced in England, winning nine of the ten events he entered, which earned him an audience with the king. In 1926, he returned to Canada and established an unrivaled string of amateur race-walking victories, including the 109-mile Buffalo-to-Toronto race in nineteen hours and fifty-six minutes, which shattered the course record.[11] In 1928, Phillip said he entered the derby "to represent Hamilton and Canada [and] I passed up one of my dearest possessions, my amateur card when I decided to enter."[12]

The Tortoise or the Hare

The press corps was convinced that the winner would come from within this assembled cast of racing stars. To most observers, the only real ques-tion was whether it would be a runner or a walker. Most believed that, like the tortoise and the hare, the race would go to a walker with a slow but sustainable pace, after the runners had burned themselves out over the long miles to New York City. Boston Marathon champion Clarence De Mar thought no living runner could run the equivalent of two mara-thons a day for two and a half months and survive.[13] Others believed the winner would be someone who used a mix of running and walking as conditions and stamina allowed.

The race would take the contestants into uncharted territory—3,400 miles of some of the most varied and difficult conditions on earth. Many wondered whether anyone would survive to collect the prize money.[14] But if anyone did, he would surely be from the cast of stars that Pyle brought together in Los Angeles.

CHAPTER 4

Men in the Shadows

WHEN C. C. PYLE PUBLISHED HIS RACE ANNOUNCEMENT IN NEWSPAPERS and magazines throughout the country, he did so with the promise that any man who braved the 3,400-mile trip to New York City would receive free food, lodging, and medical care as long as he stayed in the race.[1] He would do all this for a $125 entrance fee. This promise allowed men of limited needs to enter the race. With a sentence, the director general had let in the shadow runners—the black, the Native American, the immigrant, and the dirt-poor farmer—souls outside the mainstream far from the attention of the national press. These men were poor in funds but rich in hopes and dreams.

Most who came to Los Angeles had little training or experience with ultramarathoning. Dr. John A. Baker, a Philadelphia intern who served as the derby's physician, examined the men before the race. He found that not more than forty seemed fit enough to withstand the contest, just six had trained at more than twenty-five miles on a regular basis, and few had ever competed in long-distance events.[2] These men were mostly tradesmen or farmers. Ethnically, the Americans were mainly European immigrants or first-generation citizens, with a sprinkling of American Indians and blacks.³ They were blue-collar, roll-up-your-sleeves men, and they had often sacrificed their last dollars to come up with the entry money.

Why did these men leave the everyday world of jobs, family, and home to face stars like Arthur Newton and Phillip Granville? The answer is partly that they were dreamers, men who ignored the odds and focused on the twenty-five thousand dollars—a small fortune that would pay off a mortgage, build a new house, and ease the burden on their struggling families. Also, they believed in their own talent and luck. They answered a call for adventure that rattled around in their brains. The idea of the race ate at them until it became the mantra of their lives, until they simply decided to go.

Eddie Gardner
THE SHEIK OF SEATTLE

Edward Gardner was christened without a middle name, the eighth child of Minnie and George Gardner, who were both children of former slaves. Eddie was born in the heart of Birmingham, Alabama, in December 1897, less than forty years after the Civil War forever changed the fabric of southern life.⁴

The family had a tragic time in Alabama, caught in a wheel of birth and death that claimed seven of the eight Gardner children. In 1899, George and Minnie fled the rigid segregation and poverty of Birmingham with their sole surviving child, Eddie, and went west, following the millions of sod busters, gold seekers, and adventurers who came before them.⁵

In Pueblo, Colorado, the Gardners joined the stewpot of newcomers—the dirt-poor immigrants willing to endure the hot, dangerous work in the mills. There the Gardners lived next to an Austrian-born railroad yardman, something that would have been unthinkable in the segregated south.⁶ Drawing strength from the town's five-hundred-strong black community, the family found peace in Pueblo. Minnie had two more children there, Gladys and Helen, and both survived into adulthood. They had broken the spell of death that had haunted them in Alabama.⁷

In 1909, George Gardner caught the wanderlust again, and moved his family to Seattle where he took a job as a railroad cook. Like Pueblo,

Seattle was a magnet for immigrants and those looking for a new start.[8] These arrivals also brought disease, including one of the great scourges of the time, pulmonary tuberculosis, which killed Minnie Gardner in 1911 at age thirty-seven.[9]

Eddie was twelve when his mother died, and in less than a year his father had remarried a woman and moved to live with her in Portland.[10] Eddie stayed in Seattle for the next two years, possibly under the guardianship of a white New York socialite, Emma Hawkins.[11] For the last fifteen years, Mrs. Hawkins had raised a family of her own in the city's fashionable first hill neighborhood while her husband Erastus built railroads to the gold fields in Alaska. In 1911, death also haunted Mrs. Hawkins when her fifty-one-year-old husband died of cancer, just as the last of her five children reached adulthood.

Eddie and Mrs. Hawkins seemed to have come together in shared tragedy. Several of her servants were black, and she may have heard of Eddie's plight through them. He listed Mrs. Hawkins as his guardian when he left two years later to attend Tuskegee Institute in Alabama.[12] Why Eddie left Seattle for Tuskegee is a mystery, but he found a home in a red-brick school set among the rolling central Alabama hills. Tuskegee Institute was a technical school for blacks and the forerunner of Tuskegee University, headed by the son of a former slave, Booker T. Washington.

Gardner came to Tuskegee with very little money. He had to enroll as a night student, which meant that he had a paid apprenticeship during the day where he learned to repair and maintain steam boilers, and used his salary to cover his school fees. For two hours each evening, he studied reading, writing, arithmetic, geography, and mechanical drawing.[13] Eddie even found time to discover a talent and love for running. Three times a week, he ran ten miles before breakfast, and then reported to his job by seven. He joined the track team and set the school record for the five-mile run in 1915, won the first mile race in the newly formed black Southeast conference championship, and the black state cross-country championship of Alabama in 1917.[14]

Tuskegee gave him skill as a steam engineer, a passion as a runner, and a confidence that stayed with him the rest of his life. In 1921, Eddie returned to Seattle and started competing in the Washington ten-mile state championship. He finished buried in the pack in his first race in 1921 but took fifth in 1922, then second in 1923, and first in 1924.[15]

During the 1920s he became a familiar sight to legions of his fans with his trademark white sleeveless shirt, white shorts, and towel tied around his head, which flowed behind him as he trained for upcoming races. Cries of "oh you sheik" greeted him as he ran; the name stuck, and Eddie Gardner had become the Sheik of Seattle.[16]

On July 4, 1927, the Sheik was at the height of his amateur career. Thousands waited in the stands at the University of Washington stadium for the sight of the lead runner in this Fourth of July classic. A little before two in the afternoon, a roar went up from the crowd as wiry Eddie Gardner in his trademark outfit hit the cinder track and powered around the oval with short, powerful strides. At about five foot four, with taut muscles and his headgear flowing behind him, he was the picture of an endurance athlete. In a burst of speed, he held off his nearest competitor by twenty-five yards. The Sheik had won his third state amateur championship, cut another minute off his old state record in a time of fifty-seven minutes and forty-four seconds, and beat the best collegiate and independent athletes in the Northwest, ten years his junior.[17]

One person who was not thrilled with his running was his second wife, Mabel, whom he married in 1926. A year before, he had divorced his first wife, Henrietta, after a childless four-year marriage. Mabel brought two children to their union, and his new family lived in a twenty-dollar-per-month apartment while he worked a steady, low-paying job as a steam engineer.[18]

When she heard of the derby, Mabel said, "Here's a chance to get what we need so I guess you had better take a chance at this $25,000." Eddie seemed clear on why he entered: "My wife pushed me into this race."[19] But there was much more to it than that. Eddie had conquered just about all there was to win in the amateur world of Seattle, and he was running out of time. He was looking for a new benchmark before advancing age got in the way of his dreams.[20]

His first ally was George Curtis, a fifty-year-old black tailor, who offered to drive him to Los Angeles and serve as his trainer. Curtis had a large touring car called a "hupmobile," but he had no knowledge of training long-distance runners.[21]

Eddie cash reserves were meager, with $175 to his name. He gave $75 to Mabel, who promised to scrape by until he returned. He left town with $100 in his pocket and a cash flow problem. When he arrived in

Los Angeles in January of 1928, Eddie needed \$125 to cover the \$25 entry fee and a \$100 refundable deposit that Pyle promised to return at the end of the race, plus money for gas and supplies to get his trainer and himself across the country.[22]

He found help through a black newspaper, the *California Eagle*. The paper's editors desperately wanted to ensure that "the Negro Race" had a representative in the derby and offered to help support one black runner in the contest.[23] After an *Eagle* representative examined Eddie's running credentials, the official pronounced him "the most likely prospect on the grounds."[24]

The newspaper's editors introduced him to two African-American sports promoters: Watson Burns, and a Texan named Jimmy Akers. They agreed to cover Eddie's expenses for a 50 percent share of his winnings. The *Eagle* reported that Burns gave Eddie several hundred dollars

Figure 5. Eddie "the Sheik" Gardner, wearing his classic "sheik" outfit, in Seattle, 1928. Credit: *Seattle Post Intelligencer* Collection, Museum of History and Industry.

to support his "long grind across the country."[25] Other members of the
black community promised him free dental care for a year, a thousand-
dollar diamond ring, and a managerial job should he win the derby.[26] He
had a team in place.

The Other African Americans

Four other blacks came to Los Angeles with hopes of victory. Like
Gardner, most had left the segregated south as children and moved to
western or eastern cities.

Sammy Robinson was born in Kansas in 1896.[27] He arrived in
Atlantic City, New Jersey, in his teens, where he attended the city's inte-
grated high school and befriended the future sports editor of the *Press-
Union*, Lou Goldberg, who happened to be white and the captain of the
football team. When Robinson went out for the team, some of the white
players wanted to bar him from playing. Goldberg brushed off their pro-
tests and welcomed Sammy, who went on to win varsity letters in four
sports.[28] He served in World War I as one of the four hundred thousand
blacks who enlisted.[29] After the war, he came home to Atlantic City and
fought as a professional boxer. Robinson earned the nickname "Smiling
Sammy" because of his seemingly perpetual good mood. He was also
deeply religious, preaching an ethos of hard work and faith in God to
anyone who would listen.[30]

In 1928, Sammy had no experience as a distance runner, but he
was a superbly trained and gifted athlete. His old friend Lou Goldberg
gave him a check for three hundred dollars for training expenses and
the promise of fifty dollars for each state he crossed. This thirty-two-
year-old arrived in Los Angeles without experience or a trainer, but he
had faith in God and in himself, and enough supreme talent to see him
through the race.[31]

Toby Joseph Cotton Jr., often referred to as "T. Joseph" in the press,
was desperate to help his struggling family and he saw his chance with
the derby's twenty-five-thousand-dollar first prize. The only problem:
T. Joseph was fifteen years old and a ninth grader at McKinley High
School in Los Angeles. His father, Toby Sr., worked as a mechanic in Los
Angeles. In 1925, a three-ton truck slipped off a jack, crushed him, and
left him alive but a physical wreck with a family of three boys and four

girls facing poverty. T. Joseph, the oldest, seized on the derby as a way to save his family, and no one could dissuade him from entering it.[32]

The Cottons then formed an improbable plan to win the derby. Toby Sr. and his two youngest sons, thirteen-year-old Wesley and ten-year-old James, would follow T. Joseph across the country in their well-worn Ford touring car with Wesley driving and James providing food and water. The Cotton men loaded up their rickety jalopy and headed for the start.[33]

Less is known about the other two black participants, William Friason of Cincinnati, Ohio, and Harold Johnson of Detroit, Michigan. The thirty-five-year-old Fraison served in World War I and returned to the city where he worked as a porter in a drug store. He was an accomplished long-distance walker, reportedly covering more than 2,500 miles in 1927.[34] Harold Johnson, at fifty, reportedly looked half that age and had spent time in the West as a "crack roper, rider, movie actor, and boxer."[35] Both men apparently joined the derby without the benefit of trainers or any support crew.

These five blacks were dismissed offhand by the white press. Most southerners thought blacks had no business racing against white men, and it was a common belief among whites that Africans were only suited for short sprints, lacking the ability to concentrate over the course of a long race.[36]

People had either forgotten or chosen to ignore the exploits of great black endurance athletes of the past like the Haitian Frank Hart who, during the post-Civil War pedestrian craze, covered more than 540 miles in a six-day endurance race, winning almost $2,500 in prize money for his effort.[37] And Marshall Taylor of Indiana, who held the national bicycle sprint championship in 1898, 1899, and 1900, must have slipped their minds, too.[38] Other blacks were crisscrossing the country on foot, on motorcycles, and in cars.[39] White America simply chose not to remember.

Andy Payne

THE OKLAHOMA FARM BOY

Twenty-year-old Andrew Hartley Payne came from a small farming town in the rolling limestone hills of northeastern Oklahoma. The oldest of seven children and one-eighth Cherokee Indian, he had black, wavy hair and a copper complexion. Andy came from a struggling farm family that grew cotton, wheat, and alfalfa on six hundred acres of hard-packed ground. His father had been a life-long friend of Will Rogers—the famous cowboy humorist, pundit, and syndicated columnist—having worked on a ranch together as youths.[40]

Andy Payne's running career began over his dislike of horses. Choosing not to ride to school as the other children did, he ran the eight miles through pastures and scrub oak.[41] Andy loved school and hated farming, a bad combination for a rural farm boy. He was a scholar, earning good grades, and was a stellar member of the school track team, winning medals in half-mile and mile runs in local and state competitions. In his senior year, he fell madly in love with the new Spanish and math teacher, Vivian Shaddox, whom he would later marry. After graduation in the spring of 1927, he left Oklahoma in search of a non-farm job. They were scarce in the region, which had already plunged into depression two years ahead of the 1929 crash. He hitchhiked to Los Angeles but found no work.[42]

Broke and depressed, he read about the bunion derby in a local paper. The idea of racing across the country grabbed him. He hitchhiked back to Oklahoma and tried to persuade the Claremore Chamber of Commerce (a large community near his hometown, and home of Will Rogers) to give him the $125 entry money.[43] He convinced the chamber but he did not immediately win over his father, who called his idea "not even 'good foolishness.'"[44] Eventually his father gave Andy his blessing when he realized that "Andy weren't worth a darn when he heard about the foot race clean across the country. I couldn't get no work out of him, he sprinted from morning till night. I let him go and I think he'll win."[45]

Payne was one of the first to arrive in Los Angeles in December 1927.[46] He was fortunate to have caught the eye of Tom Young, a high school track coach from Miami, Florida, who had come to Los Angeles as a contestant. With a keen eye for his chances, Young chose instead to serve as Andy's trainer after watching him run. It was a fortunate decision for both men. Young followed Andy on his motorcycle, pacing him as he ran, and giving him drinks from a gallon jug of lemonade he carried on the back of his bike. Together they came up with the key to the

Figure 6. Trainer Tom Young and his charge, Andy Payne of Oklahoma.
     Credit: Rucker Collection, Research Division of the Oklahoma
     Historical Society.

race: "We figured it's the steady grind that will get [us] there."[47] In other
words, Young would keep Payne running at a slow but sustainable pace
over the entire cross-country trip, forgoing the fleeting glory of winning
a daily race.

Three Guys on the Wrong Side of Thirty
JOHNNY SALO, MIKE JOYCE, AND ARNE SOUMINEN

"On a bleak February day [in Passaic, New Jersey], a forlorn but determined Jackson Street shipbuilder had boarded a train for Los Angeles,
with a railroad ticket and exactly $11 and a few cents in his pocket."[48]
Johnny Salo, a thirty-five-year-old Finnish immigrant, had piercing blue
eyes and blond hair. He was of medium height and had the build of a

wrestler. Looking more Russian Cossack than Viking, he had left Finland at age fifteen and immigrated to the United States. He married his childhood sweetheart from Finland in 1917. He then served in World War I in the United States Merchant Marine, making ten perilous trips across the Atlantic on convoy duty. He rose through the enlisted ranks and at the end of the war was a commissioned ensign in the United States Navy. After the armistice, he moved to Passaic, where he "spun sea yarns like a typical salt" and worked on riverboats plying the Hudson River and as a shipyard worker.[49]

Salo came to competitive running when he was thirty-two years old. He often practiced by running around his riverboats. As an amateur, he ran several local marathons without great success until his four-man Finnish American team took first place in the 1926 Boston Marathon. When he heard of the derby, he left his wife and two children in New Jersey, and arrived in Los Angeles without a trainer and had to rely on Charley's organization for food and support.[50]

Two other middle-aged immigrants would figure prominently in the derby story. The first was a thirty-five-year-old Irishman, Mike Joyce. An obscure worker in a Cleveland auto body plant, the tiny but feisty man left his wife and his five small children behind and took "the bulk of the Joyce family funds." He had some track experience in Ireland and had competed in several distance races in the United States, but why he risked his home and family for a chance at the prize money is unclear.[51] The second was forty-year-old Finnish immigrant and physician Arne Souminen from Detroit, Michigan. He left his medical practice behind but had meticulously planned and trained for the race for four months.[52]

Peter Gavuzzi

Another man in the shadows was Peter Gavuzzi of England, who "trains on cigarettes and misses English ale."[53] The twenty-one-year-old was born in Liverpool to an Italian chef and a French woman. Peter was thin and short—about five feet, four inches—with a dark, suave look. Fluent in French, Italian, and English, he spoke with a Liverpool accent, gestured like an Italian, and had a passion like the French.[54] He was raised in the Kent countryside, attended convent school in London, and then went to sea, serving as a steward on the steamship *Majestic*. During his

Figure 7.
"Ending 43 Mile Jog,"
Chicago Tribune Photo,
May 6, 1928. Peter
Gavuzzi finishing race
in Chicago. Credit:
Chicago Tribune Photo.

fifty-two Atlantic crossings, he won every cup offered for shipboard distance-running events. In 1927, he raced on land, winning the New Market Marathon and a fifty-mile running race in England.[55]

At the urging of his godfather, Peter left England for the derby with the oldest entry in the transcontinental race, the sixty-three-year-old London bootmaker Charles Hart, who had once held the world record for the one-hundred-mile distance until he ceded the title to Arthur Newton. The pair arrived in New York City on January 10, 1928, then sailed through the Panama Canal and docked in Los Angeles at the end of the month. They immediately began thirty-mile training days to build strength and endurance. Gavuzzi seemed unaffected by his habit of smoking a pack of cigarettes during his training runs.[56] Rather, his biggest problem was his teeth. Before the race, he consulted a dentist about his mouth pains, and was told he had an infection and needed his teeth pulled. Peter asked, "How the hell am I going to eat?" The dentist replied, "With difficulty." The Englishman chose to keep his teeth, put up with his pain, and take his chances on the long road to New York.[57]

The Rest of the Pack

The remainder of the derby hopefuls came to Los Angeles with a patchwork quilt of hopes and dreams. Some, like the blond Adonis William Kerr of Minneapolis, hoped the derby would help launch a career as a film star.[58] Hollywood actor Lucien Frost, who claimed to have played religious figures like Abraham, Moses, and Jesus Christ in several major silent pictures, hoped to spark a revival. Frost had found roles hard to come by of late, and hoped to use the derby to resuscitate his declining fortunes in Hollywood. Sporting a white flowing beard that went to his waist, he looked every inch the Old Testament figure, and it was rumored he would receive twenty thousand dollars and a new film deal if he completed the race.[59]

Boxer Patrick De Marr of Los Angeles thought he would box his way east, taking on local contestants after he finished each day's run.[60] Another boxer, Mike Kelly, had preprinted business cards that he planned to pass out, which read, "Mike Kelly, marathon runner, and boxer extraordinary."[61] Teducio Rivera, a Filipino dentist, had come to America for advanced training at the University of Minnesota, expecting a Mayo Foundation scholarship. Upon arriving he found that the scholarship had not come through, so he entered the race and hoped things would work out by the time he finished.[62]

Others came to Los Angeles with the hopes of a city or an organization on their shoulders. Earle Dilks, a six-foot-tall railroad man from Newcastle, Pennsylvania, ran eighteen miles a day from home to work.[63] Sensing his talent, his hometown fans raised the funds to send him to Los Angeles and the railroad gave him leave to run. Los Angeles fireman Hoke Norville had the backing of his department's Relief Association. Norville had also played center on the fire department's football team, and two of his team members went with him on his run across America.[64] The Boy Scouts backed tiny Henry Rea, a British-born California lifeguard and troop leader who was just under five feet tall and weighed about ninety-six pounds.[65]

Still more came on a lark and alone, like schoolteacher Pat Harrison of St. Louis, Missouri. "I entered this race as an adventure. I am in it to stay and really believe I have a chance," he said.[66] Then there were the Richman brothers—Sam, Arthur, Morris, and Ben—of New York City. The brothers, all in their twenties, bought a twenty-five-dollar "ramshackle" Ford sedan and set out for Los Angeles and the race. All wanted to race, but one of the brothers needed to serve as a trainer and driver, so they drew straws. Ben lost.[67]

The derby even had a millionaire's son, twenty-year-old Harry Gunn. Harry brought along his father, F. F. Gunn, a food magnate and Union Pacific Railroad official, in his Pierce Arrow touring car, along with his brother, sister, and a personal trainer in a special equipment truck. Harry's sister would prepare his meals each day, and his trainer would hand him a bottle of soda pop every thirty minutes to keep him hydrated. Gunn planned to walk the entire way, convinced that the runners would burn themselves out. His proud father promised to double any prize money his son might win.[68]

These were the bunioneers of 1928: The brave, often naively confident group of 199 men who would face the worst of Route 66. They would traverse the incinerator of the Mojave, the howling winds and thin air of the Arizona high country, the tarpaper mud of the Texas panhandle and beyond. And at the end of it all, those who survived would surely have earned stories to tell, if not money from winning.

CHAPTER 5

The Beginning

EARLY IN 1928, A CAST OF INTERNATIONAL ENDURANCE STARS AND scores of unknown but hopeful men began arriving for prerace training. They disembarked from trains arriving from snow-bound Midwest farm towns, crammed eastern cities, and points far and wide, and stepped from the train platform into the new golden city of the West, Los Angeles—a place of dreams enveloped by old orange groves and oil derricks—which had expanded pell-mell from a half million at the start of the decade to 1.5 million by its close. By 1926, filmmaking had become the biggest industry in Los Angeles, pumping almost $250,000 into the regional economy and supplying the world with silent pictures. C. C. Pyle knew Los Angeles well, after coming with Red Grange in 1926 to make a movie amid the palm trees and glittering Hollywood lifestyle. Charley was about to leave this paradise, however, to lead his contestants on an eastward trek through hell.[1]

Three weeks before the March 4 start date for the race, Pyle took over Ascot Speedway—a dirt race car track on the edge of the city, where he had ordered the contestants to report by February 13 for a three-week conditioning program. He set up shop inside the track's oval, which quickly took on the look of a "miniature army camp."[2] There were 275 arrivals—more than double Pyle's original estimate of camp attendees.[3]

As the men assembled at Ascot Park under balmy skies, one reporter commented that it looked "like a conference of the League of Nations in athletic garb."[4] C. C. Pyle's camp cook, Bill Burcher, agreed. He had established the "Pyle-Inn Café," which he dubbed the sole grub stop for 275 men. Burcher had cooked for circuses, lumber camps, "gold strike towns, and water front hash houses," but in his long career, he had never received so many requests for different meals. He moaned, "They want 57 varieties of foods in 207 'langwidges.' . . . Them Finns want four kinds of fish, [and] oh-them [Italians]. They want their salami and spaghetti." Sam Richman wanted Hungarian goulash, some of the Blacks wanted chitlins, New Yorker Harry Abramowitz asked for gefilte fish, and a Scotsman wanted haggis. Burcher asked, "Wotinhell is haggis?" He gave the man two eggs over easy instead. "I got them bimboos with me for two months more," he said.[5]

Pyle had hired Hugo Quest, an experienced and highly regarded trainer, to supervise the camp and the task of getting the runners and walkers into sufficient physical condition to survive the race. Quest had been the personal trainer to Finland's premier distance runner, Pavvo Nurmi. Camp life began at 6 a.m., when the men awoke to the sound of Hugo ringing a giant triangle. After an 8 a.m. breakfast, they were free to follow their own training schedules, with most putting in at least twenty-five miles a day.[6] This was far too little training for endurance racing legend Arthur Newton, who was appalled that only a few of his competitors had run more than fifty miles in a stretch. In a prerace briefing, he said, "[This is a] desperately serious affair and only those who used their heads to some purpose and who also enjoyed remarkably good luck could hope to come in prominently at the other end." By the time camp was over, seventy-six men had already heeded Arthur's warning and dropped out of the race.[7]

Race physician John Baker, an internist at Philadelphia's Jefferson Hospital, painted a bleak picture for those who remained. After conducting physical examinations, he found that only 40 of the 199 men seemed fit enough to withstand the race: 21 men had significant lung and gastrointestinal tract infections, 11 had mild emphysema, 18 had orthopedic problems of the lower limbs, and he considered a full 50 percent to be physically underdeveloped for the task of running across the United States. Dr. Baker had a keen interest in the impact of long-distance running on the human body. He wanted to test the conventional wisdom that prolonged distance running would damage the body and result in premature death.[8] After the race, Baker examined the finishers and published a scientific paper that refuted this long-held belief.

Charley Pyle, always the showman, put on a brave face for the press and staged a series of fifteen-mile races—two for the runners and two for the walkers—to give the public a look at his top men. The American Indian Nicholas Quamawahu won the first running event and August Fager, an American Finn, took the second. Phillip Granville won both walking races. In the last days before the derby start, Pyle also held an open house to showcase his fleet of road-ready vehicles, tents, and other derby equipment. He was ready.[9]

CHAPTER 6

And They're Off!

Race Day

DAY 1, 199 MEN

SUNDAY, MARCH 4, 1928. IN THE MONTHS LEADING UP TO THE race, Los Angeles had suffered a prolonged drought. Catholic Bishop Cantwell, vicar to the city's faithful, had done his part by asking parishioners to pray for rain at Sunday Mass on February 26.[1] On Friday, March 2, the heavens answered with a downpour that turned Charley's training camp into an ocean of ankle-deep mud.

Undaunted by the rain or a reporter who predicted his race would be "the most colossal flop in athletic history," the director general proclaimed the derby would start Sunday afternoon, as scheduled. He maintained that control points and dates had been set across the country, and reasoned that his men would encounter plenty of foul weather on their trek. As if on command, the rain clouds parted and sunlight began to reflect off pools of rainwater—a welcome sign to the rain-soaked bunioneers who had been huddled in their tents in the middle of the oval for the last three days.[2]

As the 3 p.m. start time neared, men entered the muddy track behind their nations' flags: Canada, Estonia, Finland, Great Britain, Germany, Italy, and of course a huge contingent behind the United States flag. Each man wore a racing bib pinned to the front and back of his shirt with his race number and the words "C. C. Pyle" printed above it. None displayed their names on their clothing, a C. C. Pyle marketing ploy to force spectators to pay twenty-five cents to buy a race program if they hoped to match a number to a name.[3] Most of the contestants wore tracksuits, but some donned overalls, street clothes, and flannel shirts. The well-prepared had specially built running shoes with dozens of pairs in reserve, while others wore logger boots or moccasins or, in a few cases, no shoes at all.[4]

Several latecomers made last-minute pleas to the crowd to cover their $125 entrance fees. Finding no takers, Michael Contreras of San Bernardino abandoned the effort and settled for entering the Second Annual World Endurance Dancing Championship set for April 19 in Los Angeles.[5] A sadder tale was that of Herbert Hart, who walked 1,100 miles from Vancouver, British Columbia, to the wrong city—Santa Rosa, California—missing the derby by one day.[6]

For those in line, however, the saga was just beginning. A police motorcycle escort waited in front of the 199 assembled men, while Pyle's fleet of fifty trucks and cars rumbled behind them. The race officials divided the men into thirteen lines in descending numerical order. Eugene Germaine of Montreal, with number "1" on his chest, was the first man on the outside lane, wearing a white sleeveless vest and white shorts. Once the signal was given, Germaine and the first line would go. Two minutes later, the next line would leave and so on, until all thirteen had left—an exercise designed to prolong the start for the 5,000 fans who packed the grandstands.[7]

Charley Pyle stood in the bleachers, squeezed between the excited fans. Always a fashion play, he wore a fur-lined overcoat, spat-covered shoes, and had a bowler hat and cane clutched in his hands, his graying and receding hair slicked back above his sharp blue eyes.[8] He gave a two-minute speech and a nod to Grange, who set off a large firecracker. As the blast shook the stands, the first group was off, circling the track one-and-a-half times in a sea of ankle-deep mud, led by the police escort, sirens blaring.[9]

As the remaining groups left, a reporter said, "There was no nervous pawing at the track, and no false starts. Every entrant knew he had plenty of time to run during the next two months or more."[10] One reporter claimed that Andy Payne, the Foyil, Oklahoma, farm boy, almost missed the start. The men were already lined up when a motorcar raced to the line, Andy leaped from the car, notified a race official he was starting, and he was off on his run across America.[11]

To the sound of blaring horns, waving flags, and war whoops from some of the Native American runners, the men left the muddy oval, entered a fan-choked Route 66, and headed for Puente, California, seventeen miles to the east. After the track had cleared, Charley ushered the press corps into his two huge buses for the trip to Puente.

From the comfort of their new mobile home, the reporters watched the leaders pull away. First among them was Willie Kolehmainen, one of the favored Finns. He had worn socks over his running shoes as protection from the mud, and discarded them once he left the track.[12]

Kolehmainen blazed through the course so far ahead of the estimated finish time that the local citizens did not have time to prepare a suitable welcome for him. He passed through an archway at the finish, waved to the official timer, and flopped on a cot to be rubbed down by his brother, Hannes. Willie had ignored Arthur Newton's advice to run a conservative race. The Finn had run the seventeen miles in less than a six-minute-mile pace—impossibly fast for the transcontinental race. The *Los Angeles Times* glowingly reported that the Finn "ran the race without working up a decent sweat" and "looks capable of running fifty miles a day for the next five years," but the reporter was wrong. The effort had left his forty-year-old body tired and sore, and the next day he would need to run again, this time twice as far. His friend Gunnar Nilson finished the first leg two minutes behind him in second, and New Yorker Sam Richman, part of the racing trio of the Richman brothers, finished an unexpected third. Nicholas Quamawahu was fourth, and Eddie Gardner came in a respectable ninth. Arthur Newton, the sage of the derby, had elected to hold back on the opening race.[13]

Behind the leaders came the men who one press reporter claimed had "no business in such a strength-sapping event and the sooner they find out the better." The first man to drop out was Elton Hayes of Akron, Ohio, after finishing with aching feet and a few blisters. He had just found a job in Los Angeles and had recently become engaged to a local

Figure 8. Cover of 1928 official program. Credit: 1928 official program, personal copy, author.

woman. Hayes guessed he would give up his dreams of cross-country glory and "just settle down in the West."[14] Eugene Estoppy, who ran the course in logger boots accompanied by two dogs and a young man who played the ukulele, wouldn't last much longer, either.[15]

Andy Payne described the sight in a letter to his mother: "There were half a million people [who] saw us run the seventeen miles [to Puente] for the whole way on both sides of the road. There was not space to park another car and you could not raise your head without you facing a camera."[16] The *Los Angeles Times* called it worthy of a Hollywood movie, with cars three to four deep on either side of the road.[17]

After the race, Pyle's medical team attended to a host of blisters and ailments and supplied rubdowns to the tired men who flopped on their cots. After the men had passed through the chow line for dinner, they helped sell programs. At 8 p.m., Red Grange called the lead athletes together on the stage under the big show tent and introduced them to the assembled fans. The leaders were expected to say a few words and perform a brief act to entertain the crowd—Eddie Gardner imitated a steamboat whistle; the Spokane, Washington, jeweler John Pederson sang an aria from an opera; and Frank Chavez, a Mission Indian from California, strummed the ukulele.[18] The mood was light. The first race had been a cakewalk: seventeen miles run on a flat, well-paved road on a mild spring afternoon. But dawn would bring a new reality to the bunioneers.

Welcome to Hell

DAY 2, 198 MEN

Monday, March 5, 1928. A cold, driving rain smacked the men awake as they toed the line, most still sore from the previous day's seventeen miles. They would race twice as far today. Some of the contestants, like Willie Kolehmainen, braved the weather in "abbreviated garb," scanty running shorts and a jersey, and shivered in the rain.[19] Many made concessions for the weather with tracksuits, while others gave in altogether and wore layers of clothing, raincoats, and wool underwear. One local reporter said, "[It's] the most colorful sport feature that has ever reached this part of the country."[20]

The rainy, windswept course did not discourage the crowds who lined the highway to the finish line at Bloomington, a town in the fertile valley in the coast range.[21] Bloomington had earned the right to be the derby's second stop, after the city fathers had raised enough money—around five hundred dollars—to meet Pyle's request to help defray the expense of his adventure.[22] What the citizens received in exchange was a bit of the world. The got a chance to see their town mentioned in a dozen bylines, and to experience something new, odd, and famous—Red Grange, dancing girls, snake charmers, and athletic men speaking a dozen languages engaged in the struggle of their lives.

Before noon, the derby's heavily loaded trucks pulled into town and gangs of men started unloading tents, equipment, and baggage in the field behind the train station. Soon, Pyle's men had erected his sprawling tent city. By 3 p.m., his hot-dog stands were operating despite the weather, "the carnival barker started his marathon bark," and paying customers entered the tented carnival area. Then the two palatial buses arrived, disgorging Pyle, Grange, and the national corps of sports reporters. The trainers' cars came next with their men's numbers painted on the sides, pacing their charges as they crossed the finish line.[23] In high spirits, Charley celebrated the second day of the derby with a parade down Main Street, and local businessmen joined in with a float bedecked with advertising.

Though the rain did not dampen local spirits, it played hell with the bunioneers. After a few miles, blisters erupted as wet socks rubbed against tender feet. Gunnar Nilson, who had run so brilliantly the day before, paid for his speed with an injured knee and walked almost the entire course.[24] But his countryman and derby leader, Willie Kolehmainen, seemed unaffected. He flashed a wide grin to the crowds after he won the second race, arriving at the timers a half-hour ahead of the second-place runner. He had covered the thirty-five miles in four hours and twelve minutes, a bit faster than seven minutes per mile. The *San Bernardino Daily Sun* called Willie "a short, swarthy-skinned athlete" who appeared to be breathing easily and showed no haste in crawling into his bed after the race.[25]

Eddie Gardner took second place but looked exhausted. When he asked for a bath after the race, one of his trainers seemed unsympathetic to his request, saying, "Ain't you all had enough showers in [four] hours?"[26] Gardner had tried to stay with Willie in the early part of the race, but had faded as the Finn maintained his terrific pace.[27]

While the eyes of the press focused on the lap winners, men like

Andy Payne were taking things easy. After placing eighth and ninth respectively in the first two days of racing, Payne told his mother he was confident he would finish among the prizewinners. Soon Andy Payne would be much more than a small-town hero, but for now he was content with his status: part of the pack grinding east on Route 66. The race favorite, Arthur Newton, continued to lag behind. Some in the press attributed this to a failure to acclimate to American food and climate.[28] More likely, Newton knew the leaders' early pace was impossibly fast and unsustainable over the long haul.

While Andy Payne and Arthur Newton were content to bide their time, most men were simply hoping to survive until the next stage. By the end of the second day, five contestants had dropped out—Italian walker Frank Urgo from a painful ingrown toenail, Scottish immigrant James Fleming from cramps, Mexican American Eli Sanchez from "weary feet," Californian James Gordon from a knee injury, and Walter Brunson of Los Angeles who moaned, "my dogs [feet] are all in."[29]

The tired survivors shuffled to the medical tent where trainers massaged their "dogs" with different ointments. Then they retired to the sleeping tent, collapsing on iron beds and fearing for the dawn after that second day's carnage.

The Terrible Climb to Cajon Pass

DAY 3, 183 MEN

Tuesday, March 6, 1928. Another ten men failed to answer role call for the third day, leaving 183 to shuffle to the starting line. The contestants had only completed forty-two miles of the 3,400-mile trek to New York City.[30]

From Bloomington, Route 66 turned north as it ascended the San Bernardino Mountains, taking the path of least resistance to the crest of the range at Cajon Pass where the high peaks grab eastward-drifting rain clouds, squeeze out their water, and let the remains drift to hell: the Mojave Desert.[31] The trip to Cajon Pass covered twenty miles and 4,200 feet of grinding, muscle-screaming climbing. Those who reached the crest would then have to shift gears to descend on quivering legs as they dropped 1,500 feet down the eastern flank of the range to Victorville, fifteen miles beyond the summit.[32]

The third day of the derby started at 7:30 a.m., with a confident Willie Kolehmainen running neck and neck with his countryman, Nestor Erickson. Three miles into the race, however, Willie self-destructed when he pulled a tendon, slowed to a crawl, and began an agonizing nine-and-a-half-hour walk to the finish line. A *San Francisco Examiner* reporter quipped that Willie had just about become "a finished Finn today."[33] His brother made a valiant attempt to get him ready for the next day's race, but Willie seemed to hurt everywhere—legs, sides, hips, and a painful bruise on his left heel.[34]

Kolehmainen was not alone. Most of the men—still garbed in a mix of overalls, street clothes, and running attire—suffered a range of maladies including blisters, sprained ankles, aching knees, side and muscle cramps, and simple exhaustion. Red Grange drove a truck that came to be known as the "dead wagon," picking up the spent contestants littering the highway. Riding with Grange was "Bullet Baker," his New York Yankee teammate, who scanned the twisting, climbing road to the pass to ensure none of the men "sneaked rides on the upholstery of some obliging motor driver."[35] Though the top fifty had crossed the finish line by late afternoon, twenty-five had still not finished by 9 p.m. and continued to stagger in until midnight.[36]

Among the leaders was another Finn, Nestor Erickson, who held the lead to the top of the pass using a "low-gear walk and a high-gear run" until Nicholas Quamawahu, the Hopi Indian from Arizona, passed him.[37] Erickson eventually recaptured the lead, and held off Quamawahu to maintain Finnish honor by winning the forty-five miles in six hours and forty-seven minutes. Arthur Newton, the grand old veteran from England, finished third. Arthur was the only man who maintained a slow, steady jog over Cajon Pass and passed a large portion of the men along the way. Arthur's countryman, sixty-three-year-old London boot maker and senior derby contestant Charley Hart, ran "with a smile and an unflattering dogtrot, and received a tremendous ovation from the citizens of Victorville as he crossed the timing mark."[38]

For more than a dozen men, there would be no finish at Victorville. A host of international entries were among the departed, including Paolo Bruno, walking mate of Guisto Umek; Mike Fekete of Hungary; Carl Hess Grav of Austria; and Kurt Zimmer of Germany. All had taken the long ride with Grange, where a derby official returned their one-hundred-dollar deposit and sent them home. The slopes of Cajon Pass had ended another dozen dreams.[39]

That night, the full realization of the physical demands of transcontinental racing came crashing down on the leg-dead, three-day veterans who crawled into their iron cots beneath unwashed sheets. They had begun the fight of their lives.

CHAPTER 7

Trial by Fire

To the Edge of the Civilized World

DAY 4, 167 MEN

WEDNESDAY, MARCH 7, 1928. ONE HUNDRED AND SIXTY-SEVEN MEN shivered in the freezing morning air at the Victorville start line, 2,700 feet above sea level on the scrub-pine-covered, rain-starved eastern slope of the San Bernardino Mountains. The men would descend in a lazy curve to the east on a ribbon of pavement lashed by fierce, hot winds from the Mojave. Thirty-six miles away sat Barstow, the last town of consequence for several hundred miles until the town of Needles at the eastern edge of the desert.[1]

The race to Barstow would end the reign of the speed kings. Willie Kolehmainen and Nicholas Quamawahu had tempted fate by racing in the six- to seven-minute-mile pace. The bill had come due, and Willie paid first. Three miles outside of Victorville, the battered frontrunner dropped out of the race and rode to Barstow, where he stood at the finish line. A reporter described him as a "dejected figure" as he watched the others complete the stage.[2] Willie blamed himself for excessive speed— he simply pushed too hard, leaving the survivors with cautionary tales about the merits of a steady pace. Next, the American Indian Nicholas Quamawahu paid for racing over Cajon Pass, when he sprained his ankle and developed a painful heel blister that his physicians feared would cause blood poisoning. "He trotted and walked, fell far behind the field but grimly went on until long after dark," before he heeded his trainer's advice to temporarily withdraw from the race until the next day.[3]

As the leaders faltered, Eddie Gardner stepped into the breech and won the fourth lap with graceful strides in five hours and forty-five minutes. He ran the course at a pace of eight minutes and forty-five seconds per mile, several minutes slower than Willie Kolehmainen's fatal speed, but perhaps sustainable over the long haul to New York City. He ran in the teeth of a burning wind that "played havoc with others of the hoofing horde," the effect lessened by a gift of prescription sunglasses from a black Los Angeles optometrist.[4] Eddie appeared tired, but pleased that his victory had moved him into second place in the cumulative standings. His performance prompted a grateful *Seattle Post Intelligencer* reporter to write, "Perhaps he may not survive to be met by the cheers of Harlem's colored population, but he has already brought nation-wide publicity to this city."[5] Paul Lowry, sports columnist for the *Los Angeles Times*, marveled at the beauty of Eddie's form, and wondered how the national press corps could have missed placing him among the frontrunners before the race began.[6]

Behind the Sheik came a steady and confident Arthur Newton in second, who seemed to find his stride in rough-desert running. Tiny Olli Wanttinen followed in third and moved into first place in the cumulative standings; the effort, however, left him exhausted, and few believed he would retain the lead for long. Passaic ship fitter Johnny Salo and English ship steward Peter Gavuzzi joined the ranks taking fifth and eighth places, respectively.[7] Senior derby runner, sixty-three-year-old Charley Hart, trotted across the finish in thirteenth place to a "rousing cheer" from an enthusiastic crowd of two thousand.[8]

After the leaders came a parade of the lame and limping. At least 50 percent of the men suffered from blistered feet, moving one reporter to write, "[For] most of the marathoners, it is a case of two soles with a single thought—blisters." To compound their agony, the men had to contend with the effects of a broiling desert sun, which left most with severe sunburn and dehydration.[9]

As the derby moved deeper into the desert, it wasn't just the contestants who broke down. It became apparent that Pyle's crew of off-season football players was not up to the task of monitoring and supporting 150 men, who were often spread for miles along the road. Charley had a lunch truck and patrol cars that carried hot coffee, cold drinks, and sandwiches to the men, but his crew was overwhelmed by the job. Red Munitz, in his shoe repair truck, joined the rescue effort, passing food and drink to exhausted men and winning their eternal gratitude and friendship.[10]

The director general also failed to provide his men with sufficient amounts of high-energy food necessary to sustain transcontinental runners. One reporter said the contestants ate twice as much meat as normal men, and great quantities of bread, some "eating a loaf at a time, plus mounds of potatoes and gallons of coffee and milk."[11] Nor did Charley wash the men's clothes or bedding, forcing them to run in soiled, sweat-encrusted fabric and sleep in filthy sheets that got worse by the day.[12] These failures turned the exercise of running across the country into a bitter and unpleasant task for those dependent on his generosity.

Those contestants with trainers in vehicles who could monitor their health, supply them with hydrating fluids, and help them maintain their pace had a tremendous advance over men relying on Charley's dole. In camp, the same truth applied: Competitors with the manpower to clean and mend their clothes and augment their food supplies had a great advantage.

Into the Oven

DAY 5

Thursday, March 8, 1928. The fifth day would take these exhausted and increasingly embittered men to the western fringe of the Mojave, where temperatures hovered in the nineties. The derby had been losing about a dozen men each day, and at that rate, the race would grind to a halt somewhere in Arizona. If anything, conditions for day five were worse. Here the pavement ended and real desert running began. The men would be cut off from telegraph and telephone communication for the next 161 miles.[13]

At 9 a.m., they ran down Barstow's main street, cheered by the blare of the town's brass band.[14] They were a wild-looking bunch—nearly all had a heavy growth of beard; most wore grimy, sweat-stained clothes and covered their exposed skin in grease to protect against sunburn. Associated Press reporter Russell J. Newland said, "[They are] bronzed as desert prospectors, and their grease-coated arms and piston-like legs glitter[ed] in the bright sun [as] they plunged out of civilization into the wilderness, headed for fame and glory—or failure." In the desert, a strange assortment of spectators came to greet them: Indians, Mexicans, and grizzled white prospectors. They watched in silence as the grim procession passed, spread for miles along dusty Route 66.[15]

The men ran under a cloudless sky as an angry sun beat down in the shadeless landscape. As the sun swung south on its westerly track, it focused on the right sides of the eastbound men, and most developed severe sunburns and heat blisters—particularly on the exposed right sides of their faces. To make matters worse, the road surface gave way underfoot and emitted great clouds of dust whenever cars drove by, leaving the men gagging and coated.[16] Cleveland runner Mike Joyce said, "God, it was terrible. Not a breath of air. Blistering sand, rocky roads, with those mirages dancing up in front of us."[17] Peter Gavuzzi began to follow the advice of the local Indians, begging a large sombrero off a sympathizer, covering his face in protective grease, and running with a water bottle in each hand despite fears the extra weight would through off his stride.[18]

In these conditions, most of the men could manage nothing faster than a shuffle, except Arthur Newton, who excelled in desert running from his years in South Africa's hot and dusty Natal region. He won his first daily race, covering the thirty-two miles to the desert watering hole of Mojave Wells in four hours and forty-eight minutes—a nine-minute-mile pace. His win moved him into first place in the overall standings. Twenty minutes behind came tiny Olli Wanttinen, followed by Andy Payne, who was guided by his motorcycle-riding trainer with a jug of lemonade tied to the back of the bike. Next was forty-year-old physician Arne Souminen. The surprise of the day was the return of Nicholas Quamawahu who, in the early hours, had completed his remaining fourteen miles to Barstow, then begun the trek to Mojave Wells. A reporter wrote, "[He] broke from his lagging walk into a run and passed many of the tail-enders [and] finished in far better condition than yesterday."

His trainers believed he would be ready to resume the race in earnest on day six.[19]

That night, Pyle gave his carnival workers the night off. A handful of inhabitants of Mojave Wells did not make it worth his while to open the carnival.[20] The bunioneers went to bed early, the less fortunate in their stinking sheets, as the chill night wind of the desert rattled the flaps of their camp tents. Their bodies needed sleep, for tomorrow they would head deeper into hell.

The Heart of the Desert

DAY 6

Friday, March 9, 1928. This day, Pyle's crew of desert nomads would travel forty-two miles to the appropriately named desert town of Baghdad. The men would pass the extinct Mt. Pisgah Volcanic Crater which had once spewed lava to the edge of Route 66. They would travel past the dying town of Ludlow, with narrow-gauge railroads running north to Death Valley where miners pulled copper, silver, borax, and gold out of the baked earth. At Baghdad, the men would reach the heart of the desert, with another two days of the Mojave yet to conquer.[21]

All but a handful faded in the intense heat that day, and walkers like Guisto Umek, Phillip Granville, and Harry Abramowitz finished in the top twenty for the first time. Arthur Newton won the forty-two-mile ordeal in six and a half hours, followed by Eddie Gardner who led for twenty-one miles.[22] A reporter described him as "[n]one other than the highly brown and highly honored Sheik of the bunion derby, Mr. Eddie Gardner, the Seattle Negro, who ran with his headband streaming out . . . and the white road smoking behind him." The Sheik wilted under Newton's relentless nine-minute-mile pace, however, and finished forty-five minutes behind him, followed by Andy Payne.[23] The leaders prayed they had found a magic range—a sustainable transcontinental pace of nine to ten minutes per mile that would take them across the country.

Behind them came the walking wounded, most with bandaged legs from scrapes and strains.[24] Senior runner Charles Hart, who had finished after more than ten hours, hobbled across the finish line in the late afternoon, while the few inhabitants of Baghdad cheered him on. Nicholas Quamawahu, who gamely remained in the race with a sprained ankle, finished in seventy-sixth place after walking most of the course. Quamawahu lived in nearby Orbi, Arizona, and developed his legendary toughness with daily forty-mile runs from his ranch to town.[25] Another eight men dropped out, seven from various ailments, and one, Walter Ricketts of Southampton, Ontario, barely escaped with his life when a drunk driver hit him, broke seven ribs and left him for dead on the side of the road. He was evacuated to a Los Angeles hospital and survived.[26]

Scores of other men were on the verge of physical collapse, but pride, stupidity, or guts forced them to push beyond what they thought possible. Patrick De Marr, a California boxer who had cut his feet to ribbons in the first days of the race, gritted his teeth, found two walking sticks, and hobbled his way across the desert.[27]

Iron Men of the Mojave

DAYS 7 AND 8, 147 MEN

Day seven, Saturday, March 10, 1928. In the morning, the desert veterans pulled on their stinking clothes for a thirty-two-mile trip to Danby, a place so hot that a local joked, "A trip to hell would look good." Arthur Newton again showed his prowess as a desert runner by taking first-place honors in the stage race.[28]

Day eight would be the final day of desert running, with a fifty-seven-mile course to Needles near the Colorado River, which serves as the boundary between California and Arizona. Like the Nile River in Egypt, the Colorado is the lifeblood of the region, bringing water from the far mountains to the parched Southwest. The town of Needles had long been a center for miners and ranchers, and took its name from a group of stone spires in the Arizona Black Mountains.[29]

From Needles, cars were strung west for miles to watch the procession of desert nomads shuffle into town.[30] That day the men were blessed with a better road—wide, level, and firmly packed, providing solid footing but no respite from the heat or dust.[31]

Pyle started the race at 5 a.m. to give the men some escape from the sun, but for most it made little difference. Many needed more than twelve hours to complete the distance, and seventeen dropped out, vowing to finish the stage in the morning. The list of the fallen included Italian walking star Guisto Umek, Denver baker and marathon champion Seth Gonzales, and Hollywood actor Lucien Frost.[32]

The Mojave had done its work, and C. C. Pyle added to the burden with terrible food, unwashed sheets and clothes, and inadequate monitoring and support during the stage runs. Pyle was a pioneer in managing an endurance event, but he needed to fine-tune his organization and listen to the concerns of the men. In addition to adjusting to his poor care, there were other lessons for the contestants. The first was that the men could maintain a slow running pace that would mean defeat for the race walkers. By the time the derby reached Needles, walkers such as Phillip Granville, Louis Perrella, and Guisto Umek had began running, with the help of Peter Gavuzzi, who showed them proper form and technique.[33]

Another lesson was food. Arthur Newton found that after a week or more of running, most men settled into a standard method of fueling their bodies: They ate the biggest breakfast possible shortly before the start, and ran slowly for twenty miles. During the day they drank highly sweetened drinks for races under thirty miles, adding honey or cheese sandwiches for still longer distances, and drank every five to six miles. For the evening meal, meat was essential.[34]

The third lesson was that the successful men gave their bodies time to adapt to the rigors of cross-country running. Peter Gavuzzi hit on the correct formula: "I took it very easy the first few days; the blokes up front were racing it out every day, but I wasn't worried—I wasn't expected to do anything, you see—I just ambled along at the back with a few other chaps; we'd laugh and talk and play the banjo, and come in hours after the leaders." Gavuzzi allowed his body to adjust to daily racing, while the leaders exhausted themselves by starting too fast.[35]

The bunioneers finally reached the end of the Mojave after eight days of running. Those who had learned the lessons of pace and diet became the new frontrunners. Eddie Gardner challenged Arthur Newton for a second day, holding the lead for almost half the race before the South African shuffled past him to win. Newton, with his string of top finishes, led the field by five hours in the cumulative standings. Andy Payne held second place, overall.[36] Both men had found that the key was slow, constant running. At this point in the derby, it looked like the twenty-five-thousand-dollar prize would go to a tortoise, but a fast one—the hare had crashed and burned, and the walkers were losing ground.

That day, Eddie slipped to third place with Englishman Peter Gavuzzi taking second. Charley Hart, the ancient warrior, maintained a steady pace to pass more than one hundred men, often half his age, and finished in twenty-first place.[37] In the pack, the local favorite Nicholas Quamawahu would not give up despite twelve hours of limping on his sprained ankle. He was a gifted runner, having beaten Clarence De Mar, the country's premier amateur marathoner, in a 1927 race.[38] Pride and his competitor's spirit would not let him give up his quest to win the derby.

For the first time in days, enough people gathered for C. C. Pyle to operate his carnival.[39] All across the Mojave, he had paid for food, supplies and employees with little to fill his depleting coffers. Benjamin Franklin once said there are three faithful friends in life—an old wife, an old dog, and ready money.[40] Pyle had none of these. He had started the race with a safe full of promises and his organization had begun to come apart at the seams.[41]

In Needles, his food concessionaire quit when Pyle did not pay him the salary specified in his contract, leaving the director general to find a cook from within his ranks.[42] John Pederson, a Swedish-born jeweler and runner from Spokane, Washington, complained that Charley had promised to feed the men from a rolling commissary, but in reality, he said, "[The] dietitian was an old-time can opener from the army who would toss a lot of old meat into a pot and say, 'nice juicy steaks for supper tonight, boys.'" Pyle soon abandoned the commissary altogether and began giving his men a meager food allowance to meet their caloric needs.[43]

Those with trainers and financial backers increased their edge, for they could supplement Pyle's food allowance with their own funds. Peter Gavuzzi was glad to abandon the caravan's commissionaire and start eating at local diners. He complained that across the desert, Charley "served oats for breakfast and sour oats at that, with two hard boiled eggs so hard that you could drop them on the floor without hurting them."[44] Phillip Granville was also thankful for the change. The meals, he said, "were nothing to speak of, being totally insufficient for the needs of the racers."[45] For the pack runners, with nothing but air in their grimy pockets, dreams of transcontinental glory became increasingly daunting to attain.

CHAPTER 8

Trial by Ice

Into the High Country

DAY 9, 130 MEN

MONDAY, MARCH 12, 1928. ON THE NINTH DAY, THE MEN MADE THE
one-mile dash to the Colorado River where Indians waited to ferry them
to the Arizona shore in open canoes.[1] Ahead lay the high country, a
land of towering mountain ranges, broad valleys, and deep canyons still
locked in the grip of late-winter snow. For the bunioneers, it meant a different kind of hell from the Mojave, but it was hell just the same: howling
icy winds, gut-pushing climbs and descents, and high-altitude running,
which restricted the men's oxygen intake as they ran. In 1928, Arizona's
portion of Route 66 was completely unpaved—little more than a rutted
dirt road, crisscrossed by snowmelt streams that challenged the derby
men, along with Pyle's heavily loaded cars and trucks. A sixty-mile trip
on Route 66 typically took all day, and essential tire tools for any vehicle
included a lug wrench, patching equipment, and a tire pump. Longer
trips called for camping equipment.[2]

The first stage race in Arizona would take the men along an abandoned stagecoach route into the foothills of the Black Mountains.

Charley was forced to take his vehicles south to Toprock to find ferries big enough to transport them across the river.[3] Left on their own for the day, the men began on familiar ground—seven miles of sand-blasted desert—before the road began a steep ascent up a two-thousand-foot slope to the mining community of Oatman.[4] The town had produced almost two million ounces of gold since operations began near the turn of the century. In 1928, the mines were almost played out and Oatman's former population of ten thousand had dwindled to a few hundred, still trying to wrench gold from the well-worked earth.[5]

Oatman was one of the few towns in the world to have an official town crier, and he "bellowed forth" the names of the bunioneers as they came in.[6] The first name on his lips was the unstoppable South African, Arthur Newton, who appeared to take to mountain climbing as well as he had to desert running. This lanky, middle-aged man with his clipped mustache had opened a five-hour lead over his nearest rival, Andy Payne, and had assumed the crown of the undisputed king of the bunion derby. Newton, age forty-four, ran with a scientist's eye, having perfected his stride length and height so that he would barely glide above the surface of the road. Twenty-year-old Andy Payne held second in the cumulative standings, but only by twenty minutes, with Eddie Gardner close behind.[7]

Nicholas Quamawahu's fans had hoped for derby glory, but had to settle for admiration of his gritty determination to stay in the race despite a badly sprained ankle. When he limped into town with a thirtieth-place finish, Quamawahu received a rousing welcome, and additional cheers after he assured them his injury would improve and that he would soon be back in the hunt for the twenty-five-thousand-dollar first prize. But for most bunioneers, it was just another grinding challenge that cut their ranks by three.[8]

On the tenth day, the 127 bunioneers plunged deeper into the Black Mountains. In short order, they began a steep, winding climb, long feared by drivers as a place of breakdowns and heartbreak, to Sitgreaves Pass 3,500 feet above sea level.[9] From the summit, they descended 1,400 feet in nine miles into a long, windswept valley, before making a final climb up the Perfume Pass to Kingman, a cowboy town at 3,300 feet that served as the seat of Mohave County and a shipping center for surrounding ranches and mines.[10]

Arthur Newton turned in another extraordinary performance as he traversed two mountain passes and thousands of feet of elevation in four hours, and won his fifth stage race. He passed physical education teacher Paul Simpson of Elon, North Carolina, within sight of the finish line in Kingman, and extended his lead over second-place holder Andy Payne to more than seven hours.[11]

Back in Foyil, Oklahoma, amusement over Andy's participation had turned to pride among his parents and the local community. In his native Rodgers County, "old time farm folk" waited for any word. His mother recalled that she did not want him to go at first, "but now she desires nothing more else but that he win." The *Daily Oklahoman* began to compare him to Charles Lindbergh, who flew the Atlantic in 1927. "Like Lindy," a reporter gushed, "Andrew Payne is a mother's boy. He has written a bushel of letters, all of them interesting and many filled with home sickness."[12]

A Trail of the Battered and Beat

DAY 11, 125 MEN

Wednesday, March 14, 1928. After losing another two men on the road to Kingman, the group began the eleventh day on an imposing fifty-two-mile course to the town of Peach Springs.[13] For the first thirty-six miles, they trekked across an open plain before twisting up Crozier Canyon for fifteen miles and reaching the finish at 4,800 feet. Earning its name from the peach trees that grew around its well-used watering hole, Peach Springs served as an Indian trading post and Sante Fe Railroad station at the southern edge of the Hualapai Indian Reservation.[14]

Arthur Newton showed exceptional endurance when he won his sixth stage victory, seemingly unaffected by the massive climbs and descents that broke scores of younger men.[15] He covered the fifty-two miles in seven hours and fifty minutes, with the Finn Nestor Erickson finishing twenty minutes behind him. Newton added another hour to his lead over Andy Payne, who now had a secure lock on second after Eddie Gardner began to falter in the high country. The Sheik reached Peach Springs in almost eleven hours, tumbling to sixth place in the overall standings. Gardner had apparently pushed far too hard in the desert, and his body would not respond to the demands of high-altitude running.[16]

For most of the men, the extended run to Peach Springs was a night-mare, with fifteen dropping out before the start of the next day's race. The stage almost ended the career of prerace favorite Guisto Umek, who struggled with a sore foot but managed to finish. Canadian Osmond Metcalfe had worse luck. A race official found him delirious and wan-dering the course. The official took him to town and revived him with four sandwiches, three cups of strong coffee, and a double order of ham and eggs. After the meal, the Canadian claimed he "felt better but had lost his appetite for long distance hiking."[17]

The derby also claimed two popular members of Pyle's derby pa-rade: sixty-three-year-old Charley Hart, and Arizona favorite Nicholas Quamawahu. Both temporarily withdrew from the fifty-two-mile trek, Hart from exhaustion and Quamawahu from a painfully sprained ankle that would not heal under the stress of daily ultramarathons. Both vowed to make up the distance the next day.

In the morning, the Hopi Indian resumed the race, but "eight miles east of Seligman, he ended his marathon" when he was ordered out of the race by the derby physician.[18]

Charley Hart did no better. He credited his past success in the derby to drinking a raw egg in wine every ten miles.[19] Eggs and wine, however, did not save him from the altitude's effects on his sixty-three-year-old body. When race officials picked him up in a state of collapse outside of town, he withdrew from the race.[20] Hart remained with the derby as Peter Gavuzzi's new trainer and advisor—the two had traveled together from England and had been long-time friends. Charley Hart, who held the one-hundred-mile record before losing the title to Arthur Newton, had paced Gavuzzi for most of the race. When he was about to quit the contest, he reportedly told his young friend, "Don't mind me, Chappie. It's every man for himself. You carry on and uphold the honor of Britain."[21]

Thursday's thirty-eight-mile run to Seligman promised to add to the toll of the departed. At the start of the twelfth stage, a wild headwind roared off the mountain peaks, blasting the thinly clad men with gusts on a road that kept them consistently above five thousand feet—the death zone for endurance athletes—where the human body's intake of oxygen is only about 90 percent of what it is at sea level.[22]

These conditions prompted a *Los Angeles Times* reporter to call the day's race "[t]he most grueling [stretch yet] encountered since leaving Los Angeles." The men climbed to more than a mile above sea level, leaving the Hualapai Indian nation behind them and reaching 5,400 feet after winding up a steep grade for twelve miles. The course dropped a bit, then climbed again to 5,800 feet as the wind continued.[23] Arriving in Seligman, the derby men moved out of the Pacific Time Zone, and "found themselves cheated out of an hour's sleep."[24] In the face of these conditions, another twelve men dropped out.[25] All saw their dreams of transcontinental glory die in the howling winds of the Arizona high country.

In contrast to the carnage going on around him, Andy Payne seemed to gain strength as his body adapted, due in large part to the efforts of his trainer, Tom Young. From the seat of his motorcycle, Young had paced Andy through the last two weeks and kept him fed and hydrated. Blessed with youth, talent, and Young's tutelage, Andy surged in the stage race to Seligman, breaking Arthur Newton's amazing string of victories when he blazed through the thirty-eight miles in just under five hours and forty minutes, maintaining a pace of under-nine-minute miles. He passed a weary Arthur a few miles from the finish and beat him by eight minutes, with Arne Souminen taking third. Eddie Gardner continued to tumble out of contention for the twenty-five-thousand-dollar prize, when he finished in almost ten hours and dropped to seventh in the cumulative standings.[26] The Sheik kept up his spirits, though, assuring a reporter, "I'll make up all lost time and will overhaul the other runners when I hit the prairies." He received a steady stream of telegrams from fans, and he especially appreciated those from his hometown of Seattle. "[When] I get a wire from Seattle, I pep up a little bit more," he said.[27]

In the tiny ranching town of Seligman, the men finished in the teeth of the howling gale that had battered them since morning.[28] Despite the wind, Charley set up his carnival and concessions but couldn't attract enough townspeople to make it worthwhile. However, he did attract the unwanted attention of the Yavapai County Sheriff, George Ruffner. "Dubious of the character of the carnival followers," the sheriff went to Seligman and remained with the show until it left his county.[29]

Perhaps the sheriff had heard of Charley Pyle's troupe of artistic female dancers, who seemed to practice their art locked in the embraces of local men along Route 66. These ladies proved to be the star attraction next to Grange. They were not, as Pyle hoped, "young ladies of gentle breeding and excellent social standing." They performed the "muscle dance or kootch," an exhibition Pyle found to be "entirely out of keeping with the high athletic purpose of the enterprise."[30] C. C. Pyle's decision to retain the services of these ladies, despite his moral objections, points to the earning power of their charms.

That night, the bunioneers received a reprieve from the icy wind that howled through the sleeping tents when the town fathers let them spend the night in the local school.[31] The warmth of the building was a blissful change from Charley's flimsy tents. Peter Gavuzzi later said, "I don't known what the tents were for—the rain came through in buckets, and the mountain snows nearly froze me to death."[32] During their sojourn across Arizona, Pyle had done nothing to improve the housing and food for the men. The problems lingered and festered across the vast state, resentment building with every mile. At least for that night, the men were warm and safe as the wind moaned and rattled the schoolhouse doors. Most slept soundly, trying to forget the coming dawn.

To the Top of the World

DAY 13, 102 MEN

Friday, March 16, 1928. In the morning, the men knew what lay ahead: a forty-five-mile run that would take them on a 1,700-foot climb to the town of Williams at 6,762 feet. The entirety would be run into a howling wind with temperatures near freezing. One reporter managed the understatement, "[The course] probably will cause a great discomfort to them."[33] Eight men thought better of the attempt and quit the race before the start.[34]

Thirteen days of racing, almost half the field gone, and another day of icy anguish to conquer. Many wondered how much longer Charley Pyle could continue his creaking parade. He was already days behind schedule—his original estimate of fifty miles a day had been a pipe dream, and he would cut upcoming distances even further on the advice of the derby physician.[35]

For the 102 survivors who set their teeth against the wind and began climbing that day, there was encouragement from several carloads of spectators who followed them to the finish line at Williams. The fans cheered Arthur Newton as he regained his form and covered the forty-four miles to win in seven hours and ten minutes. But even the great South African was not immune from wind's effects, and Friday's unlucky thirteenth stage race proved to be the beginning of his undoing. Throughout the day, he favored his left leg to lessen a nagging pain in his right Achilles tendon. Arthur, with a realistic eye, said if his leg did not quickly respond to treatment, he might withdraw from the contest. His questionable status threw the spotlight on second-place holder Andy Payne, with Arne Souminen and Peter Gavuzzi close behind.[36]

That night, the town of Williams gave the tired men a welcome respite from their perpetual climb into thin air: The local American Legion post sponsored a professional wrestling contest between "Sailor Jack Lewis" and the "Terrible Turk," described in the local press as "splendid specimens of manhood." Red Grange attended the event in a perfectly creased black sombrero.[37]

The bunioneers needed to celebrate, for tomorrow they would reach the zenith of their climb into the clouds when they scaled Fortynine Hill, then the highest point on Route 66 at 7,410 feet above sea level.[38] At that altitude, the men's oxygen intake was at 80 percent, making every step its own test of endurance. That would lessen only slightly as they made their descent to the control point at Flagstaff at 7,000 feet.[39]

Nestor Erickson was the first to complete the course in about five and a half hours, with Andy Payne finishing thirty minutes behind him. Arthur Newton limped along with an injured tendon but managed to finish third, while Souminen finished fourth. Behind came the pack runners and walkers who shuffled into town often hours behind the leaders.[40] One reporter said, "[They] can't make more than three miles an hour if their lives depend on it, and a few [found] two miles an hour a terrible strain in their present condition."[41]

Those bunioneers who reached Flagstaff had completed two weeks of racing across five hundred miles of some of the most difficult and varied terrain on earth, something few of them could have imagined when they toed the line at Ascot Park. The survivors were different men after their trial of fire and ice—Route 66 had shown them its worst, and they had overcome it. They were now iron men on the long trail to New York.

Changing of the Guard

DAY 15, 100 MEN

Sunday, March 18, 1928. The men left Flagstaff for a thousand-foot descent to the high desert near Diablo Canyon, a great gash in the open plain. Just east of the canyon, Pyle made an unscheduled stop at the dying town of Two Gun Camp. He had originally planned to push twenty-four miles east to Winslow, but his medical staff warned him the men were too exhausted to attempt it after days of high-altitude racing. He settled for this former frontier town, which was on its way to oblivion before the derby temporarily revived it with an influx of visitors who hoped to catch one last glimpse of the transcontinental race.[42]

Eddie Gardner led the way, along with Pennsylvania railroad man Earl Dilks, both running the thirty-five miles in about five and a half hours. A limping Arthur Newton finished fifteen minutes behind them. Gardner's performance temporarily silenced critics who believed he had spent himself after hard running in the Mojave. United Press reporter James Powers wrote, "The dusky runner . . . looked like a million dollars as he flashed across the finish line abreast of Dilks. He was breathing without apparent effort and looked fresh enough to run another thirty miles."[43]

Lost in the pack came Andy Payne, who was in a very bad way. Days of high-altitude running under brutal conditions had reduced his resistance to infection. He had suffered a sudden and violent case of tonsillitis that threatened to become diphtheria, an acute bacterial infection of the respiratory tract which would have made breathing difficult and forced him out of the contest.[44] If Payne hoped to remain in the race, his trainer, Tom Young, needed to use every ounce of his skills to shepherd him through the next few days. In the course of two days, the second- and first-place holders were both in danger of dropping out of the derby, renewing hopes of the twenty-five-thousand-dollar and ten-thousand-dollar awards for the rest of the men. Race leaders Arne Souminen and Peter Gavuzzi smelled blood.

In camp that night, the grumbling over Charley Pyle's poor treatment of his men found a voice in Paul Rodeta, a trainer for some of the Finnish runners. He was tired of watching his men endure bad food and stinking sheets. Rodeta set about trying to organize his fellow trainers to collectively demand change. The director general caught wind of the meeting, however, quickly branded Rodeta a troublemaker, and bullied him into submission by threatening to disqualify all of his runners if he did not back down. The browbeaten Rodeta complied and the derby temporarily went on as before. But frustrations continued while C. C. Pyle traveled in his palatial bus, stayed in the best hotels, and dined in white-linen restaurants.[45]

Only well-financed contestants like the millionaire's son Harry Gunn, and others like Phillip Granville, Eddie Gardner, and Andy Payne, could escape Charley's inhospitality. These fortunate few could afford to stay in local hotels far from the noise and filth of Pyle's tent city. They could also afford to eat in local diners or buy food in sufficient quantities to meet the tremendous calorie needs of a transcontinental runner. The vast majority of the bunioneers, however, had to sleep in drafty tents and survive on Pyle's meager food allowance that left many scrounging for food from local citizens. The derby had become a race of haves and have-nots, and it was decidedly unpleasant to be the latter.

Man Down

DAY 16, 99 MEN

Monday, March 19, 1928. As the sun rose on the sixteenth day, a false calm settled over the derby: Arthur Newton and Andy Payne were ailing but still in the race, while Charley Pyle papered over his incompetence with threats and intimidation. The sixteenth stage would be an abbreviated twenty-four mile course, the shortest since opening day. It took the men to warmer temperatures and lower altitudes in Winslow, a town of several thousand at about 4,800 feet.[46] In two days the men had dropped more than 2,000 feet and were breathing easier.

The thicker air, however, did nothing for the fortunes of Arthur Newton, who quit the race after telling a race official, "My legs are gone. I know that it will be impossible for me to continue."[47] His strained Achilles tendon had forced him to overwork his uninjured leg. He said it had bothered him for months before the race, and the derby physician who examined him in Los Angeles had warned him his tendon would last only a week or so under the intense strain. The South African had started the race anyway, crossing his fingers and hoping the doctor's analysis was wrong.[48] The extreme terrain had simply pushed his middle-aged body too far. As Paul Lowry of the *Los Angeles Times* wrote, "Newton had the experience, fortitude, and the will to conquer the 3,400-mile trail. But he didn't have the legs. His years were against him."[49]

Far from being crushed by the experience, however, Arthur relished the chance to see America by foot and remain with the bunioneers. He wrote, "I live in the middle of the cheeriest bunch of men it has ever been my good fortune to meet. [These men] are the cream of the world's finest distance runners, [and] that alone is enough to make any man realize that Mr. Pyle and Mr. Grange were doing their country a very good turn when they engineered the event."[50] Pyle hired Newton as an advisor to the bunioneers he had led so brilliantly since the Mojave. The South African would be a teacher and friend to the derby men, as he tried to shepherd them across the country.[51]

With Arthur out of the race, the press would need a new hero. Andy Payne fit the bill—young, unassuming, resolute—but he was close to dropping out of the derby with tonsillitis. His brief reign as the derby leader hung by a one-hour thread after he struggled into Winslow in twelfth place.[52]

The meltdown among the leaders confirmed what many observers had always thought: Those in the front could not stand the strain of daily running, and the men who shuffled through the course, often long after dark, would collect the prize money in New York. Henry Gunn held tenaciously to that view. He prided himself on having walked the entire way, "without a blister or a skin abrasion," accompanied by a racing team headed by his millionaire father. Though more than a day behind the runners in elapsed time, Harry believed his walking pace and stringent foot care would spell eventual victory.[53]

The next day, leader Andy Payne promptly lost his new status to Arne Souminen on a thirty-five-mile race to Holbrook. Payne sweated, shivered, and stumbled into town, herded by his trainer. He looked so bad that the officials scrubbed his name from the leader board on the belief he could not continue, but Andy was determine to remain, and said, "[I'm] just going to keep stepping along for the time being."[54]

Guisto Umek, the walker champion from Italy, was also questionable, after suffering stomach problems that forced him temporarily to drop out six miles from Holbrook.[55] Even Red Grange joined the sick list with a severe case of tonsillitis. He was taken to the hospital tent

and placed under the care of the derby physician. Running a temperature of 102 degrees, he was forbidden to take part in the derby activities.[56] Despite the epidemic of bronchial infections, only three men gave
up the grind that day, including fifty-year-old Harold Johnson, a black
runner from Detroit, who had had a colorful career as a cowboy and
stunt actor in Hollywood.[57]

On Wednesday, Eddie "the Sheik" Gardner led the men to win the
forty-one-mile race to Navajo in six hours and forty-one minutes, with
a pace of just under ten minutes per mile.[58] The group ran through
the Painted Desert, a palette of soils and rocks—blue, chocolate, rose,
purple—before arriving at the railway settlement and supply post of
Navajo, Arizona.[59] Eddie's win did little, however, to stem his fall from
contention. He remained in seventh, more than thirteen hours behind
leader Arne Souminen.[60] Along the way, two more runners dropped out,
including Chicago's Guicomo Clarizo who had come under suspicion
for hitching rides. Red Grange had had his eye on Clarizo after he finished several recent races in unusually fast times. "[He] raised considerable protest when he learned that a derby patrol car had been assigned
to follow him and trace his movements," and apparently quit the race
shortly thereafter, leaving ninety-six still in the running.[61]

On March 22, the Sheik again led the bunioneers, taking them close
to the New Mexico border and back into thinner air at 6,200 feet above
sea level. They left the high desert behind them and returned to scrub
pine forest near the tiny railroad town of Lupton, the last spot of any consequence before New Mexico, at the southeastern corner of the Navajo
Indian Nation.[62] Gardner won his second consecutive stage victory in
a tie with the Denver baker Seth Gonzales. In two days, the Sheik had
jumped from seventh to fifth place in the cumulative standings, though
he was still twelve hours behind Arne Souminen.[63]

After two consecutive stage wins, some in the press thought Eddie
had finally come of age, ready to assume his rightful place among the
leaders. He certainly had the look of a champion: a beautiful flowing
form that caught the eye of the public wherever he ran. But his problem
had always been inconsistent performance. For weeks, many observers
blamed his trainers for allowing him to fall into the pattern of a brilliant
stage win followed by a day or two of disastrous shuffling as he fought
to recover strength.

One of Pyle's lieutenants claimed, "It looks like to me as if [Gardner] has too many advisers hung on him. Too many cooks spoil the broth, you know; after all, I don't believe any of them know nearly as much what to do for him as he knows himself if let alone."[64] The Sheik knew he needed to run a more consistent pace, but he ran with the instincts of a ten-mile champion rather than a runner bent on crossing the United States. He reminded himself, "Take'r easier Eddie, you're in an endurance race this time."[65]

For now, the battle was between four men: Arne Souminen, Peter Gavuzzi, John Cronick, and the ailing Andy Payne, with only five hours separating first and third place. John Cronick was further back but still in contention, with a string of consistent finishes that left him solidly in fourth place in the cumulative standings. This twenty-five-year-old cross-country runner hailed from Saskatoon, Saskatchewan. These four men would fight for supremacy across New Mexico. For the rest of the pack, the days of losing a dozen a day had ended. A few might drop out, but the hemorrhage had stopped. Charley's boot camp had done its work and, despite all the dire predictions, some in the press began to realize that a number of these sun-scorched men might actually survive to reach New York City.

CHAPTER 9

Iron Men of the Mesas

One Last Trip to the Clouds

Day 21, 96 men

FRIDAY, MARCH 23, 1928. THE MEN CROSSED INTO NEW MEXICO FOR an eleven-day journey that offered little relief from the high-altitude and primitive road conditions of Arizona.[1] The state was vast and empty with a population of just four hundred thousand, a tenth of what the state supports today.[2] The group would run for hours without seeing a car, billboard, or other sign of human habitation, and one derby man said the sight of a freight or passenger train on distant tracks was a nice reminder that other humans did exist.[3]

The derby's first stop was twenty-three miles to the east at Gallup. At 6,300 feet, it was a prosperous little town of several thousand. The railroad made it a trading and coal mining center for the surrounding area. It was known as the Indian capital of the United States, since members of many Indian nations including Zuni, Navajo, and Hopi came for supplies and to ship handcrafted wares.[4]

For the first time in days, crowds appeared to watch the derby men. They applauded wildly when stage winner Nestor Erickson crossed the line. As the derby left Gallup, an editorial in the *Gallup Independent* described the race as a "highly enjoyable event . . . undistinguished by color, caste, or creed in which physical endurance alone will win."[5] However, there was at least one dissenter. An unknown writer warned the mayor of Albuquerque, "Tie down the sidewalks and nail down the First National Bank, as [Pyle's men] steal anything that is not nailed down." This information appeared in the *Albuquerque Journal* and caused two New Mexico counties, Gallup and McKinley, to ban the bunion derby carnival from operating there. Rumors flew that the bunioneers were little better than a band of thieves, and that towns that hosted them did so at their peril. These rumors may have been spawned by the activities of some of Pyle's carnival workers.[6] Poorly paid and often of less than stellar moral character, they may have done a bit of pilfering to pad their meager wages.

Outside New Mexico, press reports about the transcontinental race were generally favorable. With Arthur Newton gone, attention focused on Andy Payne, Peter Gavuzzi, and Arne Souminen. Andy Payne's curly black hair, boyish good looks, and quiet, unassuming, and businesslike approach to running across America endeared him to the sports world and made him breakfast reading in every newspaper in Oklahoma. Peter Gavuzzi "was developing a flair and flamboyance that the organizers were heartily glad to see. . . . [He had] sewn the Union Jack on his running vest, and grew a rapidly lengthening beard, which gave his light frame a buccaneering hardiness."[7] His trainer, Charley Hart, followed him in a donated car with their nation's flag tied across the trunk. This growing Gavuzzi-Payne rivalry was building into something newsworthy: an American against the Brit sports story that newspapers loved to follow.[8]

And Arne Souminen, the middle-aged doctor, was leading the group across the country. Quiet and business-like, this methodical man was outrunning others half his age. As befitting a well organized physician, he had trained methodically for six months before entering the race.

News of the men had also filtered north of the border to Canada. In Hamilton, Ontario, the mayor had his secretary wire Hamilton runner Phillip Granville a congratulatory message on his "plucky exhibition." Granville had made a slow rise to eighth place after being well back in the pack for many days. The mayor thanked him for the favorable publicity he had brought Hamilton, and gushed that a win for the local star would be wonderful for the city.[9]

Back in the pack, far from the public eye, the lesser known men had learned to pace themselves. For the first time in twenty days of racing, none of the ninety-six starters dropped out.[10] Most of these road-tested men had given up hope of winning prize money, but they carried on anyway, happy to be in a brotherhood of strong and committed men. During a stage race, many would stop for a swim in an inviting lake or river if the opportunity presented itself; others brought fishing tackle and tried their hands at angling; and one man, Mike Kelly, became adept at catching naps in the arches of bridges during races, earning him the nickname "bridge sleeper." Some of the men even adopted stray dogs along the way. Johnny Salo had found a collie he nicknamed "Shin Splints," and another man christened a stray German shepherd "Blisters."[11]

The next morning, dogs in tow, the men made one last trip into the clouds. They would achieve the sky-high continental divide at 7,200 feet—the symbolic backbone of the United States—where waters to the east flow to the Rio Grande and those to the west to the Colorado.[12] These hardened men seemed to take the 1,200-foot climb in stride; they had reached the top of the world, the beginning of the end of their high-altitude suffering. They began their grand ascent past great red sand cliffs, then passed through a forest of scrub pine before reaching the control point at the tiny town of Thoreau, five miles east of the divide. It had been named for author Henry David Thoreau, but for convenience the townspeople pronounced the name as "threw."[13]

The first runner to reach Thoreau was Peter Gavuzzi, who blazed through the course in about four and a half hours at the breathtaking pace, by derby standards, of roughly eight and a half minutes per mile. No one still in the derby had run that fast for days, and he did it in the teeth of an exhausting climb. Race observers must have wondered about the sanity of Peter and his trainer Charley Hart—had the Englishman found hidden reserves of power, or had his judgment vanished in the thin air? Whatever the reason, he had come within an hour of second-place holder Andy Payne, and was just four hours behind leader Arne Souminen.

For the remaining placeholders in prize-money spots, prairie-born John Cronick of Canada had a comfortable hold on fourth, with a five-hour lead over the rest of the field. A real battle was brewing for the remaining spots, with just two hours separating fifth through ninth. Dwight Houfstater, a twenty-seven-year-old cross-country runner from Michigan, held fifth; Nestor Erickson, sixth; Eddie Gardner, seventh; Phillip Granville, eighth; and Johnny Salo, ninth.[14] The race was far from decided. The days of hill work were over. These men had developed stamina and fortitude. They were about to see what they would do on easier ground.

A One-Man Machine

DAY 22, 96 MEN

Tuesday, March 25, 1928. The bunioneers had their first taste of extensive downhill running on day twenty-two, losing six hundred feet of altitude in thirty miles. They would finish at Grants—known by the Indians as Nahto-Si-Ka'i, the place of friendly smoke—which had been the site of a treaty signing between Kit Carson and the Indian Chief Manuelito.[15]

In 1928, Grants was a sleepy highway town of several thousand that woke to Peter Gavuzzi creating his own smoke by blazing into town almost thirty minutes ahead of the next finisher. This was his second day of what seemed a mad assault to recapture first place for the honor of Britain, and he did it in frightening style, covering thirty miles in three hours and fifty minutes. This translated into seven and a half minutes per mile—something new and breathtaking, alarming to the walkers, and horrific to the other front-runners who had been keeping the pace in the nine- to ten-minute range. No one had seen this speed since the early days of the race when long-departed Willie Kolehmainen led the pack. The Englishman had raised the bar, pushing both Andy Payne and Arne Souminen to race faster. They did not try to keep up with him, but they did increase speed to the eight-and-a-half-minute range. They wanted to shadow Peter, and hoped he would soon burn himself out or come to his senses.[16]

The downhill continued the next day as the men lost another seven hundred feet through the Malpais, or "the evil country," an area where hardened black lava bordered either side of the highway.[17] In this tortured place, a howling wind kicked up a sandstorm, obscuring deserted pueblos and legendary lost treasures and bandit hideouts tucked into the hills. Happily for the other leaders, Peter Gavuzzi did abandon his suicidal pace, finishing thirty minutes behind Eddie Gardner.[18]

On the twenty-fourth day of the derby, the men descended another nine hundred feet to the Rio Grande at Los Lunas. By the afternoon, gale-force winds had created a series of desert sandstorms, making running dangerous as the visibility dropped to almost zero on Route 66. The derby officials flagged down cars and asked them to be cautious with the men on the road.[19] The Sheik had a terrible time with the storms, and said, "I walked six hours with both hands beside my face for protection from the sand, and I was lost off the road for about forty minutes."[20] He lost another six hours on the frontrunner, putting him twenty-two hours out of first place and eighth overall.[21] Peter Gavuzzi seemed to have avoided the worst of the storms, covering the distance in a nine-minute pace, and bumping Andy Payne out of second by about twenty minutes.[22] With ease, this one-man machine had taken on the continental divide and beat his competitors, despite thin air and sandstorms.

No Welcome Mat in Albuquerque

DAY 25, 96 MEN

Wednesday, March 28, 1928. It should have been a great day for the derby as it rolled into Albuquerque, the largest town since Los Angeles after more than three weeks of racing. But things did not work out as planned.

Albuquerque had always been a safe and respectable merchants' town. The sheriff had thrown Billy the Kid into jail when he paid a visit,[23] and the city didn't treat Charley Pyle or his men much better. Five days before the derby's scheduled arrival, Pyle sent his sixty-man carnival and concessions ahead to Albuquerque, where he hoped to earn much-needed cash from its twenty-six thousand inhabitants. When they arrived, however, town and county officials told them Charley's carnival could not operate in Albuquerque or anywhere else in the county.

Mayor Clyde Tingley claimed that city officials in Gallup had run the derby out of town—a claim contradicted by reports in the Gallup newspapers. He also said a phone call to Holbrook, Arizona, revealed that twenty-one house burglaries had occurred during the derby's stay.[24] Pyle fervently denied theses allegations, but the mayor's mind was made up. Mayor Tingley had the police threaten to arrest Charley's men if they tried to sell derby programs in town.[25] To make matters worse, two of the derby's alleged "advance men" were arrested after spending the night in the Craig Hotel and sneaking out a rear window when the bill came due. In court statements after their arrest, it turned out the two had quit the derby in Holbrook and arrived in Albuquerque unemployed.[26] This incident helped to raise suspicions about Pyle's transcontinental race.

True or not, the mayor's comments poisoned C. C. Pyle's reputation with the local business community. Albuquerque's chamber of commerce rejected Pyle's request for a two-thousand-dollar contribution to bring his racers to town. The chamber conveniently forgot that Charley Pyle had agreed to organize the race at the bidding of the Route 66 Association, with the explicit understanding that major towns along the route would contribute funds.

Perhaps the mayor was trying to get some political mileage out of this confrontation with Pyle—the stalwart mayor protecting the townsfolk from Charley's evil hordes. Mayor Tingley did have aspirations for higher political office. In 1935, he was elected governor of New Mexico, running on a "good roads" platform. When Tingley was sworn in, Route 66 was still mostly dirt and gravel. By December 1937, New Mexico's portion of the route was completely paved and the winding stretch between Grants and Santa Rosa straightened, cutting ninety-six miles off the journey.[27]

Charley was indignant over his treatment in Albuquerque. He detoured around the city, and took the men another fourteen miles up the Tijeras Canyon to an isolated camp at Seven Springs. In these early days of Route 66, Model-T Fords often overheated on the canyon climb and drivers nursed their cars to Seven Springs, where they scooped up spring water to cool their engines.[28] Charley was also boiling, but with rage—he had counted on income from the carnival and from Albuquerque's contribution. Instead, he left the city with his reputation in tatters and a pile of unpaid bills, as massive crowds lined the road, watching the show for free.

As for the race itself, the wind continued its assault, blasting the men with grit and sand all the way to the finish. The derby crew managed to erect five tents at Seven Springs, but three blew down within ten minutes. Charley abandoned his men and spent the night in an

Albuquerque hotel while his exhausted athletes carried their bedding to a local inn and slept on the floor.[29]

Eddie Gardner seemed immune to the gale after recovering from the previous day's disastrous run through desert sandstorms. He tied for first in the thirty-nine-mile race with tiny California lifeguard Henry Rea. People along the route were impressed by the Sheik. "Are you Gardner?" someone yelled as he passed a church corner in the town of San Jose. Eddie lifted one arm slightly, wasting almost no energy on the acknowledgment. He covered the course in just over five and a half hours—another amazing performance that moved him back into seventh in the cumulative standings. Arne Souminen, Peter Gavuzzi, and Andy Payne kept their first-through-third positions.[30]

Within the top ten, Johnny Salo seemed in the most dire straits. Without a trainer or money, he was forced to rely on Charley's food and lodging. In Albuquerque, he went to the local American Legion Post and asked for help.[31] Since he had served as a sailor during the war, the legion took him under its wing.[32] The Albuquerque post wired its counterpart in Johnny's hometown of Passaic, New Jersey, and he soon had himself a trainer, an escort car, and some pocket money. Granville's manager said, "Salo is the best man in the race, and if he had had a manager or trainer in the early stages of the grind, he would have been well in front by now."[33] Phillip added, "Salo had very poor attention at the start and it was not until the American Legion took charge of him that he began to show his true wares."[34]

Others were not so lucky. The derby lost two men on the way to Seven Springs: Italian Louis Alfano "decided the grind was too strenuous" after completing the brutal climb to the finish; and Frank Johnson, a steel worker from Granite City, Illinois, was an experienced marathon racer but no match for an angry spouse.[35] At camp, he received a telegram from his wife ordering him to return home. Johnson showed the note to the referee, and said, "Those are my wife's orders to hurry home, and I dare not refuse."[36]

Many who remained in the race were in tough shape. The bunioneers were a weary-looking lot with leather-brown tans, unruly beards, and sweat-stained clothes. Some barely had enough remaining shoe to cover their feet, others were heavily bandaged, and "some were so lame that they could hardly go at all."[37] One concerned citizen wrote

Figure 9. Left to right, Johnny Salo, #107, wearing his American Legion cap, and Eddie Gardner, #165. Credit: El Reno Carnegie Library.

to the *New Mexico State Tribune*, "I would like to see the race called off as unfair and inhuman and Pyle forced to pay the men in part for the misery he has caused them." Another added, "I cannot believe that Pyle could have got the runners to start if they had known how they would be treated."[38]

In fairness, the men were often their own worst enemies. Few had trained properly or brought enough clothing to get them through the trans-America race.[39] They were free to drop out whenever they wished. Charley did keep his word on some issues: His race officials drove the course to care for the men as best they could. The Maxwell House coffee truck served coffee, drinks, and sandwiches to the men; the traveling cobbler did his best to kept the men in shoes; and the physician tried to keep them healthy, but Pyle's promises of hot showers, wholesome food, warm sleeping quarters, and clothing were unkept. The men survived as best they could, begging, borrowing, or stealing additional food to keep them going and enduring Pyle's drafty tents and unwashed sheets.

This begs the question: Why did the men persevere? O. B. Harrison of St. Louis, Missouri, said the only way he would quit "is if they pick me up dead." He added, "I am in it to stay and I really believe I have a chance."[40] And Barry Richman, one of the three New York brothers, said the derby gave the men a chance to test themselves. "Every man who finishes such a race is a winner," he said. "He has shown strength of heart and purpose, which should uplift him with pride and uplift his children after him."[41] In short, each man had invested a piece of his soul in the race. The bunioneers had pushed themselves to the limits of human endurance in the company of tough and committed men, and they simply wanted to see the thing through to the end. As the first and second verses of the little derby poem "More Power to Barnum" said,

> Across the far flung nation,
> The bunion clan is sprinting,
> Toward that distant station,
> With energy unstinting,
> Though blistered dogs are aching,
> And tongues are dry like dust,
> The gang is bent on making
> the journey's end—or bust![42]

A Discontented Band

DAY 26, 94 MEN

Thursday, March 29, 1928. The dawn greeted the survivors with another
bout of freezing winds as they followed a winding road back into thin air
to seven thousand feet before making a long downhill run to Moriarty, a
small railroad town.[43] Arne Souminen won the stage and added another
forty minutes to his lead over Andy Payne and Peter Gavuzzi, who finished in a fourth-place tie.[44] Peter would shadow Andy across the rest of
the state, apparently content to let Arne build his lead. The Englishman
seemed to have made a conscious decision that his real competition
was the young, talented, and well-coached Andy Payne, and that Arne
Souminen, a man in his forties, was too old to hold on for long.

That night in camp, there was more discontent about Pyle's treatment
of his racers. Trainer Alex Finn confronted him about the filthy sleeping
accommodations. After the disaster in Albuquerque, Charley Pyle was in
no mood to hear Finn's complaints. From the comfort of his "land yacht,"
the director general snapped that he was in charge of the race, and had his
referee ban both Finn and his wife from the race. (Mrs. Finn worked as a
nurse in the hospital tent.) The embittered trainer complained to the *New
Mexico State Tribune* that he had spent three hundred dollars on food and
lodgings for his men because "both were sub-standard," adding that if
Pyle offered him ten thousand dollars to run in the race he would refuse,
"because I know the conditions the men are up against." Finn maintained
that Charley had no authority to dismiss him, but decided to withdraw in
fear the director would find an excuse to disqualify his runners.[45]

From Moriarty, the men climbed to about seven thousand feet before
dropping in a series of rolling prairie hills to the tiny town of Palma, set
among juniper and piñon trees at six thousand feet. Arne Souminen
extended his lead to more than five hours with another stage win, while
Andy Payne and Peter Gavuzzi waltzed along together in sixth place.[46]

On the last day of March, the men followed an "impassable desert
road" down a long grade to Santa Rosa at 4,500 feet, forty-five miles
to the east. The town had a population of several thousand, mostly of
Spanish descent. Here, the bunioneers entered the *llano*—the Spanish
word for plain—a vast prairie that stretched to the eastern horizon.[47]

Payne and Gavuzzi finished in a first-place tie in about seven hours,
while Souminen followed nineteen minutes behind. The rest of the field

had fallen hours behind them, with John Cronick locked in fourth and Dwight Houfstater, Johnny Salo, Phillip Granville, and Eddie Gardner bunched together in a struggle for fifth through eighth. Among these five, the press took great interest in Phillip Granville, the walking champion who had switched to running in the Mojave. Braven Dyer of the *Los Angeles Times* wrote that Granville, "with his relentless machine-like strides is, to us, the outstanding marathoner left in the great Bunion Derby." Phillip's coach and business manager W. J. Westcott added to expectations when he claimed that his man planned to hold back until Chicago before displaying his true speed and power.[48]

On April Fool's Day, the derby continued across the llano to the tiny railroad town of Newkirk.[49] Eddie Gardner led the way with an eight-and-a-half-minute-mile pace for thirty-two miles, vaulting him from eighth to sixth in the cumulative standings.[50] Despite being hours behind the frontrunners, Eddie remained hopeful. "I'll be in the finish," he said. "I'm in fine shape and the [daily] jaunts are no more than what I took in Seattle where I jogged around Lake Washington every day."[51]

Tucumcari to the Texas Border

DAY 30, 93 MEN

Monday, April 2, 1928. From Newkirk at about 4,300 feet, the derby headed for Tucumcari at the eastern edge of the great plain. Just out of town, the men crossed the Goodnight Trail where cowboys once drove herds of cattle from the grasslands of Texas and New Mexico to northern markets.[52] Tucumcari was named for the nearby mountains, whose jagged peaks were used by Comanche warriors to send smoke signals, once upon a time.[53]

Local fans were thrilled to see New Mexico-born Seth Gonzales finish their stage in first place. He flew through the thirty-four miles in just under four and a half hours. Seth was raised on his parents' ranch in nearby Harding County, though he now lived in Denver. The *Tucumcari American* called him "a gentleman, and loyal friend of the state." Though he was in forty-second place in the cumulative standings, Seth revealed amazing speed when he ran in his home state at under eight minutes per mile.[54] This was almost twice as fast as the fourteen-minute-mile pace he had averaged over the course of the race.

With Gonzales as the favorite son, Charley Pyle finally found a sympathetic venue for his derby. The local Kiwanis Club raised and paid the guarantee, as Charley requested. Reporter Cal Farley of the *Amarillo Daily News* questioned him about reports that his derby had done some salvaging in the towns they passed through. Charley joked, "Yes, we are having considerable trouble with Red; he seems to try to steal everything that is loose." Pyle then produced six letters from various chambers of commerce secretaries, stating that there "had been no trouble whatsoever from the sore-feet squad in their towns."[55]

The stage race to Tucumcari left the standings among the frontrunners unchanged, though many local sportswriters seemed convinced Andy Payne would be the eventual winner.[56] Eddie Gardner was back on his roller-coaster schedule, finishing well back but managing to retain sixth place overall.[57] A local reporter believed his erratic performance was due to his feet, which were too large and "detracted from the appearance of a finished runner."[58] The local press also ridiculed another black, Sammy Robinson, saying he ran as if he had a bad case of "hoof rot" and described young fifteen-year-old T. Joseph Cotton as a "picaninny" with an infectious smile.[59] This racist reporting was a warning that the derby was approaching Texas, where rigid segregation was the law of the land and there was great resistance to whites and blacks competing together. On a happier note, former derby runner Walter Ricketts of Southampton, Ontario, paid the men a visit on his way home after recovering in Los Angeles from seven broken ribs he received from the drunken driver in the Mojave.[60]

After Tucumcari, the men may have thought the worst was over. They had left the desert and mountains and entered the western edge of the staked plains, a place so flat that local legend claims early pioneers drove stakes into the ground to keep them on course. In the frontier days, many "pioneers had died here from thirst and Indian arrows."[61] And there was still danger in the air. In 1928, Route 66 between Tucumcari and the Texas state line was narrow and pockmarked with holes. In some stretches, there was no center strip and scores of people had died in car accidents.[62] One saying went, "There was only a few inches and a cigarette paper between you and death." True to the road's reputation, one of Charley's baggage trucks caught fire on the way out of town and sent a plume of billowing smoke high into the air.[63]

Troubled by the sight, the ninety-three men ran wearily to the tiny border town of Glen Rio. Two men dropped out there: Carl Swenson of Los Angeles with stomach trouble; and Mike Galena of Palm Beach, Florida, from a "general breakdown."[64] Among the frontrunners, little had changed. Each had a solid grip on his respective position: Arne Souminen in first, Andy Payne in second, and Peter Gavuzzi in third, with a yawning fifteen-hour gap separating them from the rest of the pack.

Eddie Gardner was the first to reach the border, putting in another of his patented first-place victories by covering the forty-four miles in just over six hours—an eight-and-a-half-minute-mile pace.[65] His performance bounced him once again from eighth to fifth, though he was still twenty-six hours out of first. At the same time, though, he was struggling in other ways as the derby knocked on the door of the Old South. Fans in eastern New Mexico began to yell racial slurs and threats at the

Figure 10. Racecar legend Barney Oldfield, unidentified woman, and Red Grange, circa 1926. Credit: Red Grange Collection, Special Collections, Wheaton College (IL).

black runners, for they were violating basic pre-civil rights tenants of behavior.[66] First, blacks and whites did not compete against each other; second, they did not live together as equals; and third, blacks did not beat whites in sporting events. Eddie Gardner broke all these rules—the Sheik and his fellow blacks were on a collision course with Jim Crow segregation in Texas.

In Glen Rio, Barney Oldfield, the greatest racecar driver of his age, met the derby as he was driving from Los Angeles to New York in his custom-built Hudson touring car. He was amazed by the strangeness of these racers. "I've never seen so many queer looking men in my life," Oldfield said. "Some of them don't wear anything but a loincloth, others have on long underwear or pajamas, and still others are bundled up with heavy clothing." He added, "I'm here to say it's a motley crew. Amarillo [Texas] or the country has never seen anything like it."[67]

Pyle's "motley crew" was about to embark on a six-day sojourn across the Texas Panhandle, a land blessed with oil and gas reserves, wheat farms, and cattle ranches.[68] In 1928, the panhandle was bursting with wealth that just might turn Charley Pyle's meager fortunes around. For the derby's black runners, however, it turned out to be a place of hate and fear—this land of milk and honey was meant for whites only.

CHAPTER 10

The Meaning of Courage

IN 1928, TEXAS HAD A LARGE BLACK UNDERCLASS OF 15 PERCENT of the state's six million citizens.[1] Before the Civil War, most blacks had worked as slaves on the coast and as field hands in river valleys growing corn, cotton, and sugar cane.[2] After the war, black units of the U.S. Army—buffalo soldiers—sweated and died protecting the Texas frontier. They built roads, escorted wagon train and cattle drives, strung telegraph wire, and patrolled against Indian raiders and Mexican and Anglo bandits.[3]

These contributions were forgotten as segregation locked black southerners into a permanent underclass. In 1909, Texas state law mandated segregated waiting rooms at railroad stations. A few years later segregated schools, libraries, pools, and restrooms became the law. In 1919, the white executive secretary of the National Association for the Advancement of Colored People (NAACP) arrived in Austin to defend the establishment of Texas chapters, where a police officer and a county judge beat him into unconsciousness. No arrests were made, and the governor of Texas publicly condoned the attack.[4] In the 1920s, Texans elected klansman Earl B. Mayfield to the U.S. Senate, and the Ku Klux

Klan dominated the Texas state legislature and the city governments of Dallas, Fort Worth, and El Paso.[5]

When the Sheik of Seattle led the bunion parade to the gates of the South, the alarm bells rang. All across the state, black runners were harassed and intimidated by white fans. A reporter from the black newspaper the *Amsterdam News* wrote, "When the crackers (white bigots) told them to scoot, they had to scoot—or else."[6] The Sheik's trainer, George Curtis, said, "We have accepted every shameful condition with silence because we knew that the main point of the great game was to stay in and win."[7]

When the men crossed into Texas, the black runners had to abandon the communal quarters and sleep in a "colored only" tent. Foreign contestants, unfamiliar with American society, thought, at first, that all the blacks had dropped out when they did not sleep in the tent that night. George Curtis said the international athletes were appalled by this enforced segregation, calling it "the most disgraceful thing they ever knew anything about."[8] No mainstream, white newspapers mentioned the appalling racism endured by the black bunioneers. The job of reporting the abuse was left to the black press—the *Black Dispatch*, *Chicago Defender*, *Pittsburgh Courier*, and *California Eagle*.

Weather

DAY 32

Wednesday, April 4, 1928. In the panhandle, spring storms come up quickly; days can begin warm and sunny but end in a violent gush of arctic air that collides with clouds from the Gulf of Mexico. In this scenario, temperatures plunge and dust swirls in the grasslands before rain turns the land to mud.[9] Such a storm—a blue norther—was brewing as the men lined up for the start in Glen Rio, half of them in New Mexico, the other half in Texas. By nightfall, dust had blocked the moonlight at the finish line in the little prairie town of Vega, thirty-seven miles to the east.[10] Someone offered five hundred dollars to the first man to cross the finish.[11] Peter Gavuzzi, who smoked a pack of cigarettes along the way, collected the money when he won the stage race in five hours and fifteen minutes, followed by Olli Wanttinen, Arne Souminen, and Andy Payne.[12] The race remained a three-way show between Souminen,

Payne, and Gavuzzi, with nineteen hours separating them from the rest of the field.

Eddie Gardner had a terrible time in the panhandle. After his victory in Glen Rio, he stumbled through the course with thirteen-minute miles and dropped to sixth place overall. This time, though, he did not return to win other races in Texas. He finished behind the frontrunners during the entire six-day crossing, intimidated by death threats and other abuses by racist whites. Gardner felt the full force of Jim Crow segregation. Texas would be his testing ground, his "time in the wilderness," where he had to decide if winning the bunion derby was worth death or injury.[13]

The next day the weather was even worse—the thirty-third stage in the derby would be seared into the memories of the remaining ninety bunioneers. At the start, clouds hung low on the horizon and a wind peppered snow across the plains.[14] At first, this seemed a welcome change for the runners because it calmed the dust clouds that had engulfed them the day before. Soon, however, it turned to sleet and rain, and the road surface turned into ankle-deep, tendon-ripping mud. Andy Payne called it the worst of the entire derby, eclipsing even the days in the Mojave.[15] Johnny Salo agreed, saying the hardest stretch was in Texas, "where the clay stuck to the soles of [our] feet and made [our] feet weigh like lead."[16] Eddie Gardner, harassed by mud and hostile fans alike, said, "The snow storm the day we made Amarillo was the worst [of the derby]. The cold tightened up a fellow's muscles, you know. I had to walk all the way that day."[17]

The only saving grace was that the last half of the course was paved, which was a reprieve from the mud and allowed thousands of motorists to watch the epic struggle of men fighting their way to the finish.[18] The caravan of fans waved and greeted the runners, except for the blacks who they singled out for abuse.[19]

The winner of the day's race was a dark horse: Patrick De Marr, a lightweight boxer who typically finished far back in the pack. During the first few days of the race, he wore ill-fitting shoes that cut his feet to shreds. Advised by doctors to drop out, he instead found two canes and hobbled along until his feet calloused over near Holbrook, Arizona, where he celebrated with a trip to the Holbrook dance hall.[20] From then on he had been advancing in the standings. Despite his heroics, Patrick De Marr would later be disqualified for accepting a ride in Missouri. De

Marr said, "It was pretty tough going, but I guess that I go along equally well on good roads and bad." Johnny Salo, one of the toughest men in the race, finished a half hour behind him in just under six hours.[21]

Andy Payne survived with a third-place finish ahead of both Arne Souminen in fifth and Peter Gavuzzi in eighth.[22] Arthur Duffy, the derby's head referee, predicted Andy Payne would win the derby. Duffy said, "[He] seems to be developing none of the physical troubles that other men have and with his mental attitude, he seems to get stronger as the days go by."[23] Payne also received moral support in Texas.[24] Joining him in Amarillo was his father and namesake, a seventy-year-old, twinkle-eyed hill farmer. Andy Sr. knew how to spin a phrase, saying he planned "to stick by that boy of mine until he trots into New York as the winner of the whole outfit." Before the race, Andy Sr. had thought his son's derby plan was not even "good foolishness," but he now had changed his tune.[25]

Others fared badly. The day's muddy road claimed David Davies from Ontario, Canada, who dropped out with a stomach aliment along with a second, unidentified man. Another six competitors temporarily dropped out and were picked up by patrol cars. They planned to make up the distance the next day.[26] The derby almost lost Frank Chavez from Pasadena, California. After he finished the stage, Frank decided to have some fun, and turned an ankle dancing at the VFW Charity Dance. His fate caused the rest of men to avoid the dance floor—once a popular place for the bunioneers to relax—for the remainder of the race to New York.[27]

Amarillo by Charley

DAY 33, 90 MEN

Thursday, April 5, 1928. Amarillo was a rich city of forty thousand, the capital of the booming oil and gas industry, the cattle trade, and a railroad-shipping center.[28] It had several grand hotels and citizens with extra cash in their pockets—prime territory for Charley Pyle and his derby show. The director general had big plans for Amarillo. He brought his portable radio station two days early and began broadcasting news of the race.[29]

Pyle choreographed the day carefully, proclaiming that his Amarillo show would be bigger and better than even the famous circus promoter

Barnum could have dreamed. His men would finish in the stadium, shortly before the start of a baseball game between a traveling team from the religious cult, the House of David, and a local team. Red Grange would serve as the celebrity umpire and announce the arrival of derby men over the loud speaker. Local businesses planned to observe a half-day holiday, and fans from throughout the panhandle were preparing to attend the game. Finally, the VFW would host the bunioneers at a charity dance—where Frank Chavez later twisted an ankle—and a football signed by Red Grange and the runners would be auctioned off.[30]

The day began well with a derby parade, the two massive buses and Maxwell House coffee truck leading the way. The hype and excitement were building, until a storm washed it away. Rain forced the cancellation of the baseball game and most of the planned ceremonies, leaving a local reporter to write, "Thus what was promised for the city as a gala sports event bowed to the weather gods in favor of the growing wheat crop."[31]

The day was bad for the derby men, too, when Pyle arranged "housing" in unheated and drafty Rock Island Railroad freight cars on a rail line next to the ballpark in the midst of a howling gale.[32] The lucky ones found lodging in barns, post offices, and jails, since any accommodation would be better than Charley's boxcar hotel.[33] Pyle's choice of boxcars points to either an appalling lack of involvement or disinterest in the welfare of his racers.

Few in the press, though, seemed concerned about Charley's treatment of his men. One reporter described the director general as a man "with twinkling gray eyes who immediately takes you in the warmth of his greeting and general good fellowship."[34] Nina Martin of the *Amarillo Globe* may have gotten a more accurate reading of his eyes, which she said "can be very hardboiled." She was taken in, instead, by Red Grange. Martin wrote, "Of course there were other men around, but after the first glimpse of him, I couldn't see them."[35]

Despite the weather, Pyle and Grange announced that they planned to hold another derby the next year. With a startling level of confidence despite the disasters that had befallen him to date, Charley promised a bigger and better race in 1929.[36] Always the salesman, he claimed he could soon recoup the thirty-five thousand dollars he had spent since the derby had left the sparely populated west and would soon enter "zones of population."[37]

Wind and Rain Storms Take Heavy Toll Over Southwest

THE AMARILLO GLOBE

Price 5 Cents   AMARILLO, TEXAS, THURSDAY, APRIL 5, 1928.   TWENTY PAGES   Fifth Year, No. 48.

FIRST RUNNERS HERE

Figure 11. Headline from the April 5, 1928, edition of the *Amarillo Globe*.
Credit: *Amarillo Globe*.

Though unprofitable, the bunion derby had spawned plans for other long-distance adventures. Irving Wallace, manager of American sprinter Charlie Paddock, announced plans to hold his own one-man derby. Wallace planned to leave from Perryton, Texas, and run to Bismarck, North Dakota, in about three weeks. He hoped to challenge the winner of Charley's derby if he completed the south-to-north race.[38] In June, plans began to take shape for a north-to-south swim of the Mississippi River. Derby fever, in one form or another, was catching hold in America.[39]

Andy Takes the Reins

DAY 34, 88 MEN

Friday, April 6, 1928. Good Friday brought a temporary reprieve from the spring storms. The sun returned and quickly dried the mud to a firm-packed course that ended forty-one miles east of Amarillo at Groom.[40] The warm weather was a blessing—the black gumbo mud around Groom was famous for trapping cars when it rained, which made a lucrative business for local tow-truck drivers and innkeepers.[41] The town was a small railroad center founded in 1902, and took its name from Colonel B. B. Groom, an Englishman who started a thriving panhandle ranch.[42]

Eighty-eight aching men ran the hardened course to Groom.[43] The stage winner was tiny Olli Wanttinen, with a winning time of five and a half hours. A revived Johnny Salo, after coming under the wing of the American Legion in Arizona, finished second and moved into fourth place in the cumulative standings, replacing John Cronick. Peter Gavuzzi and Andy Payne tied for seventh, and race leader Arne Souminen finished eleventh.[44]

In Groom, the bunioneers left another three runners behind after a total of 1,200 miles. After all they had been through, losing someone now was a bit like a death in the family. The men had forged a bond of brotherhood in the desert heat of the Mojave and thin air of the Arizona high country; they had suffered bad food and drafty tents. They had burned a thousand memories on the long road to New York. Two were out with twisted ankles: Frank Chavez, who never recovered after the Amarillo dance;[45] and Andrew Grimell, who twisted his ankle on the muddy road to Amarillo. The third man, Dick Lesage of Toronto, withdrew partly due to homesickness, and partly to a nagging infected toe. He said he simply "found the distance too far."[46]

It was a hard day for several of his countrymen: Andrew Constantinoff, Russian émigré and citizen of Toronto, underwent a minor operation for a hip infection in Amarillo but planned to stay in the race; and John Cronick of Saskatoon dropped from fourth to eighth place after shin splints dramatically slowed his speed.[47]

On Saturday, spring storms returned to lash those who made the thirty-nine-mile trek to McLean, another Texas cattle town. A blizzard blasted the eighty-seven men with snow and sleet and forced them to switch from running clothes to wool sweaters and rain gear.[48] Mud stuck to the runners' shoes, weighing them down and straining already tight muscles. It was too much for Boston's Billy Busch, who lost heart and left the race; and for Minnesotan John White, who aggravated a hernia on the slippery roads.[49]

It was also too much for Arne Souminen, who had held first place for several weeks. He pulled a tendon on the muddy course, and finished long after dark. This gave hope to Andy Payne, the farm boy from Foyil, just a day's race away from setting foot on his own Oklahoma soil. Back home, he was now a household name, and one man joked that the Republicans should nominate Andy for a political office, "simply because he could run so well." In Oklahoma City, the American Legion Post held a benefit dance for him. The band called itself the "Transcontinental Southern Syncopaters." The band took 60 percent of the receipts and held the rest for Andy—a total of $17.50.[50]

Just outside of Groom, many of Pyle's trucks and cars slid off the slick road, including those carrying the tents and bedding. This forced Charley to lodge his freezing bunioneers in local hotels for the night.[51] The storm also played hell with T. Joseph Cotton's family—ten-year-old James, thirteen-year-old Wesley, and Toby Sr.—who had followed him in their old open Ford touring car. The three were pummeled with rain and mud until Wesley managed to tie an old piece of canvas over the car as a makeshift top. Toby Sr. said later, "I can not see how we came through."[52]

For T. Joseph Cotton and the other black runners, it was anything but a celebration when they arrived in McLean. Hotels wouldn't take them in, so they had to sleep where they could—some in barns, others on the floors of post offices and jails. The townspeople considered Canadian Phillip Granville a novelty: Jamaican born and light skinned, he spoke English with the crisp vowels of an upper-class Englishman. Crowds gathered just to hear him speak, but that did not save him from having to remove his hat as he entered a McLean bank, a requirement of all blacks.[53]

Eddie Gardner's trainer, George Curtis, a black man, came in for much more sinister harassment. The fact that he owned a large touring car—an item out of the price range of many of the local whites—brought some of McLean's men to an angry boil. One threatened to set Curtis's car on fire, claiming, "They ain't got no business racing niggers against white folks."[54] In another incident, Curtis was sitting in his car when a crowd of whites gathered about him. The *Black Dispatch* recorded the exchange:

> White man: "I God! Did the desert sun tan you like that?"
> Curtis: "No, I'm not tanned. This is just my color."
> White man: "Well, what nationality are you then?"
> Curtis: "I am a Negro."
> White man: "You're a damned liar. You know you ain't no niggah. What you doin' drivin' that big car . . . Take off yo' hat and I kin tell whether you're a damn niggah." (At this point Curtis tried to end the confrontation when someone snatched the hat off his head.)
> White man: "I'll declare, he is a damn niggah."
> Curtis, with defiance in his voice: "We are out to win this race."[55]

In another instance, a black hobo told Curtis how when he reached McLean, a policeman slammed him into a boxcar, locked the door, and left him there until morning because it was against the rules to house him with white prisoners in the town jail. Curtis, though Louisiana-born, had spent his adult life in Seattle where blacks were a tiny minority and racism was more subtle. Blacks attended neighborhood schools and did not face a formal color line. He was appalled when he saw hundreds of black, school-aged children without access to basic education, calling it the "most pitiable thing I have seen on this trip." Curtis left Texas more convinced than ever that despite the threats of violence, Eddie Gardner's run was worth the risk, because it gave hope to millions of his brothers and sisters in the South.[56]

Morning Has Broken

DAY 36

Sunday, April 8, 1928. On Easter, the men spent their last day in the panhandle, following a thirty-five-mile course to Texola, "a dusty collection of buildings" in Oklahoma.[57] Twenty miles toward Texola, Arne Souminen dropped out after his strained tendon failed to respond to treatment.[58] The dejected doctor was brought into town by patrol car. His middle-aged body had failed him after serving so well in the high country. With hopes of prize money gone, the derby left him only facial scars from blisters that erupted in the searing heat of the desert.[59] Another runner, the unheralded Tony Toste of Berkeley, California, was also forced out, "a victim of exhaustion."[60] The mud and snow of the panhandle had proved too much.[61]

It was a great day for Oklahoma, however, when its favorite son Andy Payne was first to cross the finish line after officially moving into first place overall after Souminen's departure. Andy received a hearty welcome, and collected a one-thousand-dollar stage prize offered to the first man to cross into the state.[62]

Rumors had flown that Eddie Gardner would make one of his pace-pushing runs to capture this prize money, and local whites threatened Eddie's trainers with violence if he finished ahead of Andy.[63] While the Sheik made his run, someone yelled, "Get Out! You better not come into town ahead of a white man." Eddie had finally had enough and shouted back, "This race is for black and white and I am in it to win if I can." A black newspaper, the *California Eagle*, reported that one old cowboy in the crowd then mounted his horse and covered Gardner's back with a shotgun, daring anyone to taunt the Sheik again.[64]

Andy Payne finished first to the thunderous applause of his happy home-state fans. "Their Andy" had returned to the red dirt of Oklahoma. Peter Gavuzzi finished fifteen minutes behind him.[65] A yawing twenty-hour gap separated Peter from third-place holder Johnny Salo and the rest of the field. Across the next three states, it would be Peter Gavuzzi versus Andy Payne. The *Los Angeles Times* wrote: "The Englishman and the Oklahoman . . . are expected to wage a hot fight for supremacy through the Sooner State."[66] The men were equally matched: Both had talent, youth, and experienced trainers. Both men had been unknown shadow runners when they came to Los Angeles, but after a boot camp of 1,500 miles across the toughest terrain on the planet, Payne and Gavuzzi were the kings of Route 66. Barring injury, no other runner could touch them.

FIGURE 12. The front runners: Andy Payne, #43, and Peter Gavuzzi, #103, on Route 66 in Oklahoma. Credit: El Reno Carnegie Library.

CHAPTER 11

Andy Land

The name *Oklahoma* comes from the Choctaw language. "Okla" means people, and "humma" means red. This place of the red people has more Native Americans than any state in the union.[1] In the 1820s, the federal government started "resettling" southern Indian tribes including the Choctaws, Cherokee, Creeks, Seminoles, and Chickasaws on large grants of land in the Oklahoma territory. The land was then designated as Indian territory and off-limits for white settlement until 1889, when the government bought tracts for white homesteaders.[2] In the first "land run," settlers would line up on horseback, in wagons, or on foot, waiting for a cannon shot that sent them racing to stake claims for free land. The temptation to sneak in a little bit sooner than the official start time inspired Oklahoma's nickname, the "Sooner State."[3]

As former Indian land was brought under the plough, towns sprang up and railroads opened lines. A mishmash of ethnic groups arrived— city slickers from the East, immigrants from Europe, former slaves, and Native Americans.[4] In 1907 Oklahoma joined the union. In the course of about forty years, Oklahoma had blossomed from empty prairie land into a colossus with a population of about 2.4 million. In 1928, farms, towns, and petroleum reserves were sprouting to nourish the nation's new love affair with cars.[5]

Andy Payne was the Oklahoma poster boy. He was one-eighth Cherokee, humble, and tough, with a quiet, unassuming attitude that hid his sharp mind. The combination was hypnotic and drew fans like ants to honey. When he lined up for the start in Texola, he looked to the crowd and simply said, "This red Oklahoma dirt looks good to me." This inspired a rousing cheer from his fellow statesmen.[6] Andy was back with his people. Towns along the route declared holidays, closed schools and businesses, and held parades when he passed through. Today's senior citizens still remember the days they stood on some forgotten stretch of old Route 66 to watch the schoolboy from Foyil pass by.

Western Oklahoma

DAY 37

Monday, April 9, 1928. While Andy was in his glory, many of the bunioneers were wishing to be anyplace but Texola in their unwashed clothes, still two thousand miles from New York City. Most of the men were destitute, relying on handouts from fans and their meager $1.50 daily food allowance. They slept in Pyle's drafty tents when they had to, but they hoped for better options. One reporter wrote, "They felt lucky if they found a jail or a garage for a night's lodging."[7] The packmen were a drain on C. C. Pyle's nearly empty bank account—he didn't need them, and he treated them like dirt, but still they carried on. The lead runners, with their trainers and support cars, had abandoned Charley's hospitality long ago.

On April 9, the bunioneers left on a thirty-two-mile run to Sayre, a farming town on the Red River, with bearded Peter Gavuzzi pacing the field to win the race with eight-and-a-half-minute miles. He cut the gap on frontrunner Andy Payne to about one and a half hours. Johnny Salo increased his hold on third place overall, and Phillip Granville further entrenched himself in fourth.[8]

The tiny town of Sayre was bursting to capacity as thousands of fans jammed the intersection of Fourth and Main to get a glimpse of Andy Payne ramble across the finish line in ninth place.[9] The *Sayre Herald* reported, "Some came in walking a swift shuffling stride, others were trotting and some were of an inventive nature and were setting a pace that possibly only themselves could properly name." The town welcomed the spectacle, and Sayre's chamber of commerce even paid Pyle five hundred dollars for the privilege of hosting the bunion derby.[10]

Across Oklahoma
DAY 38, 82 MEN

Tuesday, April 10, 1928. The thirty-eighth day of the race took the men fifty miles east to Clinton, another farm town on the western Oklahoma plain. The conditions were ideal for cross-country running: flat road, low altitude, and mild spring weather. Eighty-two men waited for the starting gun.

As early as 10 a.m., Clinton's streets filled with fans hoping to find a good vantage point for the finish.[11] By the time the first runners arrived, the race had drawn the town's largest crowd since the Armistice Day celebration in 1918. With the streets jammed, town officials had to string ropes to keep a lane clear to the finish.[12]

Eddie Gardner arrived first around 2 p.m., with a huge three-mile lead over second-place finisher Guisto Umek.[13] The day before, an irate white farmer had ridden up behind Eddie, trained a gun on his back and dared him to pass another white man.[14] After that brush with death and the six days of abuse in the panhandle, the Sheik had reached a crossroads. He put his fate in God's hands and ignored the chance of death at the hands of white racists. From then on, he ran the race undeterred by fear. Along the way, Eddie Gardner found he had the fanatical support of 172,000 black Oklahomans who would shelter and support him across the state.[15] Undeterred by fear, the coal-skinned Sheik sped through the fifty-mile course in six hours and forty minutes, leaving the cries of "Niggah drop dead" to die in the prairie winds.[16]

The town fathers were outraged—they had not paid Charley's retainer to watch a black beat their hero. They had to wait another two hours before Andy Payne and Peter Gavuzzi finally arrived. This state of affairs put a damper on Clinton's mood, and the disappointed crowds had begun to disperse soon after.[17]

The Sheik's performance moved him from sixth to fifth in the cumulative standings and gave him front-page headlines in Oklahoma's black newspaper, the *Black Dispatch*. National black papers such as the *Chicago Defender*, the *Pittsburgh Courier*, and the *Afro-American* also reported the story of Eddie's race to Clinton and his courageous journey through the segregated south. Eddie "the Sheik" Gardner was fast becoming a household name and a symbol of hope and pride to black Americans.[18]

The trip to Clinton was anything but pleasant for Charley Pyle when his twelve-ton bus crashed through a small bridge west of town. Wary of its safety, Pyle and Grange had gotten off the bus and told the driver to nurse it across the bridge. The front end made it, but the back end did not, crashing through the structure and smashing the bus's hindquarters. The injured mammoth used its own power to free itself from the mess and proceeded to Oklahoma City for repairs.[19]

The next day, many of Andy's fans were at the start for the race to Bridgeport. They followed the eighty-two men by car, and miles of vehicles were parked along Route 66.[20] Along the course, Payne's fame started to become an irritant to him as fans relentlessly tried to talk to him, get his autograph, or pose for a picture. His trainer finally asked the county's commissioners for road patrols to give him some peace. Andy said simply, "I wish they wouldn't try to stop me and talk to me."[21]

The weather didn't help Payne's mood, as a hard, blowing wind filled the sky with sand the entire thirty-five miles to Bridgeport.[22] The town had begun in 1890 as a way station for travelers who waited for the water level to drop before fording the South Canadian River. In 1921, a nine-hundred-foot suspension toll bridge spanned the river with a hefty charge of a dollar per car.[23]

Andy Payne and Peter Gavuzzi won the race in a tie, preserving Andy's hour-and-a-half lead.[24] Johnny Salo finished third, Olli Wanttinen fourth, William Kerr fifth, and Mike Joyce sixth. Joyce, the tiny thirty-five-year-old Irish immigrant, had been making a steady rise in the standings and now was in ninth place overall. Eddie Gardner finished seventh, after leading the stage in its opening miles.[25]

The fortieth stage took the men on a thirty-seven-mile run to El Reno, the last stop before Oklahoma City. El Reno grew up along the Rock Island Railroad, which went through the area in 1890.[26] There, new faces took top honors when Niels Nielson of Denmark finished first in about five and a half hours and tiny Olli Wanttinen came in ten minutes behind him in second.[27] Andy Payne and Peter Gavuzzi returned to another day of shuffling along in the pack. A *Los Angeles Times* reporter described Andy's strategy: "Payne has not extended himself, saving his energy for the weary miles yet to be footed to New York. He has refused, however, to permit his advantage to be whittled away by those within striking distance of the first place."[28] That translated to Peter Gavuzzi, and so long as the Englishman was content to keep pace with him, Andy would let the men in the pack have their stage wins. The derby continued to lose men. Henry Swabey of Yorktownship, Ontario, dropped out in El Reno due to foot trouble, poor food, and lack of rest. Swabey maintained, "You can't live on ham and eggs while running across the continent, and you can't sleep alongside a circus Ballyhoo and get sufficient rest." At forty-eight years old, he was one of the senior men in the derby and a veteran distance walker. Swabey took a parting shot at the two frontrunners. He said they were going much too fast and "were just wearing themselves out."[29]

Figure 13. Crowd waiting for the finishers in El Reno, Oklahoma.
Credit: El Reno Carnegie Library.

Figure 14. Left to right, Andy Payne, #43, Patrick De Marr, #188, and
Bill Kerr, #7, finishing in El Reno, Oklahoma. Credit: El Reno
Carnegie Library.

For the weary black runners, El Reno was a welcome respite from
the days of abuse and harassment. Throughout Oklahoma, strong, tightly
knit black communities shepherded the men east, feeding and housing
them, and supporting them with cash contributions. In El Reno, Eddie
Gardner led them into town, where he met a black doctor who slipped
him some pocket money and said, "Come in first. I'm depending on

you." That night, the black runners and their trainers were dinner guests at the home of Mrs. George Green, a leading black townswoman. Sammy Robinson especially welcomed the home-cooked meal and the chance to bathe—something he had been unable to do for days because most public facilities were closed to blacks.[30] In a sign of trouble to come, Canadian Phillip Granville turned down Mrs. Green's invitation and stayed at a white YMCA. Phillip, light skinned with European features, began referring to himself as Jamaican Indian—"anything but black"— and distanced himself from the group. After Texas, Granville had apparently had enough of being on the wrong side of Jim Crow segregation in the south.[31]

Friday the Thirteenth in Oklahoma City

DAY 41

Friday, April 13, 1928. It was not the best time to race to Oklahoma City. Like Amarillo, it should have been a huge payday for old Charley. More than 350,000 strong, the city was brimming with new oil money and served as the political and economic center of the state.[32]

The city adored Andy Payne, and the business community had planned a mile-long parade. Thousands of fans would pack the state fairgrounds at fifty cents a head, and the city's chamber of commerce had raised five thousand dollars for the privilege of hosting the derby. Pyle's grand plans, however, quickly unraveled. The herald of disaster was a cold blast of air that sent the mercury sliding toward freezing.[33] By late Thursday evening, the temperature had dropped from seventy to thirty degrees Fahrenheit. In the morning, the men shivered at the start in El Reno. After a three-hour delay, they finally began at 10 a.m. for the thirty-three miles to Oklahoma City.[34]

To ensure good profits at the fairgrounds, the chamber of commerce had Charley divert his men off Route 66 to a parallel road, hoping to force roadside fans to pay the price of admission. However, the organizers had not counted on a helpful truck driver who spread the word to the thousands who lined the highway. They simply moved, en masse, to the alternate route.[35] Hoppe Williams of the *Daily Oklahoman* wrote, "Horny-handed farmers were gathered with their wives and their almost unbelievable flocks of children, along the edges of the great highway,

Figure 15. Race start, El Reno to Oklahoma City.
Credit: El Reno Carnegie Library.

No. 66. Most brought their lunches, and children ran about smearing the landscape with peanut butter and bread crusts and decaying bananas."[36]

The state's new hero was not enamored of his newfound fame. He kept to his pace, and would not be drawn into a stage race for the benefit of his fans. Payne said, "I'm out for the [twenty-five thousand dollars] and I expect to go to New York a winner by a great big margin."[37] He also grew weary of the press that hounded his every step. He often simply outran them, as he did to Hoppe Williams, who tried to jog alongside, though the conversation was brief:

> Williams: "Lo' Andrew. I'm a newspaperman."
> Payne: "I knew you were."
> Williams: "How, Andrew?"
> Payne: "They look alike, kind of worm eaten."
> Williams: "How would you like to come over to my office

tonight, and we'll go out and get a highball somewhere? You look like a party man to me."

Payne: "Never touch it."

At this point, Williams couldn't keep up, and stopped in the road, breathing hard, as Andy pulled away.

Payne: "Well, so long. I'll see you in the funny papers."[38]

While Payne battled both fans and reporters, Oklahoma City organized a parade to welcome him home. At 12:30 p.m., an assortment of floats, marching bands, uniformed high-school track teams, and derby trucks assembled on West Main for a procession to the fairgrounds.[39] The local merchants tried to make the most of the derby run by tying their products to the theme. The Sipes' Foods advertisement is a typical example:

It's the day-in and day-out effort that will win the Coast-to-Coast Marathon. And so it is with Sipes' prices. Not just a few leaders some days, but every day, everything on our clean, well-stocked shelves is priced low. Sipes' leads in the race for lower prices.[40]

Huge crowds followed the parade to the finish, eager for a glimpse of Andy Payne.[41] It was meant to be an orderly affair, with fans paying fifty cents for a seat in the grandstand.[42] Instead, it was chaos. Pyle and the chamber had not fenced the perimeter of the fairgrounds, and thousands of freeloading guests avoided the ticket booth and flooded the track, which was supposed to have been kept clear for the racers. The derby men had to thread their way for the last three hundred yards of the race. Charles Brill of the *Daily Oklahoman* estimated that only two thousand of the five thousand fans who entered the fairgrounds actually paid the admission. It was a sad state of affairs for the chamber, because Charley Pyle had promised to use gate receipts to offset the chamber's five-thousand-dollar derby contribution. Instead, he collected just one thousand dollars, leaving the chamber with a four-thousand-dollar deficit.[43]

As for the racers, the first man to fight his way through the mob was the Finn Nestor Erickson, who collected the first-place stage money with a fast pace of just over seven minutes per mile. Andy Payne and Peter Gavuzzi entered the jammed fairgrounds together more than an

Figure 16. Advertisement in the April 13, 1928, edition of the *Oklahoma City Times*. Credit: The Oklahoma Publishing Company, © 1928.

hour later, tied for fifteenth place. They ran the course at a respectable nine-minute-mile pace.[44]

After the crowds dispersed, the men were free to wander the city—a novelty after weeks of jogging in the vastness of the American West. The bunioneers walked the streets, "soaking up the gaiety and the hero worship accorded them by the youngsters."[45] The excitement of the city did not stop Pyle's bunioneers from complaining bitterly about their leader.[46] John Pederson, a Swedish born runner from Spokane, claimed Charley had fed them badly and little, and had them sleep in "chicken barns, granaries, and stables." He added that their blankets were so dirty that one Texas town made Pyle burn them.[47] William Kerr, the blond stockbroker from Minneapolis, even appealed to the city's Shriners organization to pressure Charley to improve conditions for his men, since he owed them "a square deal."[48]

After reviewing the day's events, the *Oklahoma City Times* concluded, "[The] show was a flop. There is nothing interesting in seeing a mob of sun blackened runners straggle in miles apart." Despite the fiasco at the fairgrounds, C. C. Pyle must have felt secure—at least he had the $5,000 chamber contribution. That triumph was short-lived, too, however. That day, Ralph Scott of Illinois filed suit against him in the District Court of Oklahoma, alleging Pyle owed him $4,433.50 for unpaid services as a player and coach on Charley's New York Yankee football team. The judge duly attached a certificate of garnishment to Charley's $5,000, whose hopes of a big payday were put in legal limbo.[49] In a backdoor move to collect the money, Pyle signed an agreement with the chamber, releasing it from its obligation to pay the debt on the grounds that he had failed to bring the derby to Oklahoma City on the specified date. The chamber president then appeared in court and informed all concerned that his organization did not owe Charley the money. The suit was withdrawn and the matter was closed.[50]

Pyle still hoped to collect his money, but when he went to the chamber and suggested a private settlement, the president refused to comply, claiming he would perjure himself if he paid. The *Oklahoma City Times* wrote, "The chamber came away with more than $1,000 in gate receipts and Pyle went east a wiser and poorer man."[51]

The derby's black runners were taken to the black-run Great Western Hospital, where they were given baths, rubdowns, and medical treatment.[52] This visit was especially welcome news for Sammy Robinson, who had suffered stomach trouble for weeks. A writer from the *Black Dispatch* had found him lying in a ditch a few days before, doubled over with stomach cramps. Always optimistic, Sammy told a crowd that the best he could do for the last two weeks was to "keep on smiling."[53]

The men then went to a reception hosted by the Oklahoma City Negro Business League, where Eddie Gardner was asked to say a few words. "I haven't much to say tonight," he said. "I want you to know that I am not thinking much about the money to be gotten out of this race. My idea is that it would be a wonderful thing to win this test of endurance for [black America]. . . . I told my father before I left Seattle that I was going to pray and run, and that is what I have been doing."[54]

Phillip Granville apparently changed his mind about distancing himself from the black runners. He attended the reception, telling the group that, "There is no question that the odds are against a colored man in this race. . . . I am running everyday with a knowledge that if you just give the black man half a chance, he'll come out triumphant."[55]

You Can't Beat Ed Gardner

DAY 42, 81 MEN

Saturday, April 14, 1928. An icy wind whipped the deserted state fairgrounds, setting eighty-one sets of teeth chattering as the men lined up for one of the longest stretches of the derby—a fifty-two-mile trek across red clay hills to Chandler.[56] From Oklahoma City, Route 66 heads northeast into the heart of Andy Payne country, then through Kansas and Missouri to its terminus in Chicago nine hundred miles away.

With temperatures hovering at freezing, the race checker quickly ran through the list of starters.[57] The bunioneers pushed on to Chandler, a farm town of several thousand known for the honey and pecans it shipped from surrounding farms.[58] The first man to reach the town was the Italian Guisto Umek, who covered the distance in seven hours and forty-five minutes. Peter Gavuzzi followed ten minutes later, and then came the resilient Hawaii-born Johnny Vierra, who on many occasions had struggled to stay in the race. Next was Canada's Phillip Granville in fourth, followed by Andy Payne and William Kerr in a tie for fifth, more than an hour behind Gavuzzi.[59]

In the first few miles that day, the derby lost a rising star when a speeding car hit Mike Blaze and broke his leg, ending the cross-country odyssey of the twenty-three-year-old Californian. His wife had joined him several days before, and he had begun to move up in the standings under her care.[60]

Two Nordic runners—Nestor Erickson and August Fager—also dropped out. They had had enough of Charley's parade, and announced that they would need "daily prize money to induce them to pound the pavement another mile."[61] Pyle offered none, so he lost the two who were disgusted with his food and lodgings and knowing they still faced another 1,700 miles to New York.

C. C. Pyle had his fill of complaining that day. A lot of it had come from William Kerr, the urbane Minneapolis stockbroker. Like Johnny Salo, Kerr had the backing of his American Legion Post, and avoided Pyle's lodging by staying at posts along the route. Born in Harland, Wisconsin, he had served as a machine gunner in the Great War for eighteen months and wore the American Legion symbol on his running shirt. Possessing a college education and movie star looks, he had become the informal spokesman for the pack runners. In towns and cities along the route, he had complained bitterly to reporters about Pyle's treatment of his brother bunioneers. After facing near financial disaster in Oklahoma City, Charley was in no mood for an articulate dissenter in his ranks. C. C. Pyle had had quite enough of William "Bill" Kerr.

While soaking in his hotel bathtub, Bill heard a knock on the door. It was the director general and Red Grange. The two entered with doleful expressions on their faces. Charley did the talking:

Pyle: "How do you feel, Bill?"
    Kerr: "I'm fine."
    Pyle: "I'm afraid I've some bad news for you," he said, handing a telegram to Bill. "Your wife is dead."
    Kerr: "There must be some mistake, Mr. Pyle. My wife died several years ago."[62]

Pyle looked annoyed, but expressed ignorance about the source of the telegram, signed by one "Mrs. Gallagher." Charley's trick had failed.

Kerr would not be catching the next train to Wisconsin as Pyle had hoped. He was stuck with Bill for the remainder of the derby.

The black runners were not partaking of Charley Pyle's hospitality that day, either. As they entered Chandler, students at the "separate" Frederick Douglass School welcomed them with signs plastered on every possible space on the school terrace facing Route 66.[63] One read, "Welcome, Ed Gardner"; a second, "Gardner, Our Boy Must Win"; and a third, "You Can't Beat Ed Gardner." At 8 p.m., Eddie, Sammy Robinson, and T. Joseph Cotton came to the Douglass School to address a packed house of four hundred hero-worshipping students in the school auditorium. Robinson proved to be the favorite.[64] He told them, "Don't smoke, don't chew, and don't use strong drink. . . . If you want to be at your best, live clean, wholesome lives."[65] A reporter for the *Black Dispatch* said, "Sammy has a way that really gets over with a crowd."[66]

Across Oklahoma, black communities in towns like Chandler collected money for the men, which they used to buy extra food and other necessities. This support raised their spirits.[67] Phillip Granville even received a telegram from his track club in Hamilton, Ontario: "All of Hamilton pulling for you to win. Everybody interested. Olympic Club officials send best wishes."[68] These simple things—a telegram from home, a little pocket money, a good meal, the chance to take a bath and sleep in clean sheets in a warm place—kept the black bunioneers going in the face of so much racially motivated hate.

Ed Gardner did not disappoint his young fans at Douglass School.[69] In company with Peter Gavuzzi, he took first place on day forty-three in a thirty-six-mile run from Chandler to Barstow, an old Creek Indian trading post that went from rags to riches after drillers struck oil in nearby fields. Gardner and Gavuzzi motored over the rolling hills of eastern Oklahoma, at a pace of about seven-and-a-half-minute miles, in front of fifty thousand avid Andy Payne fans.[70]

Andy stuck to his game plan of running between nine- and ten-minute miles and would not be drawn into a stage race for his adoring fans. It ate at him, though. "Shucks, I was showed up today by Gavuzzi," he said. "He was trying to show me up and he sure did."[71]

Things did not improve for Andy the next day, either, on the forty-one-mile course to Tulsa. Peter Gavuzzi blazed over the rolling hills to

Tulsa in a seven-minute-mile pace. He was flying, and Andy would have to change his game plan if Peter did not let up soon.[72]

As Peter moved farther ahead, Andy became increasingly irritated with his fans as they chased him on foot or from exhaust-belching cars. While he was running, any rural school remotely close to Route 66 was dismissed for the day so everyone could get a glimpse of "their Andy." As he approached the finish line in Tulsa, a motorcycle police escort had to clear a path for him through the mob. "I'm just one of the bunch," Payne said. "I wish they would let me rest a bit."[73]

The chamber of commerce of oil-rich Tulsa had hoped for something more. Like Oklahoma City, Tulsa had paid the five-thousand-dollar contribution, and there was no lawsuit to help them wiggle out of the bill. For once, Charley Pyle had some money in his pocket.[74] Tulsa could afford it—surrounded by a sea of oil, the wealth filtered to all layers of society. The arts flourished; art deco houses went up; and Greenwood, the black district torn apart in the great Tulsa race riots of 1921, was transformed into a hotbed of jazz, blues, and relative prosperity.[75]

Black Tulsa turned out in force to welcome its bunioneers. Eddie Gardner finished fifth, despite a hail of insults—one white fan screamed that he should "be picking cotton, coon, back in Alabama!" The Sheik had learned to tuck the fear in his pocket and let the words fade in the smoke that rolled off his heels. He knew if the white world hated him, the black world embraced him.[76] That night Gardner, Granville, Robinson, and T. Joseph Cotton were the guests of honor at a reception hosted by Tulsa's black business league, with music from the thirty-two-piece Booker T. Washington high school band. Sammy told a group of women that he had only had four baths in forty-seven days, with three of them in Oklahoma. At the end of the reception, the business league gave the men a purse of money to split between them.[77]

Homecoming

DAY 45

Tuesday, April 17, 1928. On this day, Andy Payne would make his triumphal return to Foyil. He had left four months before without his father's support and had returned as Oklahoma's hero. Andy arrived home in good condition except for his right arm and back, "which are showing the effects of so much back slapping and hand shaking." His trainer warned him to avoid further handshakes.[78] Thousands of people lined the fifty-mile course, and motorists followed him en masse, three abreast, making Route 66 a rolling one-way road.[79]

Andy Payne had never raced for the crowd, except on that day, when he led the derby through Claremore, the largest town near tiny Foyil, at the thirtieth mile of the fifty-mile race. "I always said I'd be in Claremore first if I had to bust a lung," Andy said.[80] The Claremore town fathers had painted a huge white line across the pavement in the center of town to mark what they believed was the halfway point across the country, at approximately 1,650 miles into the race. As Payne reached the city limits, a squad of cadets from the Oklahoma Military Academy formed a bodyguard around him and jogged with him, in formation, until they reached the white line. The academy's corps of cadets apparently fired off a twenty-two-gun salute, one more than is given to the president of the United States.[81]

Andy paused for a moment on the line, as an official greeted him in the name of the Claremore Chamber of Commerce, which had sponsored him on his derby run. The man pressed a one-hundred-dollar bill in his hand.[82] Will Rogers, one of the greatest political satirists of his day and a friend of Andy's father, was also there to meet Payne when he entered town. Rogers topped the chamber with a $250 contribution. Shortly before the race, Rogers told Pyle that he wanted to offer a $500 prize for the first four men to reach Claremore, with $250 going to the first finisher. Charley refused his offer, but Rogers gave the $250 to Andy anyway, for "civic pride and because he wanted to keep the money in Claremore."[83] A syndicated columnist in 350 newspapers, this forty-eight-year-old cowboy had the ear of the common man in America.[84] Rogers joked that he felt kind of jealous that he had been replaced as the favorite son of Claremore.[85]

Foyil was ten miles east of Claremore, and Andy ran up the curving road and entered his old hometown. He took a few minutes to sit with his family outside the country store,[86] made his goodbyes and headed off to Chelsea, arriving at the control point a winner despite the endless interruptions from well-wishers. Payne managed to finish the course in about seven and a half hours and regained first place in the cumulative

Figure 17. Andy Payne running in Oklahoma. Credit: Rucker Collection, Research Division of the Oklahoma Historical Society.

standings. After "insistent demands for a speech," Andy mounted a dry goods box and expressed his thanks for the welcome he received.[87]

Close behind him came John Cronick of Canada, who had recovered from his shin splints and was moving back up in the standings. Andy's rival, Peter Gavuzzi, paid for the previous day's sprint by staggering through the course and finishing three hours behind him. Rumors began that the Englishman was having heart trouble and would soon drop out.[88] Another frontrunner, third-place holder Johnny Salo, temporarily quit with a stomach disorder, but vowed to make up the distance the next day. This moved Phillip Granville to third and Eddie Gardner to fourth, though the Sheik trailed Phillip by three and a half hours.[89]

The derby's roster then dropped to seventy-six when George Case of Reno, Nevada, withdrew from the race. The forty-three-year-old runner had been plagued by stomach trouble and weight loss, which left him too weak to continue.[90] As Case packed his bags, J. H. Mulroy of Cleveland was unpacking his with reinforcements for Mike Joyce, the little Irishman from Cleveland. Without financial support, a trainer, or any real racing experience, the thirty-five-year-old immigrant had simply decided that he could win the twenty-five thousand dollars for his wife and four children. He had taken a leave of absence from his job at the Fisher auto body plant, left his family at home with very little cash, and gone to Los Angeles to follow his dream. Despite impossible odds, he had prevailed, held seventh place, and now had a trainer who would follow him on the remaining miles to New York. "Mike is no flash," said Mulroy, "but he's a good consistent runner. He runs a steady uncomplaining race and always turns up in the money. He can have my shirt."[91]

The next day was the last stage race in Oklahoma. The course was a fifty-one-mile trek to the mining center of Miami, where prospectors had searched in vain for fabled Spanish gold mines in the surrounding hills, but had eventually found zinc and lead.[92] Seventy-six men left Chelsea that morning. Peter Gavuzzi seemed to have recovered, and set an eight-minute-mile pace to win the stage—fans were amazed to see him run with a tobacco pipe between his teeth. After the previous day's stage win, Andy's trainer, Tom Young, told him, "Let Gavuzzi have it."[93] So Payne ran a ten-minute-mile pace, vowing not to tire himself again to please his home-state fans.[94]

Nonetheless, thousands of Oklahomans came to see Andy Payne: Twenty thousand fans packed the eight blocks near the finish and fifteen thousand cars lined Route 66 outside of Miami.[95] When Peter Gavuzzi reached the outskirts, the old fire house siren sounded and a flying escort assembled around him. Motorcycle policemen led the way in a sandwich of boy scouts and policemen, pacing the Englishman to Main Street where town officials had roped off a path to the finish.[96] The crowd had to wait more than an hour before the next man arrived—Johnny Salo of Passaic, New Jersey, who had recovered from a bout of stomach trouble—followed by ninety-six-pound Olli Wanttinen and New York runner Louis Perrella. And then at last, at 3:45 p.m., the weary crowd caught a glimpse of "their Andy" as he trotted across the line with Eddie Gardner by his side.[97]

Across Kansas

DAY 47, 76 MEN

Thursday, April 19, 1928. At 6 a.m., a crowd gathered on Main Street to watch the men for the last time in Oklahoma. Charley passed though the lines, giving each runner a word of encouragement and the promise of a chicken dinner when they reached that day's finish line in Joplin, Missouri. This evoked a cheer.

From Miami, the men followed a rolling, concrete road until mile sixteen, where they crossed the southeast corner of Kansas before entering Missouri.[98] All across Route 66, the bunioneers met swarms of people spilling from cities along the highway.[99] The crowds broke up under a violent storm that swept the highway with rain, sleet, and hail. To keep off the chill, the runners applied motor oil to their bodies, threw blankets over their shoulders, and donned oilskin slickers and heavy sweaters.[100] The downpour forced Andy Payne to change his socks twice, despite his all-weather, double-soled shoes. One runner got as far as Commerce, Oklahoma, before the rain set in. He did not like the looks of the threatening sky, so he found shelter in a hotel for five hours before resuming the race. Another runner called it, "the most goshaw-fullest race they ever ran."[101]

As Andy Payne crossed the state line, his former track coach at Foyil High School handed him an Oklahoma state flag to carry with him to New York City. Andy accepted the flag, said goodbye, and happily stepped into Kansas. "It's pretty hard keeping pace up in your home state when everybody wants to stop and shake your hand or take your picture while you're running," he said.[102]

Figure 18. Runners stopping for water in Oklahoma. Andy Payne, #43, Patrick De Marr, #188, and Peter Gavuzzi, #103, in photo. Credit: El Reno Carnegie Library.

CHAPTER 12

Duel across the Ozarks

THE NEXT NINE DAYS WOULD TAKE THE BUNIONEERS ACROSS
Missouri to St. Louis and the mighty Mississippi River. The men would
spend much of the journey in the foothills and river valleys of the
Ozark Mountains.[1] The region is vast, covering about fifty thousand
miles, including a small slice of Oklahoma and much of Missouri and
Arkansas—the only major highland between the Rocky Mountains and
the Appalachians. The mountains are just 2,500 feet tall, covered with
thin soil but filled with springs, lakes, rivers, and caves.[2]

Before the Europeans arrived, the area was dominated by the
Osage Indians. As the settlers pushed west, Cherokees on the Trail of
Tears to Oklahoma passed through and intermarried so strongly with
white settlers that many could count Cherokee blood on both sides.
During the Civil War, the region became a wasteland as it was torn
apart by guerrilla bands, outlaws, and union and confederate forces as
they vied for control.[3]

Joplin versus Carthage

DAY 47, 76 MEN

Thursday, April 19, 1928. Joplin was the first stop in Missouri, albeit unplanned. Historically, it was a strategic prize for both sides in the Civil War as a crucial source for bullets from surrounding lead mines. After the war, Joplin rebuilt and entered a wild recovery stage, with seventy-five saloons to relieve miners of their hard-earned pay. By 1928, the city had grown into a leading financial and supply center for the surrounding mining district, though Joplin retained some of its former frontier feel.[4] The city's civic leaders were not above stealing Charley's race from their archrival, Carthage—a smaller but rich neighboring town seventeen miles to the east along Route 66. Several nights before the race was set to stop in Carthage, Joplin's chamber of commerce paid one thousand dollars to have it stop there instead.[5] A cash-strapped C. C. Pyle obliged with the flimsy excuse that the fifty-seven-mile race

Figure 19. Missouri's home state favorite, John Gober, #36, and Eddie Gardner, #165, on Route 66. Credit: El Reno Carnegie Library.

[to Carthage] was "too long and feared that many of the runners would be unable to finish."[6] He had conveniently forgotten that his men had twice run fifty-mile stages in the last week. Cash and Carry Pyle lived up to his name: He took the cash and left Carthage out to dry, ruining the town's long-planned derby celebration.[7]

The bunion derby gave local fans something to cheer about when Missouri's own John Gober won the forty-one-mile race to Joplin.[8] Gober had struggled in the past but told his home-state fans when he reached Missouri, "Watch my smoke."[9] He lived up to his words, and finished in just over five and a half hours.[10]

Because of the short notice, Joplin had little time to establish crowd control. Gober had to bulldoze through the mob at the finish, in the rain, with the help of a motorcycle escort, where he had a wet reunion with his wife and their two children.[11] Payne, Granville, and Tom Ellis of England finished an hour later in a three-way tie. Andy's trainer, Tom Young, vowed to keep his young star on a consistent pace in the nine-to ten-minute range, saying, "We figure it's the steady grind that gets them there."[12] Andy's rival, Peter Gavuzzi, should have followed Young's advice. He stumbled across the finish line almost two hours later, once again paying for the previous day's speed.[13]

The citizenry of Joplin seemed especially enthralled with the derby's deputy director, Red Grange. A favorite activity that day was the "Grange hunt," especially among the town's young women. A reporter from the *Joplin Globe* wrote, "Almost anyone with red hair and a well-built body . . . is likely to be the object of many unreserved hero-worship stares, and several persons in Joplin have received such attention." One young woman asked a red-haired newspaper correspondent if his name was Red Grange. He jokingly answered in the affirmative, but then the girl took one look at his body and turned away in disgust. "Oh, raspberries," she said. "If you're Red Grange, I'm Rudolph Valentino."[14] Naturally gregarious, Grange had a way of endearing himself to a crowd. He never tired of meeting people and seeing new towns. "The trip hasn't gotten a bit old yet," he said. Most people he met wanted to talk football. With typical self-deprecation, he kept reminding his fans that football is played by eleven men and the problem is that most people "don't watch anyone but the fellow who is carrying the ball."[15]

Grange could have said as much for his own men. For the boys in the pack, it was another day of slogging it out far from the public eye, scrounging for food to supplement Charley's allowance, and trying to avoid a stay in his "no-rest hotel." A reporter from the *Carthage Evening Post* asked a limping runner where he might find the deluxe cafeteria described in Charley's derby program. "Hell, we ain't had no lunch wagon since Arizona," the runner said. "Damned good thing we haven't. Those hot dogs and [sour] kraut were terrible." The reporter was outraged to learn that Pyle and Grange "wasted no-time going to their suite at the Conner [hotel], leaving the racers to arrive with or without blankets, their joints creaking like rusty hinges."[16] Many men found novel ways to avoid the meager food and lodging. Patrick De Marr, a Los Angeles boxer, fought for prize money in towns along the route; and German-born George Rehayn held an impromptu concert from his "improvised sleeping quarters" on a Joplin street corner. Rehayn sang a medley of songs he composed about his life as a transcontinental runner.[17]

Compared to those desperate men, frontrunners like Andy Payne had a very easy time indeed. In Joplin, Andy followed his routine of dining at a local restaurant with his trainer. He sat quietly eating at the counter while admiring patrons looked on and commented on how much he could pack away. Payne and his trainer spent the night in the comfort of a local hotel.[18]

As the bunioneers left Joplin for the forty-seventh stage of the race, the clouds returned and it began to rain. They headed east, crossing a landscape of desolation—lead mines and piles of mine tailings—that gradually gave way to farmland before reaching Carthage at mile seventeen.[19] This tough little town wanted to make Charley pay for the prior day's betrayal.

Peter Gavuzzi led the men into Carthage around 9 a.m., where motorists threatened to run him down and angry crowds booed.[20] Kids pelted Pyle's patrol cars with rotten eggs, and city police arrested one of the derby's program vendors as he hawked programs.[21] It was noon before the last runner showed his heels to that angry town. An editorial in the *Daily Oklahoman* did not blame the citizens of Carthage for egging Charley's cars, but thought it unfair they took it out on the "hapless runners," who had to negotiate another thirty miles in the chilling rain before reaching the control stop at Miller.[22]

Soaked to the skin, John Gober won his second stage race when he reached the finish line in seven hours. With his two-day performance, he jumped to thirty-fifth place overall.[23] Peter Gavuzzi followed close behind, and complained bitterly to the press about the unsportsmanlike motorists who threatened to run him down.[24] He still managed to beat Andy Payne by more than an hour and came within thirty-six minutes of recapturing the lead. The rest of the men spent a good deal of the time walking in the freezing rain to Miller. Wearing sweaters and raincoats, the bunioneers tramped into town and headed straight for lodging in privates homes or the school gymnasium, which the town opened as a sleeping quarters.[25]

The day's tough grind claimed four men. Harold McNutt of Alberta, Canada, who had walked to the start in Los Angeles as a training exercise, finally found the going was too tough. He simply said: "I could not stand up under it."[26] Head referee Arthur Duffy disqualified both Carl Willberg of New York and Frank Nagoski of Seattle when they failed to reach Miller by the midnight cutoff. The boxer, Patrick De Marr, thought he would avoid the mud and rain by accepting a ride, but he was caught in the act and disqualified the next morning.[27]

Into the Heart of the Ozarks

DAY 49, 73 MEN

Saturday, April 21, 1928. At 6:30 a.m., the men left the mud and rain for Springfield, the third-largest city in the state and self-proclaimed "Queen of the Ozarks." Springfield was a military prize for both sides during the Civil War, as a gateway between the union-held Mississippi River port of St. Louis and the lead mines of Joplin and Carthage.[28] The union army maintained a telegraph line along what would become Route 66 to St. Louis, and the rebel forces cut the line at every opportunity. The route became known as the Old Wire Road, and for years after the war, wireless poles "stood as grey totems to the war."[29]

Pyle had threatened to bypass this historic town after the chamber of commerce rejected his demand for a $1,500 fee. D. D. Rayfield of the *Springfield Leader* urged the chamber to reconsider, claiming, "Anything that will attract attention, bring crowds, keep something going on and entertains the public is good for the city. It prevents dry rot."[30] In response, fifteen local businessmen contributed $100 each, and Charley dutifully arrived in Springfield several days before the stage race.[31]

Canadian Tom Ellis was the first to arrive in town. Though buried in the pack, he had managed to win the thirty-four-mile stage in about four and a half hours, with John Gober close behind.[32] Out on the course, a reporter from the *Springfield Leader* found Peter Gavuzzi and Andy Payne jogging along steadily. He asked the pair if it worried them they were more than a mile behind John Gober in the stage race. Andy said, "What do we care? We're ahead of him by 400 miles in elapsed time. He's not worrying us yet."[33] The two finished in a tenth-place tie. And despite the standard fare of death threats and racial slurs, the Sheik ran hard into Springfield and cut Phillip Granville's hold on fourth place to just two hours.[34]

By 3 p.m., thirty-three men had arrived in Springfield, with the rest straggling in until midnight.[35] Most disappeared to their hotels or nearby lunch stands, but a few early finishers reappeared during the afternoon to exchange banter with girls and bask in their hero worship. The men had a rare treat when the local YMCA offered free showers and swimming in the club pool. Left unsaid was that the YMCA had not extended the invitation to blacks, for Jim Crow ruled in Missouri through segregation laws every bit as draconian as those found in Texas. The white *Springfield Leader* newspaper noted, with dramatic under-statement, that Missouri fans have "shown antagonism to runners that are not Native Americans [white] and have not been pleasant to them, especially to the Negro runners." As they had done across the south, the black runners would have to look to their own people—a quarter of a million Missourians, representing about 6 percent of the state's 3.6 million.[36]

Gardner versus Granville

DAY 50, 73 MEN

Sunday, April 22, 1928. On the fiftieth day of the race, hundreds of Springfield residents braved a heavy rain to see the men depart for the small community of Conway, forty-three miles to the northeast. The course took the men along the northern fringe of the Ozarks, past quiet agricultural communities intermixed with tree-covered hills and fish-filled streams. By noon, Conway's usually quiet streets were lined with cars and spectators, until torrential rains shut down the concession stands and sideshows, leaving Conway a rather forlorn place as sheets of rain danced on the nearly deserted city streets.[37]

Guisto Umek was the first to finish the course, which he did in six hours and twelve minutes. He was followed by Johnny Salo, Eddie Gardner, and Sam Richman. Eddie opened his offensive to cut Phillip Granville's hold on fourth place, reducing the margin separating the two men to just one hour. Andy Payne and Peter Gavuzzi finished together in another of their trademark ties, more than an hour behind Guisto.[38]

The derby left Conway early Monday morning for Waynesville, fifty-one miles into the heart of the Ozarks. Waynesville was renowned for its water, said to offer relief "for all the ills to which human flesh is heir to."[39] At mile eighteen, the runners cut off Route 66 for a brief run through the town of Lebanon after its chamber of commerce had contracted with Charley for the detour.[40] New York's Sam Richman and his three brothers knew the town well; they had passed through Lebanon on their way to Los Angeles in January, where they had had a fatal run-in with a mule. It belonged to local farmer George Haynes, who hauled the brothers to court to seek reimbursement for his loss. The Richman brothers told the judge they had little extra cash, after spending most of it to purchase their old Ford sedan in New York. After Haynes threatened to seize their car for the money, the brothers agreed to pay him eight dollars and signed a note for the unspecified balance, which they presumably paid on their return visit to Lebanon.[41]

Eddie Gardner and Phillip Granville led the race to Waynesville, tying for first place in seven hours and forty-two minutes—a nine-minute-mile pace. Phillip held his slim margin on fourth place in the cumulative standings.[42] Behind them came ninth-place holder Olli Wanttinen, who had clawed his way back among the frontrunners after almost dropping out in Oklahoma with stomach trouble. Gavuzzi and Payne jogged along together for another day of easy running, finishing in a ninth-place tie, more than an hour and forty minutes behind the lap winners. One reporter wrote, "Thirty-six minutes still separate the pair, and neither appears to be expending any great amount of effort, other than keeping track of the other."[43]

At 7 a.m. the next morning, the seventy-three men left Waynesville for a thirty-two-mile race to Rolla, where Federal troops had maintained a fortified camp during the Civil War. That night, the bunioneers

Figure 20. Three Legionnaires with the American Legion emblem
on their shirts: left to right, Johnny Salo, #107, Bill Kerr, #7,
and C. R. Brown, #193. Credit: El Reno Carnegie Library.

would reach the 2,000-mile mark in the 3,422-mile race.[44] Granville and
Gardner continued their duel for fourth, tying for first in about four hours
and forty minutes. The racist assaults continued, and the *Black Dispatch*
reported that "much [ill] treatment had been dealt to the runners" and
"[they are] keeping close together as a matter of protection."[45]

During the early part of the stage race, Phillip and Eddie sprinted
up to Andy and Peter, who quickly matched them stride for stride. The
four raced each other for about a quarter of a mile before the derby leaders dropped back, breathing hard. Granville thought this little victory
"may be a sign that they have cracked."[46] More likely, it was a game of
cat-and-mouse. Andy Payne and Peter Gavuzzi had a bank account of
thirty-five hours over third-place holder Johnny Salo, and forty hours
over Phillip Granville. Andy's only opponent was the bearded wonder

from Southampton, and if both men could avoid injury, the rest of the racers were just background noise.[47]

In Rolla, the derby pitched its tents at the Masonic lodge opposite the post office. That night, the Rolla Theater ran free movies.[48] However, the treat was not enough to pacify Bill Kerr, recipient of Charley's bogus telegram, who had had enough of "unwashed blankets and haphazard housing conditions," contacted Rolla's Board of Health, and had it take action against Pyle for his filthy sleeping quarters.[49]

Another day in the green, rolling hills of the Ozarks took the men to Sullivan, near beautiful, seven-thousand-acre Meramec State Park.[50] On this leg, reporter Bill Witt decided to get a taste of derby running with Andy Payne and Peter Gavuzzi. Witt found things easy enough over the first few miles, but it grew progressively worse for the reporter. He quit after ten, and said, "I began to think my chest was bursting, my feet were on fire, my muscles like red-hot wires, drawing tighter at every bounce." As he sat nursing his swollen legs, he said, "This isn't a race at all—it's a miracle."[51]

On the road to Sullivan, Gardner saw his dreams of fourth-place glory die when he failed to match Granville's speed and paid dearly for the attempt. Spent and exhausted, the Sheik staggered through the course at an almost fifteen-minute-mile pace, lost three hours on Granville, and dropped to sixth overall behind Bill Kerr.[52] Granville, however, blazed through the forty-three-mile course in almost half the time to take first place. He was "so far in the lead that he had time to change his clothes and sit in the grandstands to watch the other runners go by."[53] Peter Gavuzzi ended his extended truce with Andy Payne, taking second-place stage honors and claiming the frontrunner title with a thirty-minute lead over his Oklahoma rival.[54]

In Sullivan, however, much of the attention was centered on the return of hometown hero Pat Harrison. Long after the leaders had finished, he crossed the line with his head held high. He had gone through hell to get there, and this was his moment in the limelight. Harrison was hustled into a car and taken to his mother's house for his first home-cooked meal since he had left for the race four months ago. That evening, he gave an impassioned talk in the local high school auditorium. Harrison said he had fainted twice on the course from exhaustion, "[but] I could not see the word quit," he said. "I felt that I was the chosen one to carry the banner of Sullivan to New York."[55]

To the Mississippi

DAY 54, 72 MEN

Thursday, April 26, 1928. Sullivan marked the end of the derby's sojourn across the deep valleys and wooden hills of the Ozarks. Ahead lay the bright lights of St. Louis and the vast Mississippi River—the division between east and west. On the road, the runners met metropolitan traffic as they dodged and wove through lanes of exhaust-belching cars.[56] The forty-six-mile trip took them to the finish line at Hillside View Hotel, an isolated spot on the western outskirts of St. Louis. The men followed a dirt road to the hotel where they had a hearty, low-priced meal of veal, gravy, and mashed potatoes.[57]

Charley had envisioned a glamorous evening in the city, but the St. Louis Chamber of Commerce had refused his twelve-thousand-dollar demand, so he settled for the isolated inn atop a windswept hill—another in a long line of failed payoffs. The next day, he would route the derby through the outskirts of town, avoiding the business district that had betrayed him.[58]

It had been a good day for Peter Gavuzzi, having won the forty-six-mile stage in an eight-minute-mile pace, extending his lead over Andy Payne to almost two hours. Peter trotted up to the Hillside Hotel at 1 p.m., knocked loudly on the door of the official timekeeper, gave him his number, and said, "This looks like a dull village. Not even a movie to take up a guy's time. Guess we'll turn in early tonight. Oh, well, we'll be in New York soon and we'll do our stepping out there." Peter then went to the hotel, washed his face, combed his beard, and strolled out to the lawn to watch his friends finish.[59]

Andy Payne had the handicap of a cold but still finished in a tie for fifth with Eddie Gardner, in a pace of under-ten-minute miles.[60] Both men hoped their rivals would pay for the prior day's speed; Granville, like Gavuzzi, ran strong. The Ontario star burned through the course to take second place, opening an offensive against Peter Gavuzzi. Gardner lost another two hours on the Canadian and saw the gap between fourth and fifth widen to seven hours. He did manage to regain his hold on fifth by displacing a struggling Bill Kerr.[61] Granville, however, no longer worried about the Sheik. He had set his sights on bigger things, and opened his offensive against the Englishman from Southampton.

Phillip vowed to lead "Gavuzzi every day from now on."[62] He really had no choice if he hoped to capture first place—more than thirty hours behind, he had to cut Gavuzzi's lead by an hour a day for the remaining thirty stages.[63]

For Eddie Gardner, who was engaged in a fading effort to capture fourth, everyone from Pyle himself to the derby physician blamed his demise on his trainers, George Curtis and James Akers. "Neither of the men are former athletes or trainers of athletes, hence at times their liberal advice proves to be harmful," one reporter wrote.[64] But ultimately, Eddie had no one to blame but himself if he chose to stick to a failed strategy.

In the pack, the men continued to hope the leaders would wear out. Harry Gunn, the millionaire's son, still fervently believed he would lead the race into New York City despite his 108-hour deficit. His father drove the course in a high-powered car, "watching for signs of weakness among those in the lead."[65] But most of men knew, in their hearts, that they were engaged in wishful thinking; the lead runners were getting stronger as they went, and life in the shadows continued to be a daily struggle. Their only goal was to hold on until the end of the transcontinental rainbow in New York. "Fitfully they struggle from hot dog stand to hot dog stand, striving to put strength in their stomachs and hoping their legs will come alive again," one reporter wrote.[66] Their lifelines were the shoe repairman who answered sixty-four requests each day,[67] the medical staff who patched them together, the attendants in the Maxwell House Coffee truck who gave them coffee and sandwiches, and Pyle's race patrols.

At 8 a.m. the next morning, seventy-two men left their hillside retreat west of St. Louis for the thirty-two-mile grind to East Saint Louis in Illinois. St. Louis, the largest city between Los Angeles and Chicago, had a population of eight hundred thousand. Founded in 1763 as a furtrading post, St. Louis is shaped by the Mississippi, halfway between its headwaters and terminus in the Gulf of Mexico. After the 1803 Louisiana Purchase stretched the United States territory to the Rocky Mountains, St. Louis became the gateway to the west. The city motto is, "The world passes through St. Louis."[68]

Charley, however, tried to "pass through" quietly and without fanfare. But the word was out, and scores of fans sat along the road to watch the bunioneers race by.[69] They clapped and shouted encouragement. Eddie Gardner was the first to reach the river, followed by Johnny

Salo and Phillip Granville. By the time Guisto Umek came into view, the crowds had started to grow, and by noon the pack threaded its way down Chateau Avenue as thousands of workers were taking their lunch breaks. The crowd had grown to six deep, forcing the runners to dodge both cars and people.[70]

The derby lost one man on the trip to East St. Louis. Nick Perisick of Long Beach, California, dropped out from exhaustion after surviving for nearly two months.[71] Lucien Frost, the biblical actor, almost joined him. "I feel like hell," he said, as he suffered through a heavy cold, and added, "I'll be tickled to death if I ever get to New York."[72] Another runner, Thomas Ellis of Canada, was brushed by a car in East St. Louis, which left him hobbling for three days as derby trainer Hugo Quest nursed him back to health.[73]

The loss of any man continued to be a rare event at this stage in the race. Pyle claimed, "The runners now are in fine physical condition and some are actually gaining weight," despite running the equivalent of almost two marathons a day. Head referee Arthur Duffy agreed, saying that "sometimes I think half the contestants are getting a little bit light in the head from the constant pounding on the pavement, but the next minute I am equally convinced that no man with the tenacity of purpose and the capacity for hard and constant work in the face of such difficulties can be anything but in the very best shape mentally as well as physically." He added, "Maybe we're all cuckoo, myself and the runners, but I think that some day the public will come to realize that this cross country foot race is one of the greatest athletic achievements of the age."[74]

CHAPTER 13

Last Legs to Chicago

Into the Land of Lincoln

DAY 55, 71 MEN

Friday, April 27, 1928. On Friday, the derby entered Illinois, the land of Abraham Lincoln. Lincoln spent much of his adult life here before assuming the presidency and was laid to rest in Illinois soil after his assassination. This was also the first state in the Old Northwest—land proclaimed forever free from slavery under the old Northwest Ordinance of 1778.[1]

The nine-day state crossing would take the men to the end of the great road in Chicago, 2,402 miles from Los Angeles. The days of desert heat and mountain climbs were behind them, and the men who remained would run the last 300 miles of Route 66 on a flat, concrete surface, embraced by gentle spring weather—a heady mix for speed as they crossed through the state's fertile farmlands and industrial cities and towns.

The first stop was East St. Louis, a gritty industrial town, with an infamous reputation for American blacks. On July 2, 1917, white rage exploded as waves of southern blacks arrived in the city to fill wartime jobs. After several blacks allegedly killed two white police officers, white mobs rampaged through the black community, burning two hundred homes and killing at least thirty-nine residents. They killed indiscriminately, shooting blacks as they fled from their burning houses. They lynched one injured man while chanting, "Get hold and pull [the rope] for East St. Louis," and hurled another into a burning house.[2]

Eddie Gardner led the derby into the heart of this racially charged town, flying through the short twenty-nine-mile course in about three and a half hours. Mislabeled as a "16-year-old negro school boy of Seattle," he was followed in short order by Johnny Salo and Phillip Granville. For all his effort, the Sheik gained just ten minutes on Phillip.[3]

The frontrunners, Peter Gavuzzi and Andy Payne, coasted to a twentieth-place tie, content to spend a bit of their lead over the field that day. Payne said, "I can take my normal pace and certainly finish in the money. I have only got to watch Gavuzzi and can lose more than an hour a day every day to every other man in the race from now on and will still win." The Englishman, for his part, believed he had the legs to beat Andy Payne to New York City. He told the press, "I will win the race. I haven't begun to run yet."[4] This confidence must have raised an eyebrow or two in the press corps, however—Peter Gavuzzi had tried to break away by running seven- to eight-minute miles for a stage race or two, but always exhausted himself in the effort and quickly lost all the time he had gained. His Oklahoma rival was still very much in the game, and Peter had yet to find the pace that would leave Andy in the dust.

The next day, in the forty-two-mile race to the coal-mining town of Staunton, Peter tried once more to push the envelope. He finished the race in about five and a half hours, blazing through the course at a pace of about seven and a half minutes per mile. He crushed Andy, doubling his cumulative lead to three and a half hours. Ten minutes behind him came Johnny Salo and Phillip Granville. Eddie Gardner lagged behind in a fifth-place tie with Mike Joyce of Cleveland, and saw his deficit with Phillip increase to eight hours.[5]

Among the pack runners, the derby lost one of its most eccentric stars when Lucien Frost, the actor with the long white beard who portrayed biblical characters on the silent screen, was disqualified. A derby official found him in the trunk of an obliging fan's car, dragged him out, returned his one-hundred-dollar deposit, and drummed him out of the derby. Arthur Duffy had been suspicious of Frost for weeks, but until now had not caught him in the act.[6] One eyewitness said the actor was "crying like a child" after his ousting from the derby. Another runner, John White of Oklahoma, explained the cause of those tears: He was forfeiting a twenty-thousand-dollar payment the National Film Company had promised him if he finished the race, which would likely have led to a film deal about his life on the road.[7] Frost pleaded, "Let me make up the mileage. Add plenty of time penalty, too. My foolishness means curtains for my movie career."[8] But he was out.

Gavuzzi's Run

DAY 57, 70 MEN

Sunday, April 29, 1928. Sunday was anything but a day of rest for the derby's surviving seventy bunioneers. They set their sights on the coal-mining town of Virden forty-four miles away, as thousands of spectators jammed the route.[9]

Peter Gavuzzi achieved another day of eight-minute-mile racing and arrived in Virden at 1 p.m. Andy Payne limited the damage by tying Phillip Granville for third, allowing Gavuzzi to add just thirty minutes to his overall lead.

In contrast, one man who felt no pain that day was George Jussick of Detroit. He had arrived in the little town of Nilwood where a man offered him a pint of corn whisky, "where upon Mr. Jussick absorbed the entire pint." A local reporter wrote, "Shortly thereafter his lope slowed to a walk, then degenerated into an aimless shambles, which resembled nothing so much as a one-man snake dance." Then Jussick started hiccoughing. When the "juiced" George Jussick arrived in Virden, derby officials assessed him a twenty-hour penalty for drinking alcohol—an illegal act in this time of prohibition. A Virden reporter mockingly called it "a manifest injustice, because a man who can run from Nilwood to Virden after consuming a pint of present-day corn whisky deserves a far better fate."[10]

Virden inspired other sentiments, too. Several days after the derby left town, local mechanic Bob Gaddie decided to hold his own one-man race from Burris' Garage in Virden to the nearby town of Thayer. He bet a group of onlookers twelve dollars that he could complete the run. A passing hobo, thinking he was part of the transcontinental race, told

Gaddie he was two days behind the derby and that he had better speed up if he hoped to catch them. Gaddie told the man to mind his own business. A group of small children tried to follow him, as did a pack of barking dogs that snapped at his heels, and off he went.[11]

As for the derby men, the fifty-eighth stage took them to Springfield, the state capital and final resting place of Abraham Lincoln.[12] A fit and trim Johnny Salo was the first man to reach this historic ground. Escorted by a cadre of motorcycle policemen "with sirens screaming," he blazed through the course with seven-minute miles and finished in front of the Springfield Elks Club, where hundreds waited to see him.[13] Peter Gavuzzi arrived next, as the new undisputed king of Route 66. He had completed his third day of racing in the seven-minute-mile range. No one had done this before and survived. Payne did not give chase, and slipped more than four hours behind the bearded ship's steward from Southampton, England.[14]

The short race gave the men a rare afternoon to themselves, which most spent soaking in the Elks Club pool. The club treated all the men well, opening its facilities, providing lodging, and holding a cabaret dance on the roof garden.[15]

C. C. Pyle, however, was not having a pleasant afternoon. On the brink of financial ruin, he had handed control of the derby's financial affairs to F. F. Gunn, the millionaire father of derby contestant Harry Gunn. F. F. Gunn was a businessman and made immediate changes—for the first time, the derby walled off the finish with a high canvas fence that forced the curious to pay an entrance fee.[16] Charley's demise as the business manager was understandable. He was not a detail man. He was a promoter. He was about making deals, about convincing powerful people to buy into his plans, and about getting someone else to pick up the pieces when his grand vision was caught in the light of day.[17]

There were some pieces Gunn couldn't pick up, however. Two deputy sheriffs presented Red Grange with papers that sought twenty thousand dollars' worth of attachments, issued by the County Circuit Court at Champaign for creditors who alleged Pyle and Grange held two unsecured notes from the defunct Illinois Trust and Savings Bank of Champaign. A reporter wrote, "Red warmly greeted the deputies and grabbed the writ like a forward pass," but claimed he did not owe any bank anything and would have paid it if he did. He suggested the officers talk with Charley, and said he had no property with the derby. He conveniently forgot his title as "Assistant Director General" of the race and claimed to have "no official contact with the derby and was merely a spectator."[18] While the deputies searched for Charley Pyle, the show went on.

On May 1, seventy men left for Lincoln, the only town in America to take the name of a U.S. president while he was still alive. As a young lawyer, Lincoln had drawn up the articles of incorporation for the town. When the developers told him of their intention to name the town after him, Lincoln said, "[I] never knew of anything named Lincoln that amounted to much." He then baptized the town by spitting a mouthful of watermelon seeds onto the ground.[19]

Lead runner Peter Gavuzzi and Denver baker Seth Gonzales led the thirty-two-mile race into town, arriving before 11 a.m. They covered the distance in seven-and-a-half-minute miles. Gavuzzi made derby history with a fourth day at sub-eight-minute-per-mile pace, which was deeply troubling for Andy Payne.[20] Peter was raising the bar for every runner in the race, and consequently, everyone was running faster. On the flat, well-paved roads of Illinois, it was a new ballgame—the old days of plodding along at ten minutes a mile were done. It was now a time for fast-paced racing among fit young men.

Andy Payne had run at a reasonably fast pace of under nine minutes per mile, but still saw his deficit with Gavuzzi widen to five hours. For Eddie Gardner, it was even worse. To stay with the leaders, he had to keep pace consistently day after day. He had never learned to do this and paid dearly for it in Illinois. After running the course in an eleven-and-a-half-minute-mile pace, he fell to seventh, with Mike Joyce in fifth and William Kerr in sixth. His gap with Phillip Granville had grown to twelve hours.[21] The Sheik of Seattle was fading off the radarscope as a serious contender.

For the men in the pack, the tonic was pride. At the end of the run to Lincoln, Mike Kelly of Indiana was in last place, having covered 2,230 miles in 767 hours—more than ten days behind Peter Gavuzzi. *Chicago Tribune* reporter Edward Burns explained Kelly's persistence as due to brain damage: "Mike, a pugilist, has taken many a wicked punch to the head in his 22 years of life."[22] How do you make someone understand soul, or what it means to sink your teeth into a dream and hold on through hell, for no money or reward other than the thrill of the journey? Kelly was not brain dead. He was proud, iron-tough, and focused on the far end of the transcontinental rainbow in New York City.

In Lincoln, F. F. Gunn's involvement was again apparent. The stage race finished under a large canvas tent, and fans who wanted to see the runners had to dig in their pockets for twenty-five cents. For their coins, they got a chance to meet Illinois' own Red Grange, as well as Charley's oddball carnival attractions: the fat lady, the man with collegiate mottoes tattooed on his torso, the corpse of an Oklahoma outlaw; and, of course, the derby men.[23] People came, and people paid. Gunn had begun to turn things around.

Whiskers and Lawsuits

DAY 60, 70 MEN

Wednesday, May 2, 1928. The next day marked an end to Peter's four-day rampage through the flat cornfields of Illinois. He was out of steam, and finished "a very groggy sixteenth" in the run from Lincoln to Normal—birthplace of the Republican Party in 1856—and reduced his lead over Andy Payne to five hours.[24] He had shaved his beard and cut his hair the night before, and fans wondered if he had, like Samson of the Old Testament, lost some strength along with it.[25] "What the hell came over you?" Pyle asked him, referring to his hair. He reminded the Englishman his fans would have paid good money in Chicago for a peek at those whiskers. "Here I've been working like a dog, getting things ready for a swell Chicago ballyhoo, and you spoil my plans by getting those whiskers shaven just when they were getting nice and flowing and curly at the ends," Pyle said. "All I asked you to do is to run and grow whiskers and now you shirked half of your responsibility. And me working like a dog. That's gratitude for you." Pyle turned down Gavuzzi's offer to wear fake whiskers.[26]

While Peter struggled, Johnny Salo turned in another day of speed, finishing the thirty-five-mile run with seven-minute-and-forty-second miles.[27] Johnny had reestablished his hold on third place with a comfortable lead over Phillip Granville, while his former rival, Eddie Gardner, revived enough to recapture sixth place in the cumulative standings.[28]

As the men finished the race, they were again greeted by crowds, but their leader, C. C. Pyle, was not among them. Red Grange explained the absence:

Grange: "Champions of the long trial, I have an announcement to make."
Unidentified runner: "Make it after we eat—my dogs [feet] will feel better then."
Second unidentified runner: "Tell it to Oscar," referring to the embalmed Oklahoma outlaw in the carnival.
Grange: "No, my news cannot wait. Our leader, Charles C. Pyle, has sustained a loss."
Runners: "Hurrah!"
Grange: "A deputy constable working for the railroad magnates seized his $25,000 bus this afternoon at Joliet, and it is now parked behind the jail house."
Peter Gavuzzi: "Is Charley in or out [of jail]?"
Grange: "He's out."
Runners: "Too bad."

Red promised that Charley would now lead the men on foot, which brought a hail of snickers.[29]

Pyle had gotten himself and Grange into this legal mess by investing heavily in the Illinois Trust and Savings Bank of Champaign, with money made in professional football. He then used their investment as collateral to borrow twenty thousand dollars from the bank, in the form of an unsecured note.[30] Their plunge into banking turned sour when one of the bank officers cleaned out the vault and allegedly fled to South America, leaving their stock worthless. When the bank went into receivership, lawyers for the bank's creditors drew up a writ of attachment on Pyle's bus, *America*, when he returned to Illinois. After the deputies seized his bus, Charley returned to Normal in a rented car while opposing lawyers argued the case for the next three days.[31] Pyle maintained that he was only renting the bus from his brother, and therefore it could not be seized.[32]

As the director general's legal sideshow continued, his bunioneers were burning up Route 66. On the sixty-first stage run to Pontiac, a gritty industrial town, tiny Harry Rea of Los Angeles covered the thirty-four-mile course in just over four hours with seven-minute miles.[33] Rea had recently risen in the standings to thirteenth place. Thirty minutes later came Peter Gavuzzi, revived after the prior day's struggle; then Johnny Salo, Olli Wanttinen, and Eddie Gardner, all running at a pace under eight minutes per mile.[34] Gavuzzi had once more abandoned the razor and sported a day's growth of stubble. He extended his lead again to more than five hours, quieting a critic who thought he had cracked under the strain of daily sub-eight-minutes-per-mile racing.[35] Johnny Salo also showed his iron-man credentials when he finished a fourth day of sub-eight-minute-per-mile racing and opened a five-hour lead over Canadian Phillip Granville. Granville's hometown paper, the *Hamilton Spectator*, dryly noted, "The leaders, whom Phillip threatened to run into the ground, are still in the race and increasing their margin daily."[36]

As the lag between the leaders and the pack grew, money-conscious F. F. Gunn was anxious to jettison the slower entourage and bring his money-losing derby to an end as soon as possible. He decided to increase the daily distance and strictly enforce the midnight cutoff rule. Charley said, "The pace will be hot, and the iron men will survive to the finish."[37] One derby runner the management could not shake off, however, was Blisters—a nondescript shepherd dog that had joined the race in Navajo, Arizona. He had traveled with the derby until Missouri where he became lost. He reappeared in Pontiac, five hundred miles later, a bit dirty but unharmed after having "embarked" on his own one-dog derby.[38]

On Friday, May 4, the sixty-second day of the race, the men had their first taste of the longer distances. They left for a fifty-nine-mile run to Joliet, an industrial town on the old Illinois and Michigan canal.[39] They began at 6 a.m., cheered on by early morning crowds. Eddie Gardner took an early lead in the intermittent rain.[40] Fan-packed cars were parked the length of the course.[41] Many passengers offered food, drinks, and lumps of sugar, prescribed by Pyle as "a cure-all" for fatigued athletes. One uninvited contestant passed the bunioneers "like a comet." He was professional roller skater Asa Hall, on a solo race from Kansas City to New York, via Chicago. Hall did not believe "these fellows" would make it to New York.[42]

In a driving spring rain, Eddie was the first to cross the finish line, three miles ahead of the nearest competitor. The director general's forecast that thousands would greet the finishers was "slightly awry," although Eddie did receive a feeble cheer from a crowd of several hundred fans.[43] The Sheik had won the race in the fast time of about seven hours and forty-five minutes, at a sub-eight-minute-mile pace. His effort nudged him into fifth place, though he still trailed Granville by ten hours. Next came Guisto Umek, followed by Peter Gavuzzi, Olli Wanttinen, Roy McMurtry, and Johnny Salo in a four-way tie for third. Andy Payne arrived a distant seventh.[44]

That night, Pyle announced that he would close down his money-losing sideshow acts, putting his troupe of dancing girls, the tattooed man, the snake charmer, and other novelties on the unemployment line. He said he was considering replacing them with an athletic show, more in keeping with the spirit of the cross-country race.[45] He also claimed his bus would soon be back in the derby. Charley, without a hint of shame, told the press he had been named in almost one hundred attachments and he had "never lost an action as a result."[46] The next day he produced documentation that he merely rented the bus, and he soon regained the flagship.[47]

Chicago

DAY 63, 69 MEN

Saturday, May 5, 1928. Ahead lay Chicago, a behemoth of three million people on the shores of Lake Michigan. In 1928, it was a manufacturing powerhouse that took the bounty of the region and processed it into thousands of products for the world.[48] The city also hosted mobster Al Capone, who reportedly pulled in seventy million dollars each year from his bootleg liquor trade.[49] Some of the runners feared that Capone's machine-gunning mobsters might shoot them before they passed through the city.

On May 5, thousands of Chicagoans lined Route 66. They were ten deep as the runners darted in and out of traffic and raced down Michigan Avenue to the finish at the National Guard Armory.[50] The first man to reach the city was Johnny Salo of Passaic, New Jersey, who had emerged as a star in recent weeks. Since leaving Los Angeles, this deep-water sailor had shed sixteen pounds, revealing the steel-cord body of a wrestler. He was fast, but he came to his speed too late in the race to overcome the vast gap between himself and leaders Andy Payne and Peter Gavuzzi. But right then, at the peak of his powers, he was more than a match for the two and could keep it up for the remainder of the race. That day in Chicago, Johnny sprinted up to the timer's desk at 1:15 p.m., checked in, then walked over to a hot dog stand and ate heartily before he posed for photos for the press corps.[51]

His fading rival, Phillip Granville, followed him twenty minutes later. Then came Olli Wanttinen, despite being knocked down by a car and fracturing a rib a few blocks from the armory.[52] Sam Otis, sports editor of the *Cleveland Plain Dealer*, wrote, "Such courage is not surprising, however, when one stops to consider the indomitable nerve required to hot-foot it all the way from the Pacific slope."[53] Peter Gavuzzi and Andy Payne finished together in fourteenth place.[54]

For the black runners, it was a joyous day. Blacks had always been part of Chicago: The first homesteader, Jean-Baptiste Pointe du Sable, was a West Indian "negro." After 1910, waves of southern blacks left the cotton belt and immigrated to Chicago looking for work. Most lived in the southeastern section of the city, and they turned out in force to cheer their bunioneers.[55]

Eddie Gardner took Chicago by storm. His reception started fourteen miles outside the city as a line of cars followed him to the finish. As he neared the heart of the city, he was met by the greatest black entertainer of his age, William "Bojangles" Robinson. He paced Gardner down Michigan Avenue, sprinting backwards while the Sheik ran "amid cheers of the people who lined the avenue and shrieks of sirens and honking of automobile horns." Over the years, Robinson had perfected the art of backward sprinting, which he called "freak running."[56] In his travels on the vaudeville circuit, he gained a lot of free press for his unusual running style, often challenging local sprinters to a well-publicized race. He beat most of them and held a world record for the backward hundred-yard dash.

Eddie Gardner was also a celebrity in the black community. He had stepped over the color line to compete one-on-one against the best white athletes in the world and on any given day, he beat them. He helped explode the myth that blacks lacked the endurance for long-distance events.[57] Humming spirituals as he went, Eddie was the quiet hero in the war for black equality in America. He had earned the respect of Charley

Figure 21.
"Please Stand By, Red Grange (left) broadcasts feats of Peter Gavuzzi (center) leader in Pyle's Derby, Charley Hart, Gavuzzi's trainer, at right." *Chicago Tribune* Photo, May 6, 1928. Credit: *Chicago Tribune* Photo. All rights reserved. Used with permission.

Pyle and his fellow bunioneers as well. In Chicago, Pyle was standing behind Eddie at a lunch counter. The attendant handed Charley his food before serving Eddie, to which Pyle said, "Serve the men as they come," and waited until Gardner had been served.[58]

Pyle decided to bring his derby to Chicago despite the business community's refusal to pay him.[59] Chicago was the last of a long line of great cities that reneged on their pledge to support his trip across Route 66. By one estimate, Charley had missed sixty thousand dollars in pledges, while a string of unsettled legal issues dogged his heels.[60] As the derby reached Chicago, Pyle was in Joliet making a five-thousand-dollar payment on his twenty-thousand-dollar note, held by the creditors of the defunct savings and loan. He left Joliet with his bus after he promised to pay off the remainder of the note in short order.[61]

In Chicago, Red Grange led the welcoming ceremonies in Pyle's

Figure 22. Niels Nielson, #126, left the race in Chicago.
Credit: El Reno Carnegie Library.

absence. One *Chicago Tribune* reporter wrote, "Grange used to be a shy, modest youth who abhorred making a speech." Under C. C. Pyle's tutelage, however, he had become "a typically ballyhoo man." Shortly after 8 p.m., Red began introducing the runners to the thousand spectators that milled about the raised stage, as a vaudeville team did a few chair tricks in the middle of the floor.[62]

That night, most of Pyle's men slept soundly on iron cots in a partitioned section of the armory, content that they had proven themselves in the long road to Chicago. Five decided not to go further: ice skater and boxer Walter Grafsky of St. Paul, Minnesota; runner and boxer William Meyers of Missoula, Montana; A. G. Barnes of Ohio, who survived to Chicago despite joining the race on a whim without training or experience; Chicago's own Niels Nielson, who had finished second in the opening race of the derby; and David Davies of Sandwich, Ontario.[63] With no chance for prize money, they felt having run the length of Route 66 was adventure enough. In addition, Arthur Duffy quit his duties as head referee and returned to his newspaper job in Boston, and Red Grange took his place as referee.[64]

The runners who remained had another thousand miles to go before reaching the skyline of Manhattan. But much had been decided after two months and 2,402 miles on the ground. Barring injury, it was a two-man show: Either Peter Gavuzzi or Andy Payne would win the twenty-five-thousand-dollar prize. Johnny Salo had third place locked, and Phillip Granville had fourth. Gavuzzi had shown what he could do; it was up to Andy Payne to make the next move.

CHAPTER 14

Across the Heartland

A Dime a Dozen

DAY 64, 64 MEN

Sunday, May 6, 1928. Sixty-four bunioneers plunged into America's heartland, Indiana—the second state in the Old Northwest and the eighth for the bunioneers. Two home-state boys—the one-armed Robert McMurtry of Indianapolis and John Stone of Marion—led the pack into the great steel-producing town of Gary on the shore of Lake Michigan. Stone and McMurtry broke out of their typical dogtrot pace to tie for first on the twenty-eight-mile course, covering the distance in a seven-minute-mile pace.[1] Skeptics wondered if Charley had "arranged" this all-Indiana finish to drum up local interest in the race. Perhaps it was either pride or the incentive of under-the-table local money that put the fire under their feet.

Hot on their heels came Johnny Salo, Peter Gavuzzi, Phillip Granville, Eddie Gardner, and Andy Payne, all in under an eight-minute-mile pace.[2] Andy had seen the writing on the wall—if he had any hope of beating Peter, he needed to run consistently under eight minutes per mile from then on. Eddie Gardner had to do the same, but

Figure 23. Indiana's favorite sons John Stone, #28 (pictured), and the one-armed Robert McMurtry (not pictured) tied for first place in the first stage race in their home state. Credit: El Reno Carnegie Library.

his body could not stand the strain. After Gary, he developed a painful case of shin splints, which would force him to hobble for the next six days.[3]

Others were struggling, too. On the road to Gary, the derby almost lost Harry Rea, who was stricken with stomach cramps near the end of the race. Unwilling to give up, the thirty-six-year-old was found crawling on his hands and knees in a roadside ditch before he agreed to be taken to a local hospital. He recovered enough to finish the race.[4] Guisto Umek was also stricken with stomach problems, though the cause proved much more sinister—Guisto had attended a dinner in Chicago, and shortly thereafter became very ill. Physicians who treated him said he suffered from the effects of a sedative "evidently administered in his food." Columnist George Shereck of the *Seattle Post Intelligencer* believed gamblers might have been trying to influence the results by putting the Italian out of the derby. "The race, like a title fight, would not be complete without plots and poisons," he wrote. In Arizona, Guisto had also been warned to quit the race—the Italian seemed to have made a few enemies during his trek.[5]

F. F. Gunn continued to run the financial show, and the men soon saw the results of Gunn's cost-cutting regime. The twenty-eight-mile race to Gary would be the last day of easy running for the bunioneers—there would be no more breaks between the already-increased distances. The new goal was to reach New York City as quickly as possible to stop the hemorrhage of red ink. By further increasing the daily runs, Gunn again hoped to shake off any remaining plodders in the rear and reduce the number of mouths to feed, once and for all. "There are too many [bunioneers] sticking around, and they're eating too much," said Bill Pickens, one of Charley's lieutenants. Derby management hoped no more than forty men would finish in New York City. The order came down: "[The] boys will run fifteen miles more a day."[6]

For the next sixteen days, the men would average fifty-four miles each day—sixteen miles more than they had averaged so far.[7] The next day's run would be the longest yet: sixty-six miles to Mishawaka, a manufacturing city of cars and tires, on the banks of the St. Joseph River. Named after an Indian princess, the town called itself the peppermint capital of the world, from the mint grown on surrounding farms.

Mishawaka proved a tough target—runners battled a clogged road with the help of police patrols. Louis Perrella finished first, after more than nine hours running eight-and-a-half-minute miles. To one local reporter, Louis looked "none the worse for the grind . . . [and] went to the showers in high spirits." Soon after, he returned to the finish and watched his competition arrive.[8] Salo finished next, forty-five minutes later, followed by Gavuzzi, Payne, and Granville in a third-place tie after eleven hours and twenty-five minutes. Eddie Gardner had had a disastrous day. Suffering from his shin splints, he clenched his teeth and staggered in before the midnight cutoff, but tumbled from fifth to eight in the cumulative standings.[9]

The derby had originally planned to stop in South Bend, four miles to the east, but town leaders balked at Pyle's request for a contribution. Mishawaka's chamber of commerce stepped in, sponsored the stop, and gave the town of twenty-eight thousand an unexpected holiday.[10] People lined the highway and it was mayhem as overburdened police tried to clear a path for the runners.[11] The crowd roared when home-state boy Mike Kelly crossed the line. Local newspaperman Jack Urban had followed him across the country. To Urban, Kelly was a survivor who liked to take his time and had a few odd habits. Kelly made a point of stopping at every filling station along the way, where he passed out preprinted

Figure 24. Tough and talented Olli Wanttinen, #238, dropped out of the derby in Indiana. Credit: El Reno Carnegie Library.

business cards to all who would take them. The cards were inscribed, "Mike Kelly, marathon runner and boxer extraordinaire." He was also the "bridge sleeper"—adept at curling up under the arch of a bridge for a quick nap.[12]

The remaining men were strung along the road for forty miles, and three of them did not reach the city before midnight.[13] Neither tiny Olli Wanttinen of New York nor Harry Rea of Long Beach made it. These men had often been among the leaders in stage races, but after Olli had been hit by a car outside Chicago, his fractured rib slowed him dramatically. And Rea had literally crawled to Gary on his hands and knees before he was taken to a hospital for treatment. Both tried desperately to stay in the derby, but this time, distance and injuries conspired to put them out of the contest. On a good day, both men could match the best of the derby in speed and stamina. Wanttinen and Rea had nothing to prove now. They were tough as nails and would forever be iron men of the long trail to New York. The derby also lost John Wilson, an Army veteran from Oakland, California. He was a "tail ender who dropped out with severely blistered feet."[14]

The next day, May 8, the sixty-one remaining men were weary. One reporter said that the previous day's sixty-six miles "clear took the wind out of the sails of the runners." They had an easier time with the day's forty-one-mile course to the quiet farming community of Ligonier, and a recovered Guisto Umek won the stage in six hours. Indianans Roy McMurtry and John Stone followed an hour later in second and third, quieting skeptics. Payne and Gavuzzi spent a few hours of their massive lead when they finished in a tie for thirteenth, two hours behind Guisto Umek. Salo, Granville, and Gardner—who continued his painful battle with shin splints—collapsed into the pack and were not seen or heard of in press reports.[15]

The frontrunners returned to form on the next day's sixty-seventh stage race to the university town of Butler. Phillip Granville led the pack on the forty-two-mile jaunt, finishing in about five and a half hours, with Johnny Salo thirty minutes behind. Eddie Gardner fought through another day of excruciating pain to complete the forty-two miles in just over thirteen hours, dropping to ninth in the overall standings.[16]

A Sad Demise

DAY 68, 61 MEN

Thursday, May 10, 1928. John French, sports editor for the *Toledo Blade*, positioned himself nine miles west of Wauseon, the first control stop in Ohio.[17] His first sign of the derby was the appearance of a large automobile with the words, "Official Program Car" painted on its hood in gold and blue letters—the colors of the University of Illinois—driven by Red Grange. Then a few cars with California license plates arrived and, as they passed him, storm clouds appeared on the horizon and petals from spring cherry blossoms rained pink out of a blustery sky—a herald of trouble for the leader of the bunioneers, who was suddenly extremely sick and tormented by an ulcerated tooth.[18]

Peter Gavuzzi's rivals caught the scent of change in the air. Johnny Salo was quick to bounce on his rival's weakness, hitting a near suicidal pace for hours, and opening a four-mile lead over the field.[19] The New Jersey Finn had been pushing the pace for days, forcing the frontrunners behind him to go faster than they thought safe to go, into the injury zone that had undone so many before them. When Johnny's trainer had left the race a few days before, some of his rivals saw a chance to taunt the unescorted speed king. In one instance, a trainer paced him, pretended to offer him a drink, dumped the water on the road in front of him and then sped off. Johnny sent a telegram to the American Legion, complaining that some of the bunioneers and their trainers were "doing everything to tantalize and break him down." The Legion responded by promising to send two security men to meet him in Cleveland and escort him the rest of race.[20]

French next saw Andy Payne as he jogged over the horizon with Phillip Granville and Louis Perrella. They stopped in front of the reporter and took a drink of water from Granville's trainer, Bill Westcott. French was startled to hear the brown-skinned runner speak in the well-modulated tones of an Englishman when Phillip asked Westcott, "How much further to that town? I can't remember the name." Westcott replied it was about nine miles, and told them there was one more water stop. Andy said, "Okay, let's go," and the three jogged away again, as chummy as a group of college kids.[21]

As men continued to pass by alone and in groups, French saw how important the automobile escorts were to them, providing water, food, or a change of clothes. When rain clouds threatened, the trainers, following a well-oiled routine, drove up with emergency outfits—yellow slickers, mackintoshes, waterproof trousers, and rubber caps.[22]

Many runners loped by before Gavuzzi finally came into sight, with Richard Thomas, another British-born runner, nursing him along. French wrote, "No grotesque, gaunt, bewhiskered individual, but a beautifully built little fellow, with a gait that was the poetry of motion, with brown eyes that flashed clear and steady, with a little moustache neatly trimmed, whose eyes gave no sign of the nausea which was gripping him, nor the jumping pain in his ulcerated tooth." However, on another stop on the race, Peter vented his frustration on a group of photographers as he stopped for a drink. When they tried to take his picture, Peter wheeled around and threw his big, waterproof hat at them.[23] Frustration and gloom whirled around his camp, like the rain-laden clouds that hung in the sky on that dreary day in Ohio.[24]

Johnny Salo won the forty-five-mile race to Wauseon, beating the trio of Andy Payne, Phillip Granville, and Louis Perrella. Gathering storm clouds chased the three to the finish line and let loose "a heavy torrent of rain" just as they crossed the line. Eddie Gardner again struggled to complete the stage by the midnight cutoff, and tumbled another spot in the standings to tenth—the last money spot in the derby. The derby lost Kenneth Campbell of Ranger, Texas, twenty-four miles west of Wauseon, when arch trouble forced him out of the race.[25]

That night in Wauseon, Charley Pyle suddenly revived his sleazy carnival sideshow. Perhaps Pyle had had a change of heart after its colorful members threatened him with a lawsuit or, more likely, he saw that gate receipts had fallen off after its departure. He gave no reason for its return, and all the men knew was that the carnival barker's cries had returned to disturb their sleep.[26]

That night, Peter Gavuzzi had his gum lanced, which gave him some relief from the pain.[27] But it did not improve his fortunes. For two weeks, the pain had forced him to abandon solid food. He had survived by drinking soup and sucking hard candy—a diet that could not supply the massive calorie needs of an ultramarathoner. Peter literally ran of gas. The next morning, his distraught trainer, feisty little Charley Hart, made a pathetic plea to sell his shares to Peter's prize rights to anyone he saw, including a reporter for the *Cleveland Plain Dealer.* There were no takers, however, for Peter's stock had crashed. The iron man from Southampton was finished. "It just made me sick," said his sad manager.[28] The end for Peter Gavuzzi came nine miles west of town where he was found sitting in a ditch, doing what he loved best: smoking a cigarette. He told the press, "My teeth. They have been threatening me for two weeks. They finally got me."[29] Asked about his future plans, Peter said, "I guess I'll go on the program-selling crew."[30]

The exhausted Englishman traveled by car to the control point in Fremont, climbed out, staggered into the press bus, and announced that he had quit. With tears streaming down his face, Peter checked out of the race. He then pushed himself through the crowds just as fans began to cheer for Mike Joyce, the little Cleveland Irishman.[31]

The ship's steward from Southampton had a right to shed some tears. He had the twenty-five thousand dollars in his grasp after sixty-eight days of gut-busting racing. More than that, he had pushed the sport of ultramarathoning to a new level and took the frontrunners along for the ride. He had shown his toughness in the thin air of Arizona and the prairie mud of Texas. When he had a chance to run unencumbered in Illinois and Indiana, he showed the speed of a god, swift, graceful, and resolute. As *Toledo Blade* reporter French said, "This beautifully built little fellow" ran with the "poetry of motion."[32]

Peter Gavuzzi's end meant a chance at first for Johnny Salo, though Andy Payne had a cushion of twenty-four hours that he hoarded like gold. With less than two weeks to go, Johnny would need to burn up the course every day, running seven-minute miles if he had any hope of catching Andy. It would be tough. Barring injury, the Foyil farm boy had already won.

Cleveland Welcomes Mike Kelly Home

DAY 69, 60 MEN

Friday, May 11, 1928. The news of Peter Gavuzzi's departure spread among the bunioneers strung along the sixty-four-mile course to Fremont, an old Wyandot Indian village on the colonial trail from Detroit to Pittsburgh. The course followed Highway 20 across Ohio, skirting the bustling Lake Erie port of Toledo.[33] The runners were grateful to Frank Smith, a gas station owner, who passed out a cold bottle of soda pop to each contestant who passed by. One thankful bunioneer said Frank's pop "was the first thing he had gotten gratis since he left California."[34]

A reporter from the *Toledo Blade* painted a vivid picture of the men: "Faces burned by wind and sun, muscles taut, eyes weary, arms and legs swinging easily in constant rhythmic motion, gave the joggers a pictur-esque appearance as they continued on quiet highways bordered with blos-soms and spring flowers."[35] Another reporter came upon Guisto Umek, the famously temperamental Italian, sitting on a large rock by the side of the road. Guisto was in the middle of a sit-down strike against his trainer. The reporter listened to the trainer beg Guisto to reenter the race. When he finally did, he took things easy for five miles before shifting into high gear.[36] The reporter then met Cleveland's Mike Joyce, the little Irishman. At just five feet tall, he described Mike as "a little green frog in a green gym shirt." Joyce announced that he felt great and had never had so much as a blister since his trainer and friend Jack Mulroy had joined him in Oklahoma.[37]

Johnny Salo was the first to reach Fremont at 3 p.m.[38] He had cov-ered the distance in eight-minute miles—not nearly fast enough to catch Andy. Hours later, Andy Payne and Phillip Granville finished in a tie for sixth, with Mike Joyce close behind. Eddie Gardner continued his battle with shin splints, arriving later after hobbling across the Ohio country-side. Latecomers, like Gardner, had to deal with a drenching rain that left them soaked to the skin and shivering when they finished.[39]

With the extended mileage, many of the men in the pack had to push hard to arrive before the midnight cutoff, now rigidly enforced by Red Grange. The head referee promised to disqualify them if they missed the deadline by one minute. Red was proving to be a bit of a tyrant, and said, "Speed is the thing that counts now, and all men know that they will be dropped at the least show of indifference."[40] Indifference, after 2,600 miles. The bunioneers had fought through hell to run the length of Route 66, and froze in Pyle's drafty tents while folksy Red Grange traveled in style and stayed at the best hotels. It was simply a crime to push exhausted men to the breaking point after all they had been through.[41]

The next day, the 59 remaining men had a 63-mile race to Elyria, which made 173 miles in three days.[42] It also brought them close to Cleveland, the manufacturing powerhouse of 900,000 at the mouth of the Cuyahoga River on Lake Erie.[43]

To the bunioneers, it seemed that every car in Cleveland was on the road to greet them and, in particular, Clevelander Mike Joyce. Much like in Oklahoma, fan-filled cars felt free to idle along with the men, clogging the roads and forcing contestants to weave through their gridlock.[44]

When the bunioneers reached Elyria, the crowds were still thick and the runners had to thread their way to the finish. The first man to negotiate the jam was Guisto Umek, who arrived at 3:30 p.m. Johnny Salo followed fifteen minutes later with Harry Abramowitz in third, and Andy Payne, Phillip Granville, and Louis Perrella in a tie for fourth with just thirteen days left in the race.[45] Andy Payne still held a massive twenty-four-hour lead over Johnny Salo—the New Jersey Finn needed a miracle.

When Mike Joyce crossed the line, his fans didn't recognize him until "they finally got wise that the tiny fellow in the green gym shirt was Joyce." After finishing the race, "Midget Mike" went ahead to Cleveland to visit his wife and children. When he knocked on his own front door, he received a rather cold welcome from Mrs. Joyce, until she realized that this wiry little nut-brown man was her husband. He did not fare much better with the children. They cried at the sight of him and dove under their beds.[46]

There are no reports on the status of Eddie Gardner at this point, except that he was still in ninth place overall. For Charley's "dime a dozen" pack runners, it was another day of struggling to beat the midnight cutoff under the stern eye of Red Grange. Reporter Phillip Porter wrote, "Nobody can say what keeps them in the race except habit and the hope that the first ten or fifteen will drop dead before they reach New York."[47]

The next morning, fifty-six bunioneers left Elyria on a pleasant morning for a fifty-one-mile run along the Lake Erie shore to Arrowhead Beach. They would be passing through Cleveland, and had to thread their way through another day of gridlock down the lakeshore. In the western suburbs, people stood shoulder-to-shoulder and many "planted themselves in chairs for the afternoon."[48] The *Cleveland Plain Dealer* even penned an ode to the racers:

Hark! Hark! Their dogs go bark! Pyle's cuckoos are comin' to town.

   With addled brains and aches and sprains and arches breakin' down.[49]

Unfortunately, without crowd control and with cars packed along the route, the forty-nine-year-old ex-Alaskan musher, Harry Sheare of San Francisco, was nearly killed just east of Elyria when a car ran him down. He was taken, unconscious, to the Elyria Memorial Hospital with a possible skull fracture, a wrenched pelvis, and contusions. This tough old prospector had been more than a match for many men half his age, having finished in the top fifteen in stage races at least five times, with his best showing being a fifth-place finish in the forty-one-mile run to Ligonier, Indiana, but that was it for his derby racing.[50]

While Harry Sheare lay in the hospital, the crowd scanned the road for their hero, Mike Joyce. He had left a steady job and five small children to follow a dream—that at age thirty-five, he could take on the best of the distance world over the long trail to New York. Like Johnny Salo, Mike Joyce learned that sometimes dreams do come true, despite the odds. His struggling family survived, and as he moved up in the standings, "[F]unds started to pour into the family treasury as Mike's game showing opened the purse strings of the Cleveland public."[51] The *Cleveland Plain Dealer* wrote that Mike was surprised to find that his hometown considered him a hero, "the Hon. Mike Joyce, ex-factory toiler."[52]

Mike was not about to disappoint his Cleveland fans, yelling to fellow bunioneer Paul Simpson, "It's a poor man who can't run first into his home town." As he entered Cleveland, the city's Irish swarmed the road and almost stopped the race with their celebration. Thousands were applauding, shouting "Atta boy," and "Hooray for the Irish!" Fifty of Joyce's co-workers from the Fisher auto body plant were on hand to cheer him on, as well, and they gave him a $100 donation from the company's athletic association.[53]

The course ran through Mike's neighborhood, and Mrs. Joyce and their five children were waiting for him. When he reached his family, his kids were crying out to him and he said, "Lo, kids, there, there, Sh! Sh! Dadda's here."[54] Mrs. Joyce had brought a larder of food with her to help sustain him on the remaining days to New York—two dozen eggs, a cake, three roast chickens, a pound of butter—which he gave to his trainer to carry. He stopped for a few minutes and posed for a picture with his youngest child in his arms, which appeared on the front page of the *Cleveland Plain Dealer*.[55] Then he scooped up another child as surging fans nearly knocked him down. He waited a minute for the chaos

Figure 25. Philadelphia's Arthur Studenroth, #88, and Cleveland's new
hometown hero Mike Joyce, #83. Credit: El Reno Carnegie Library.

to subside, said his goodbyes, and headed down the road. People threw dollars bills at him and he collected thirty-five dollars as he ran.[56] He was the only bunioneer on the course—the reunion had brought traffic to a standstill, and those behind him were stuck.[57]

Last Legs in Ohio

DAY 71, 57 MEN

Sunday, May 13, 1928. Charley Pyle's choice of Arrowhead Beach was testament to his skills as a salesman. While scouting for a control stop, he passed through the pleasant lakeside community and said, "This looks like a pretty good place. Guess I'll stop here." As he pulled off the road at 5:30 p.m. that Thursday, May 10, Mr. R. N. Russell, real estate developer, was sprinkling his lawn.

The great director general stepped out of his bus, ambled over, and began to talk with him. Russell told a reporter from the *Cleveland Plain Dealer* he was a pretty good salesman himself, but had been outclassed by Charley Pyle. When Pyle began to talk, Russell had no intention of working with him, "much less of paying any guarantees." Russell first advised him to meet with the city fathers of the nearby town of Painesville, which they did together that evening at a dinner meeting at a local tavern. As the Painesville businessmen warmed to the idea of hosting the derby, the "warmer [Russell] got to" the idea of having it at his town. By 11:45 p.m., Russell had written a $1,000 check to Pyle. Like a bad hangover, Russell woke up in the morning wondering, "What do you get for the thousand dollars?" He hoped the event would make Arrowhead Beach "a bit more famous."[58]

By 2 p.m. Sunday, Red Grange had arrived and begun to set up the tents, the sideshows, and the canvas fence that walled off the finish area.[59] The first to arrive was Johnny Salo, as he continued his long-shot drive to catch Andy Payne. He covered the distance at a pace of just over seven minutes per mile and narrowed his gap with Andy to twenty-two hours, with just twelve days to get rid of the rest. Thirty minutes later came Eddie Gardner, having overcome his bout with shin splints.[60] His finish moved him from tenth back into ninth, but his six-day struggle had sealed his fate: He could possibly rise to seventh, but beyond that, he was stuck. Louis Perrella had a virtual lock on sixth with a thirteen-hour cushion.

Eddie was running for pride now, a brilliant athlete, badly coached, with the heart of a sprinter and the courage of a lion.[61]

Mike Joyce finished next and made a little speech to the crowd. "Ladies and gentlemen, it's wonderful the reception I got in Cleveland. Of course I'm sorry I couldn't win this lap, but I was first into Cleveland. There were a lot of fellows I knew started in Los Angeles, but old Anchor Man Mike is the only one left now. It's a wonderful reception. I couldn't talk in other states, but I can now for I know I am home."[62] With that, he flopped on the grass for a little rest. Earlier that day, a reporter had asked him what he thought about F. F. Gunn and Charley's decision to increase the distances each day. Mike laughed and said, "Pyle's speeding the race up to weed out the bums, and that's just what I wanted all the time.[63] The little Irishman had a solid hold on the $2,500 fourth-place prize money, with a five-hour lead over Guisto Umek in fifth.[64]

On Monday, the last race in the Old Northwest took the men on a forty-one-mile jaunt to Ashtabula, a Lake Erie port for off-loading shipments of iron ore and coal to fuel Ohio.[65] A true port town with some of the largest shipyards on the Great Lakes, it was rumored to have had more saloons in its pre-prohibition heyday than any port but Singapore.[66] In 1928, the town was in holiday spirit, festooned with American flags and red, white, and blue bunting decorating downtown buildings. Schools were let out, farmers left their plows, and Highway 20 was again a parking lot. Policeman waged a losing battle to clear a path for the men. On this obstacle course, Johnny Salo called a temporary truce in his drive to wrest the twenty-five thousand dollars from Andy Payne. The pair covered the forty-one miles together in six hours, and Andy retained his twenty-two-hour lead.[67]

The big surprise of the day was the fifth-place finish of Sam Richman, one of the four brothers from New York, who held forty-seventh place overall. With a cumulative time of 801 hours, Sam was two weeks behind Andy Payne.[68] His performance, though, gave a hint of the untapped talent that brewed within him. Sam had the nickname "sexy" for his legendary good looks. Eddie Gardner ran at a twelve-minute-mile pace, but still clung to ninth.[69]

And while the remaining runners continued to struggle, a few acts of kindness padded the way. For Louis Perrella, Ashtabula was a miraculous place. His brother had been hitchhiking from New York to meet him at the finish, and planned to accompany Louis the rest of the way to New York City. Just east of town, one ride short of Ashtabula, a local motorist picked him up. When the man heard of his plans, the unnamed driver got out of his Ford in Ashtabula and gave him the keys, telling the startled brother to return the car at the end of the race. This incredibly kind man gave from his heart, sensing the magnitude of the accomplishment in crossing the United States on foot.[70]

Cowboy humorist and Andy Payne's friend Will Rogers echoed those feelings in his nationally syndicated column. Rogers was fed up with snide comments of sports reporters, blinded by Pyle's unsavory reputation, who could not acknowledge the Herculean efforts of his bunioneers. Rogers wrote:

It's all right to kid and call it bunion, but no athlete in any branch of sport could get up every day for three straight months and run 40 to 70 miles a day. Sports writers write pages over some football player's 70-yard run. There is not a golfer who could have stood the same trip in an automobile. You'll find it's the grit and heart that's doing this more than bunions, or growing toenails. So be fair and give 'em a break.

Yours from Claremore,
Will Rogers[71]

CHAPTER 15

Salo Country

Eddie Gardner's Return

DAY 73, 56 MEN

Tuesday, May 15, 1928. Rogers had it right. These fifty-six men were exceptional. No one would have guessed that this mix of outcasts—an aging Passaic shipyard worker, a black man from Seattle, a starry-eyed Oklahoma farm boy, a Cleveland factory worker, and a handful of converted walkers—would beat the world's greatest runners to New York. They had to stay on their feet for another eleven days and six hundred miles, and they were home free. After all these men had been through, nothing would deny them the satisfaction of reaching New York City under their own power.

The bunioneers had left Ohio and entered the cradle of the nation— the original thirteen colonies, first to Pennsylvania, where brilliant men drafted the Constitution of the United States, then through New York and New Jersey for the final laps to the finish. For now, the men would stay on Highway 20 to Erie, Pennsylvania, a port town lined with dry docks for ship repair. The city had been the fledging U.S. Navy's hub when battling the British for the Great Lakes.[1] As in Ohio, interest in the race was huge, with cars and spectators jamming the course. A police guard escorted the first runner along the route, like an icebreaker, parting the crowds.[2]

The *Erie Dispatch Herald* sent one of its reporters, Barbara Hawley, to cover the arrival of the men. The first man she saw was Eddie Gardner, running with "trousers under his trunks." She kept hoping to get a picture of "the main body of runners," but she soon realized they were spread for miles "walking, trotting, loping, cantering, jogging . . . in twos and threes, but mostly singly on their lonely jog east."[3]

Eddie led the derby to the finish at the Erie Elks Club.[4] In a show of grit and determination, the Sheik had survived his six-day ordeal with shin splints and had found his stride again. "My dogs are just right again," he said, having covered the forty-five-mile course in six hours. He recaptured eighth place from John Cronick, who had developed his own case of shin splints.[5] Tenth-place holder Harry Abramowitz of New York developed the condition as well.[6]

Andy Payne and Johnny Salo tied for second, which maintained Andy's twenty-two-hour lead. After the finish, Payne told reporters he was taking nothing for granted. "I remember what happened to Gavuzzi just the other day. He had a comfortable lead over me," he said. "Then things went wrong and he was out. Before him Willie Kolehmainen, Arthur Newton, Charley Hart, Olli Wanttinen and other great runners met misfortune. The last 600-odd miles are the hardest. Anything may happen."[7]

But Andy's fans had more faith, and their main concern was whether Charley would be able to pay the prize money. "The many suits and attachments, which have been tossed this way ever since the caravan left Oklahoma City, is food for concern," wrote Charles Brill of the *Daily Oklahoman*.[8]

Salo could also see the handwriting on the wall for his chances of winning the race. In Erie, Johnny said, "Payne has a nice edge. I'm still going ahead and hoping that I'll carry somewhere in the money division."[9] He was not quite ready to cede victory to Andy just yet, however, and would continue to cut time off his deficit. He also told his fans in Passaic, New Jersey, that he had a good lead over his third-place opponent, Phillip Granville, and "[I] will hold it."[10]

As the derby neared New York, local attention shifted to Johnny. He was another rags-to-riches story as Mike Joyce had been for Cleveland.

He was the quintessential American success story—a lowly immigrant who risked everything for a dream. He started the race broke and alone, overcame incredible hardships with the help of the American Legion and, by Pennsylvania, had become a juggernaut with an escort car, a trainer, and his own personal reporter from the *Passaic Daily Herald*. He also had his own motorcycle police escort, supplied by the Passaic superintendent of public safety.[11]

In Passaic, civic pride in Salo's gutsy performance was reaching the bursting point. The editors of the *Passaic Daily Herald* invited Pyle to bring his derby to Passaic. Charley asked for $1,000, the amount was quickly raised, and Passaic began preparing for Johnny Salo's homecoming celebration. The town, just twelve miles from New York City, would be the last stop before the finish.[12]

On the stage race to Erie, the derby lost Bill Downing of Los Angeles to a knee injury. His withdrawal turned out to be a blessing for the men. He decided to stay with the derby for the trip to New York and, as a new member of the race patrol, he promised he would do his best in "herding the troupe in before midnight."[13] The men also had comic and practical inspiration from Juri Lossman, Estonia's Olympic marathon star, who had fallen days behind the frontrunners. He was now more emotionally helpful than anything else, and "rated as the prize jester of the caravan."[14] Next-to-last place in the contest, Lossman in a thick accent said he is "not making any money but having lots of fun." Arthur Newton was there as well, following the men on the course and encouraging the stragglers to keep up the pace.

With these reinforcements, the remaining fifty-five men would make it to New York, without exception. Reporter Barbara Hawley marveled at the resilience of these athletes and said, "I wish every one of those men could win. Will Rogers is right. They deserve it."[15]

The Last Long Legs in New York
DAY 74, 55 MEN

Wednesday, May 16, 1928. After Erie, the derby crossed into New York State with just ten days to go. The sixty-mile course would take the men through a pastoral scene of hills and farms to Jamestown, New York, a city noted for its furniture-making industry. The route skirted the southern boundary of Pennsylvania, where the dark, rolling Allegheny Mountains loomed against the overcast sky.

Even though he knew it would be almost impossible to overtake Andy Payne in the cumulative standings, Johnny Salo won the stage race to Jamestown in eight hours and forty-six minutes, cutting Andy's lead by an hour and a half.[16] Before he crossed the state line into New York, Johnny did a gracious thing: He slowed down to give New Yorker Sam Richman the honor of entering his home state first. "Thanks a lot, Johnny," said Richman. "That's all I wanted, and now I'm satisfied."[17] In Jamestown, a now-normal police escort cleared a path for Johnny, through a crowd of flag-waving fans, to the finish at the American Legion.[18] Forty-five minutes behind him came Guisto Umek in second, putting to rest a rumor that he had collapsed on the course. Sam Richman followed forty-five minutes later in third.[19]

In Jamestown, Charley Pyle's money-hemorrhaging derby finally found itself in the black—evidence of F. F. Gunn's involvement. Gunn denied credit for this, but admitted that he had handled the business end of the derby for the past several weeks. He called Charley "a brilliant promoter, [but] a poor business man."[20] Gunn's modesty notwithstanding, the money was finally coming in. The Jamestown Chamber of Commerce had paid Pyle's $1,000 fee and, in the end, the derby pulled in 1,868 paying customers and the derby left with $1,223 for the night.[21] Red Grange did his part to draw in the fans, standing at the finish line for hours, in the rain, fighting off a cold and autographing everything in sight. He signed "envelopes, copy paper, and non-descript papyrus" until he could barely move his wrist.[22]

With the edge of desperation off the race, Pyle abandoned the midnight cutoff time. Even Red seemed to mellow a bit, hinting to the boys in the rear that they still might get a little prize money at the end of the race.[23] Arthur Newton said, "The stamina of the entire lot [of the bunioneers] is almost superhuman."[24] Grange added, "I never cease to marvel at these runners."[25] Even Charley Pyle was impressed by the heart of his men. He said, "They have plenty of guts to keep up this pace." He also dismissed reports that his men were skin-and-bones, saying that half of them had gained weight since leaving California.[26]

On May 17, these survivors continued to follow the Liberty Highway along the southern border of New York, through the foothills of the

Allegheny Mountains.²⁷ They finished at Bradford, Pennsylvania, for a brief return to the Keystone State. Charley did so at the invitation of the sports editor of the *Bradford Era*, who did not want his readers to miss a chance to see the "most interesting race in all of athletic history."²⁸ With the derby bringing in money and towns clamoring to host it, Pyle began to think that, with some refinements, he might yet make a profit off transcontinental racing. He began planning to hold the second installment of the race in 1929, and hoped to include distance runners from the 1928 summer Olympic games.²⁹

On the road to Bradford, "sexy" Sam Richman continued his run with the derby leaders, winning the forty-four-mile race in six hours and forty-seven minutes.³⁰ Two minutes behind came the surging Californian Frank Von Flue in second, who had also broken into the top ranks in recent days. An hour later came Johnny Salo in third, immediately followed by Andy Payne.³¹ Andy was taking nothing for granted, despite his lead. "I have run all along, and will right through to the finish. If I am beaten, I will be the first to congratulate the winner," he said.³²

The next day, the men had another long run through the mountains to Wellsville, New York, with its fine old homes built by tycoons made rich from the surrounding oil fields. As they approached the end of their fifty-mile run, they met the usual contingent of schoolchildren given a holiday to watch the derby's arrival. At the city limits, Boy Scouts lined the road to greet the bunioneers.³³

There was no blinding speed displayed that day, as Johnny Salo and Eddie Gardner shared first-place honors with nine-and-a-half-minute miles. With no police supervision at the finish, the duo had a difficult time threading through the happy throng until Johnny's Passaic motorcycle police escort cleared a path, sirens blaring. The Sheik's finish secured his hold on eighth place, with a six-hour lead over Canada's injured John Cronick. Beyond that, though, Eddie could go no further— a yawning eight-hour gap separated him from William Kerr in seventh.

On May 19, the men had covered more than three thousand miles and the finish line was just four hundred miles away. They braved another day of hills on a course assaulted by torrential rains, making a fifty-two-mile journey to the aptly named town of Bath.³⁴ Johnny Salo renewed his assault on Andy when he led the pack to the finish in eight hours, cutting his deficit to eighteen hours. Californian Frank Von Flue finished ten minutes behind him in second, followed by Andy Payne in third. Unfazed by Johnny's performance, Andy turned the race into a victory parade, waving to the crowds at the finish and telling them, "Howdy. Feeling fine, thanks." It really was over now. During the last ten days, Salo had only managed to cut Payne's lead by six hours—he had seven days left to eliminate the remaining eighteen.[35] Phillip Granville's manager, Bill Westcott, acknowledged that the positions of the leaders were unlikely to change, noting, "[Granville] is in wonderful condition, however . . . only an accident to either Payne or Salo could result in his finishing better than third."[36]

Sunday found the men fighting through fifty-eight miles of winding mountain roads to Waverly, New York. Pyle had intended to stop in nearby Elmira, but its "blue laws" made it impossible to hold the race there on Sunday. The town fathers said, "[We] would be pleased to welcome you on any other day of the week."[37] The business and professional men of Waverly were glad to step in and host the derby instead.[38]

Paul Simpson of Elon, North Carolina, won the fifty-eight-mile race in nine hours, almost an hour ahead of the next finisher. Simpson, a physical education teacher, had overcome his "eleven-week battle with blisters and other inconveniences." After the race, the happy North Carolinian told the press, "I do not know whether I'll keep on with pro racing or not. I've a yearning to go back to Carolina where the sweet taters grow, but anyhow, I did my stuff for one day."

Salo, Payne, and Gonzales followed in a three-way tie for second; the two leaders were not going to risk injury in such tough conditions in the waning days of the race.[39] Frank Von Flue finished next, bumping an injured Harry Abramowitz of New York City out of tenth. His performance amazed the derby physician, who said, "Frank has no outstanding style or anything in his favor. He has carried on by putting his all into every day's run."[40] Frank next set his sights on John Cronick in ninth, who was engaged in a losing battle with shin splints. For his part, Cronick vowed, "[I'll] crawl before dropping below the money division."[41] For the rest of the men, the road to Waverly was a nightmare of wind, rain, and hills, forcing many to stagger through the darkness to the control station long after the now-defunct midnight cutoff.[42]

Things got worse the next day on the route to Deposit, New York. The seventy-five-mile course was the longest in the derby, run under a blistering sun on a winding mountain road. The derby had planned to stop in Binghamton, but its Better Business Committee turned down a $1,500 request, so Charley pushed on to Deposit where he found the town's leaders more receptive to his monetary demands.[43]

Johnny Salo won in twelve hours and thirteen minutes, cutting Andy Payne's lead to sixteen hours. He told the press, "Those were some hills, no fooling."[44] A *Binghamton Press* reporter captured Johnny's gutsy effort and wrote, "There was an expression on his face that conveyed a sense of deep concentration and determination. His eyes seemed to project a bit from his sockets, giving the impression that his mind was outdoing his body in his desire to break a record or assure a victory."[45]

Frank Von Flue finished next after being bowled over by a hit-and-run driver, which left him with slight contusions on his left leg. Race officials thought the injury might put him out of the race, but the Californian shook it off and finished second, forty-five minutes behind Johnny.[46] Thirty-five minutes later came Andy Payne, who told reporters, "Those miles seemed unending, the most maddening thing that I've covered so far. But I'm here and it's all over."[47]

For those with nagging injuries, the race was torture. The heat, hills, and winding road aggravated many ailments. Twenty-year-old Norman Codeluppi of Pasadena, California, who had struggled through the past several days with a wrenched knee, broke into tears as he reached Deposit, after being on the road for twenty hours. Norman told the press, "I felt my knee give way several times and on any number of occasions I had to sit down for several minutes and rub it so I could stagger on again. Each step was agony, but I've come this far and will go on."[48]

There was no reprieve the next day, either, with a heartbreaking pull of fifty-nine miles over the Catskill foothills to Liberty, New York.[49] In Liberty, Guisto Umek arrived first at 6 p.m., after ten hours of running. He received an ovation from the appreciative crowd as he ran down Church Street, which had been roped off to provide a path to the finish.[50] Another roar erupted when Johnny Salo and Frank Von Flue finished in a tie for second. Salo cut his deficit with Andy Payne to under sixteen hours, and Frank moved from tenth to ninth place, replacing John Cronick who continued his battle with shin splints. Andy Payne finished next, thirty-five minutes behind his rival.[51] Soon after, a torrential downpour let loose and washed out the evening's entertainment.[52]

So Close, So Far

DAY 81, 55 MEN

Wednesday, May 23, 1928. Though the mountain route continued, the run to Middletown, New York, marked the end of the extended distances. With the short thirty-eight-mile course, Pyle even gave the men an extra hour of sleep and set the start for 9 a.m. When the derby got underway, several members of the Monticello High School cross country team paced the bunioneers to the end of town before the racers returned to the tortuous winding hills of Sullivan County.[53]

Eddie Gardner, who had not been among the frontrunners for several days, won the lap in six hours. His erratic performances spawned rumors that he sometimes intentionally held back at the request of an alleged betting clique, though derby management flatly denied these rumors.[54]

Welshman Tom Ellis, who had shepherded Peter Gavuzzi on his last run to Fremont, finished three minutes behind the Sheik, with a surging Frank Von Flue taking third. A slew of slower men finished in the top ten that day, as the leaders chose to hold back. Two former frontrunners, Louis Perrella and Harry Abramowitz, continued to fall as their injuries deteriorated. Louis "finished far in the ruck" with a bad case of sore feet, and Abramowitz showed "unmistakable signs of wear and tear."[55]

Andy Payne finished in a tenth-place tie with Phillip Granville and one-armed Roy McMurtry from Indiana. Andy regained two hours on Johnny Salo after Johnny developed a chafed foot.[56] The *Oklahoman City Times* wrote, "Nothing save a complete collapse can prevent Payne from winning first money."[57] Payne's Oklahoma fans were putting plans into high gear for his finish in New York City. The airplane *Will Rogers*, piloted by family friend Charles Parker, would follow Andy for the last twenty miles of the race. Painted in white letters on the underside of one wing was the legend, "Greetings, Andy Payne," and on the other, "Will Rogers."[58]

With just three days to go, no one in the derby wanted a fellow bunioneer to drop out. Stronger runners helped the weak finish, and the midnight cutoff continued to be ignored. A reporter from the *Passaic Daily Herald* said, "There is real sportsmanship being displayed by everybody associated with the marathon."[59]

The next day's race to Suffern, New York, got under way at a bit past 9 a.m., held up by a camera crew taking pictures of the starters. The bunioneers had another short day: thirty-eight miles from Middletown to Suffern on "the concrete roller coaster over the Catskills."[60] On the road to Suffern, a large contingent of cars full of Passaic fans paced Salo, shouting words of encouragement and sending representatives to run by his side. Fans sat on fences and cheered, waved handkerchiefs, tooted car horns, and thrust paper and pencil into his hands for autographs.[61]

While the men ran, the derby trucks with canvas tents rolled into Suffern in the morning in a familiar routine practiced for the last eighty-two days. About noon, Red Grange arrived, and program men began peddling the twenty-five-cent programs. And then, one reporter wrote, "Shortly after two o'clock, the pulse of the little town quickened. There were cries of 'here he comes.' Small boys scurried around on bicycles, necks were craned, traffic policemen assumed new dignity, and presently a sun-scorched figure in dusty running trunks came trotting into town." It was the Denver baker and Rocky Mountain marathon champion Seth Gonzales, racing for pride. Small boys crowded around and watched him check in at the broadcasting bus and receive his $1.50 food allowance from the clerk. He had come in fast, covering the thirty-eight miles in five hours—a pace of less than eight minutes per mile. His efforts counted for little in the standings, however, moving him from sixteenth to fifteenth.[62]

Forty-five minutes later, others began to arrive. The ten prize holders had slowed for a second day, hoping to avoid injury that might cheat them of their prizes. They left the frontrunner glory to the rest of the pack, and forty-third-place holder Thomas Ellis finished next, despite having been struck by a car.

Out on the course, Johnny Salo's crew found him sitting in a ditch after being knocked off the road by the ill-timed opening of a car door. John McCarthy of the *Passaic Daily News* wrote, "There was nothing we could do but slap him on the back as he started off again." Johnny was followed by twenty-sixth-place holder William Morady of New Jersey; nineteenth-place holder Arthur Killingsworth of California; seventeenth-place holder George Rehayn of Germany; and thirteenth-place holder James Pollard of Nevada.[63]

Buried in the pack came Andy Payne in nineteenth, leading Johnny Salo by just four minutes. When they crossed the line, the crowd cheered.

And a surprise was waiting for Salo: his wife and two children. Passaic's superintendent of public safety, Benjamin Turner, had brought them, and told the press, "It was a real treat to see the look of joy that came over [Salo's] face when he saw his family."[64]

The rest of the men pushed doggedly ahead. Louis Perrella threw his hip out on the course, walked it out, and then sprained his ankle but still trudged stoically to the finish. To some, the derby men looked "like escaped lunatics," but beneath this rough facade beat the hearts of heroes who, come hell or high water, would reach the end of the trail in New York City.[65]

When darkness fell, Pyle's enclosure took on new life and "a tawdry brilliance." Emmet Crozier of the *New York Sun* wrote, "As the light came on, the portable radio station caught some jazz out of the air and sent it echoing among the tents. A brass drum began to beat and the barkers shouted the amazing wonders of the mummified outlaw and the snakes of Siam." Several hundred people paid their twenty-five cents and entered the enclosure. Red Grange came out on a platform and described the derby and introduced some of the runners. "One by one," Crozier wrote, "they stepped into the limelight, said hello to the crowd, listened to the patter of hands clapping and then climbed stiffly to the ground." Then Red and the runners disappeared, replaced by the carnival. Charley's derby had just two days to go.[66]

Welcome Home, Johnny

DAY 83, 55 MEN

Friday, May 25, 1928. Tensions were running high the day before the end of the derby. The men were heading to Passaic, New Jersey, Johnny Salo's hometown, filled with partisan fans hoping for a miracle to give him the twenty-five-thousand-dollar prize in New York. Andy Payne feared violence at the hands of Johnny Salo zealots, and said so publicly. Passaic's superintendent of public safety acted quickly to calm his fears by detailing a police officer to watch over Andy on his run to town. "We are going to give Andy Payne all the protection he should and ought to get," the superintendent said, going on to assure Andy's father that if anyone threatened his son, that person would face "swift justice in New Jersey."[67]

With threats of violence swirling, the race got off to a nervous start at 10:30 a.m. for the short twenty-four miles to Passaic. The group looked different, too—Charley wanted the men to look sharp for their final runs, so he dug deep in his pockets and bought uniforms. Into the trash bins went the stinky, thread-bare attire of the packmen. Pyle also had the men shave off weeks or months of beards, leaving many barely recognizable in the morning light.[68]

Among the ranks of the newly uniformed and shaven bunioneers was *New York Post* reporter F. Raymond Daniell, who had decided to run the Passaic leg of the race. He had only gotten three hundred yards into the race when a large truck pulled alongside him and none other than Red Grange leaned out:

> Grange: "Hey, where do you think you're going?"
> Daniell: "Passaic."
> Grange: "You're not in this race. You'll have to get out."
> Daniell: "Don't be a meanie, Red. You remember me don't you? Go on, let me run. I like to run. Besides, if I win, I'll split the prize with you."
> Grange: "[Why didn't you join us] in Los Angeles?"
> Daniell: "I know that part of the country already, and besides, I'm already too thirsty to try marathoning across the desert."

Grange paused for a moment, and Daniell thought he might leave him alone. But suddenly Red lost his legendary charm, and the big halfback grabbed him like a forward pass, pulled him into the truck, and gave him an enforced one-way trip to town. While the reporter sat glumly under guard, the rest of the men got on with the business of racing through the cheering thousands that lined the course to Passaic.[69]

This was a doubly sweet day for Johnny Salo. He turned thirty-five that day and was coming home. Salo ran through gridlocked traffic that forced many men to abandon the road for the sidewalk.[70] Despite a painfully chafed right foot, he was determined to lead the derby into town. However, thirty-ninth-place holder Richard Thomas forgot his racing manners. He sprinted by Salo two miles from town, forcing the Finnish American to race him as they neared Passaic. Thomas was no match for Johnny's speed, however, and the Finn left Thomas gasping for breath by the side of the road.[71] No one was going to deny Johnny his triumphant return home. The town declared a half-day holiday in his honor and, with factory whistles blowing, crowds cheering, and American flags flying, Johnny Salo reached the Passaic city limits at 1 p.m. The *Passaic Daily Herald* wrote, "If the President of the United States were to have visited Passaic today, he could not have had a warmer reception nor a bigger crowd than Salo found when he came loping down Lexington Avenue this afternoon."[72]

When Salo entered town, he ran methodically, stone-faced, but as the cheering increased, he finally broke a smile and waved. Near the finish, a mass of humanity ten deep parted to open a lane for him. At the finish, a brass band played, and Red Grange was there "autographing everything but an offside kick."[73]

A beaming superintendent of public safety, Benjamin Turner, was there to meet his new employee, Officer Johnny Salo. Late the night

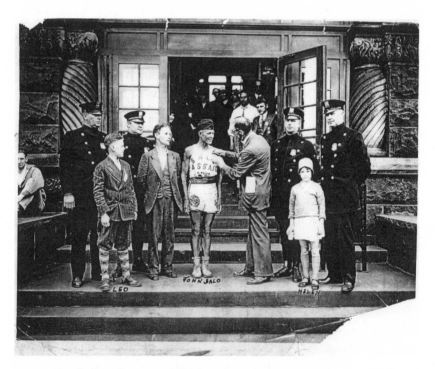

Figure 26. Johnny Salo receiving his commission as a Passaic police officer. Son Leo and daughter Helen look on. Henceforth, Salo was dubbed the "flying cop from Passaic." Credit: *Passaic Daily Herald*, May 25, 1928.

before, Turner had appointed Johnny a member of the Passaic Police Department before he turned thirty-five, the cutoff age for joining the force. Turner said, "For what John Salo has done for Passaic, I feel Passaic can scarcely do enough." The superintendent had sounded out Mrs. Salo and she assured him her husband would accept the offer.[74] Johnny had found spotty employment in the shipyards in recent years, and the prospect of a steady job and a modest $2,100-a-year salary meant a guaranteed income for the family.[75] Salo was grateful for the offer and said, "I'm glad to know that I'll have a job after my vacation," but quipped, "Does C. C. Pyle split with me on my salary?"[76]

Johnny then stepped up to the portable microphone and said, "This is the greatest and happiest day of my life. It almost makes me cry to see what the people of Passaic are doing for me." When asked why he entered the race, he said, "I did it for the wife and kiddies."[77] And when asked for his thoughts about Andy Payne, he said, "I am proud to run second after Andy. He is a great runner. He is a better runner than I am."[78]

Payne graciously left the limelight to his Passaic friend. He finished in a fifteenth-place tie with William Kerr and lost an hour to Salo, but still held an unbridgeable sixteen-hour lead with one day to go. In a radio broadcast, he gave his thoughts on Johnny's appointment as a police officer. "Oooh," he joked, "I beat him to it. I was made an [honorary] captain down in Oklahoma."[79] And despite fears of violence against Andy, his trainer, Tom Young, had nothing but kind words for Passaic: "Andy received a bigger welcome down Main Avenue than he did when he ran down his home state, Oklahoma."

Eddie Gardner finished seventh, and his old rival Phillip Granville finished tenth and was all smiles. Back home in Hamilton, Ontario, his wife had just given birth to an eleven-pound baby boy.[80] Smiling Sammy Robinson was a happy man, too. The *Atlantic Union* newspaper had paid him fifty dollars each time he crossed a state border, so the race to Passaic had just padded his pocket. Sammy planned to return to Atlantic City the next Sunday, stick his feet in the ocean, and say, "Dawgs, drink yo' fill."[81]

Pyle Problems

Friday, May 25, 1928. That night in Passaic, Red Grange sang the praises of Charley Pyle and his bunioneers from his raised platform in the center of Passaic's high school stadium.[82] However, controversy continued to follow the director general, for two main reasons: Runners were unhappy about a recently added plan to finish the race with a two-hundred-lap run in Madison Square Garden when they reached New York, and they were worried Pyle would not be able to pay the prize money.

In Passaic, six runners, allegedly led by Charley's old nemesis Bill Kerr, threatened to seek a court order to force him to drop his plans for the two hundred laps. Pyle told them, "If you don't like the race, go home." Charley's warning seemed to scare off Bill Kerr. Fearing Pyle would remove him from the race, Kerr tried to downplay his part in the rebellion, saying, "I've been blamed for more than I'm responsible for." He acknowledged his opposition to running in the garden but said he would "be foolish to destroy my chance at sixth-place money by not competing in the race."[83] C. C. Pyle seemed undisturbed by the runners' negative reports to the press. "Front pages are front pages, whatever comments are on them," he said.[84]

The second issue was the prize money. Pyle tried to calm the fear, promising to deposit the $48,500 in prize money in a New York bank, and to pay his winners on May 29 at the start of his latest money-making scheme: a twenty-four-hour footrace, composed of two-man teams from the bunion derby.[85]

That night, the fifty-five men slept on the road for the last time. The morning would bring an end to their toil—they would reach the end of the 3,400-mile, transcontinental rainbow in New York City. The ten money winners prayed Pyle could come up with the pot of gold.

PART III

THE END

℮‍‍⌒

CHAPTER 16

End of the Rainbow

Two Hundred Laps in the Garden

DAY 84, MAY 26, 55 MEN

Saturday, May 26, 1928. The last day of the derby started late, at 4 p.m., from the Passaic High School stadium. The men would make a ten-mile run to the ferry terminal at Weehawken on the Hudson River, take a ferry to West Forty-Second Street in Manhattan, and then race across Eighth Avenue to Madison Square Garden and begin Pyle's dreaded two-hundred-lap, twenty-mile race around a slippery track for the benefit of the derby's New York fans.[1]

Along the ten-mile route to the terminal, thousands of Salo fans packed the course. As the men neared the ferry, many were stunned by the sight of the soaring Manhattan skyline they had dreamed of for so long. Tom Ellis, who had forced Johnny to sprint into Passaic, reached the terminal first just after 5 p.m., with the last man arriving at 6:30 p.m.[2]

At 8 p.m., the men posed before a battery of motion picture cameras, and then boarded the ferry for the quick trip across the Hudson River. At 8:19 p.m., the bunioneers leapt from the ferry onto the Manhattan shore, to the cheers of New York's residents. The runners were so suntanned by

Figure 27. Tom Ellis, #206, shown here with Charley Pyle, led the derby to the ferry terminal on the New Jersey side of the Hudson, the last stop before New York City. Credit: El Reno Carnegie Library.

months of running that one reporter from the *Afro-American* newspaper had trouble distinguishing the whites from the blacks.[3] Curious New Yorkers lined the course to the finish. As they neared the garden, shouts and sirens from the police motorcycle escort sent thousands more to jam the entranceway.[4]

The first to enter the arena was Pyle's battered fleet of cars and trucks. After taking a lap around the track, his smoke-belching parade parked in the center of the arena, joining a brass band that was doing its best to entertain the crowd. The car exhaust barely had time to settle before the runners arrived for their final twenty miles on the composite tile floor.[5]

The runners arrived to a nearly empty stadium. Swallowed up in the vast arena were, at most, four thousand fans who had paid the swollen sum of $1.65 to watch the men shuffle around the track. About half were Johnny Salo supporters, who cheered wildly when he appeared.[6] Another contingent came from Harlem to cheer Eddie Gardner, Sammy Robinson, and T. Joseph Cotton.[7] As one reporter put it, C. C. Pyle's "wind-up would be staged before row upon row of barren, empty seats in the huge arena."[8] Pyle felt he made a great blunder by having his men run from the ferry to the arena, rather than loading them into taxis. "As it was, we allowed thousands to see them free of charge on the streets of New York," he said. "I'm still Cold Cash Pyle, but I pride myself on having given the world its greatest free show."[9]

On the track, the bunioneers were forced to slow down at the corners to avoid slipping on the slick surface. Many, including Guisto Umek, were content to take the two hundred laps at a fast walk, which allowed them to nibble on food as they raced. The fans in the stands felt half the distance would have been enough for a show. Tired of the boring, shuffling affair, one spectator offered a hundred-dollar prize to the winner of a one-mile sprint. The race was temporarily halted while the men lined up, and all fifty-five started off at a brisk pace, but the majority soon fell back to walking. Five or six sprinted for the prize, and seventeenth-place holder Alan Currier won the hundred dollars.[10]

The slow pace upset the director general. "Come on, you fellows. Streak it boys, streak it. Show 'em what I've brought to New York," he said. There was a brief, feeble spurt, but that soon ended as well.[11] After the ten money winners finished their laps, Pyle mercifully waved the remaining men off the track, given none could hope to break into the money-winning spots.[12]

Johnny Salo finished ahead of Andy Payne, then the two came off the track together. Charley congratulated them for their achievements, and gently reminded them they were still under contract for a year.[13]

Andy Payne
DAY 84, 3,400 MILES

Andy had nothing but praise for C. C. Pyle that night and said, "Mr. Pyle is good as gold. And I am satisfied with his handling of the race. I expect to get my $25,000 Friday night."[14] Payne had finished the race a few months short of his twenty-first birthday after covering 3,400 miles in 573 hours. His speed averaged ten minutes per mile, all the way across America.[15]

A delegation from Oklahoma was on hand to present him a $500 check and a telegram from Stanley Draper of the Oklahoma City Chamber of Commerce. Draper gave him the happy news that the chamber would award him $4,097, reflecting the $5,000 that Pyle had forfeited in the court action in Oklahoma City. After the chamber had deducted its expenses, $4,097 remained.[16]

There was family news, too. When his mother heard he had won the race, she fainted. She worried that the victory might make him "big headed."[17] His father downplayed rumors that he would force Andy to use his winnings to pay the mortgage on the family farm. He told a reporter, "The time had not come when he had to call on his boy to pay off any mortgage for him."[18]

Andy Payne had won the derby by heeding his trainer's advice: Maintain a pace in the nine- to ten-minute-mile range, and ignore the temptation to race for stage victories.[19] Phillip Granville went so far as to say, "I might say that Payne's manager won the race for him, using the greatest judgment in everything connected with the race and nursing his man along so as to hold his lead all the time."[20] Andy's trainer, Tom Young, gave the credit to Andy. "Andy is a wonderful bunch of flesh. He goes to the starting line each morning quietly. But when he gets the word 'go,' he is off like a flash and [he doesn't] let up until the finish." Young marveled at the endurance of his charge, claiming that even after a sixty- or seventy-mile run, Andy's heartbeat was normal. He added, "I cannot place a limit on his endurance. . . . To me, there has been only one runner in the race, and he is Andy Payne, the greatest marathon runner in the world."[21] A bit of the afterglow left his face when a doctor, believing the conventional wisdom of the time, examined Andy and pronounced him in good shape, but thought the strain had probably shortened his life by a decade.[22]

The Money Winners
DAY 84, 3,400 MILES

Johnny Salo lost the derby by fifteen hours, and settled for the ten-thousand-dollar second prize. He was immensely talented and tough, but he entered the race unprepared for transcontinental running. He may have had more natural talent and speed than Andy, but he didn't have Tom Young. He did, however, have a dream. At thirty-five, when most men's athletic hopes had died, he led the bunion derby across the East in what proved a futile but gutsy effort to overtake Andy Payne. Despite his loss, his effort earned him the respect of his city, a better life for his family, and newfound employment as a police officer. Johnny Salo had become the "flying cop from Passaic."

Phillip Granville took third place and the five thousand dollars. He made the transition from walking to running too late in the race. He, too, was a tremendous competitor, blessed with a massive, powerful body accustomed to mile after mile of race walking. This and his champion's heart saw him through the race. He joked that he gained fifteen pounds during the trans-America crossing: Five he added himself over the course of the event, and the other ten from his newborn son born just days before the finish.[23] Phillip called the race "a wonderful event" despite facing death threats and verbal abuse in Texas, Oklahoma, and Missouri. Often thought of as black, Jamaican-born Phillip claimed he was "Indian" and anything else but black, which earned him the wrath of some black Americans.[24] The black newspaper *Amsterdam News* scolded its readers, however: "Why [should] a person with more white blood than colored [be forced to call himself part of a race] which only a chump would deny is the most despised race in America. . . . Go ahead and choose your own companions, Mr. Granville; we are only interested in your work as a runner, and if you do well there it will give others inspiration."[25]

Mike Joyce took the $2,500 fourth-place prize home to Cleveland, and it was nearly midnight when Mrs. Joyce heard the news that her husband had won. She was ironing the last of a basket of clothes for her five small children. When a reporter asked her about her plans for the money, she put down the iron and said, "What am I going to do with it? Wait'll I get it. I haven't seen the cash yet. I heard Mr. Pyle didn't have the money to pay the boys." She started ironing again, and then said, "Yes, we're going to move. Get a nice place to live in and decent clothes for the kids. Some square meals would be nice, too."[26]

The rest of the top ten would get a thousand dollars apiece.

Feisty little Guisto Umek won fifth place. Like Phillip Granville, he began as a walker. By the end of the race, the Italian revealed himself to be a gifted runner who seemed to gain strength with each stage race. But like Phillip, he abandoned walking too late to challenge the leaders.

Sixth place runner William Kerr had long been the voice of the underdogs, the men in the rear, and the bane of Charley Pyle's existence. And he had more on the line than prize money—before the race, he placed a $50 bet at fifty-three-to-one odds with a Los Angeles book-maker that he'd finish the race in New York. He now hoped to return to California to collect his $2,650 winnings.[27]

In seventh was Louis Perrella of Albany, New York, another con-vert to running. He showed amazing heart when he fought through shin splints over the rolling hills of New York. He also received a lot of support through the kindness of a stranger in Erie, Pennsylvania, who allowed his brother to follow him in a donated car and nurse him through the last weeks of the derby.

In eighth place was Eddie Gardner. He had used fourteen pairs of running shoes to cross the country, and now it was over. He was the true winner for black America, but he wasted his talent in spurts, which gave him the highest number of first-place stage victories but only a thou-sand dollars for his efforts.[28] Nonetheless, in black communities along the route, he offered inspiration to the thousands of children who saw him pace the world's greatest distance runners. For black Americans, this was victory enough.

Frank Von Flue came in ninth, and John Cronick in tenth. And that was it. No one else would get paid. For those out of the money spots and running for pride, the end came with little official respect. Sammy Robinson chewed gum steadily and read letters as he ran around the track and thought about home. Eugene Germaine from Montreal wore the faded "1" on his back and chest and "limped endlessly around the garden floor." From his knee to his ankle, his left leg had swollen to twice its normal size from shin splints. Wildfire Bill Thompson from Arkansas abandoned Charley's uniform and stumped around the track in filthy flannel underwear.[29]

Most New York City reporters balked at this spectacle, and branded Pyle's race as little more than a cruel parade of battered and exhausted men. *New York Post* reporter F. Raymond Daniell wrote, "It may be all right for some people to see the tortured faces of these men who have pounded their way from Los Angeles to the edge of New York with their feet blistered, bones aching, and their lives shortened, perhaps, but if the race is all right, I don't see why humane societies make such a fuss over bull fighting."[30]

There was no pot of gold at the end of the rainbow for these hardy men. Rumors of endorsement deals and a share of the gate receipts fell through.[31] They might win something in the upcoming two-man-team race Pyle had devised, but the only certain money coming their way was the $100 deposits they had paid at the start—enough for a return trip home to the world of work and family they had left three months before. However, though cash poor, they returned changed, filled with a thousand memories from the road—the smell of sage in the prairie wind, the glow of a desert sunset, the majesty of snow-capped peaks. Each man had also learned courage and fortitude, and joined a family of brothers on the 3,400-mile trail to New York.

CHAPTER 17

The End

SUNDAY, MAY 27, 1928. FOR THE FIRST TIME IN EIGHTY-FOUR DAYS, Andy Payne did not have a race to run. He had sat up in his hotel room late into the night, discussing the race with Tom Young and other friends. In the morning he was out of the hotel by 9 a.m., eager to see the sights of New York, for the next day he was off to Washington, D.C., as the guest of the Oklahoma congressional delegation.

Some of the bunioneers made quick trips home in the five-day interim before the two-man race. Smiling Sammy Robinson received a heartfelt welcome when he stepped off his train in Atlantic City at 1:45 p.m. Sunday afternoon. A sea of people swept aside a security detail and surged onto the platform to greet him. One large man plucked Sammy from the crowd and carried him to the waiting car of Mayor Anthony Ruffin Jr., who paraded Sammy through city streets to a welcoming ceremony at the Ambassador Hotel.

Another twenty-three men postponed hometown visits, instead opting to take part in an assessment of the effects of the derby on their bodies at Jefferson Hospital in Philadelphia. They did so at the request of derby physician and Jefferson Hospital internist James Baker. Baker and his colleague, Dr. Gordon, examined the men and conducted many tests, including x-rays of their hearts and limbs. Contrary to the prevailing wisdom that the men had permanently damaged their health, doctors found no evidence of enlarged hearts, abnormal bones and joints, or other ailments beyond what would be expected in a normal population. They concluded that a normal body with adequate food and rest could handle prolonged exercise without serious untoward effects. Baker said, "In the main, [there was] nothing more alarming than abnormal normalcy."[1]

As the week wore toward Friday, the day scheduled for the two-man race and the money awards, the ten prizewinners worried about Pyle's ability to pay them, and for good reason—Charley was slow even to repay the $100 deposits he had promised to refund. To make matters worse, he was subject to a slew of new lawsuits filed to recover equipment rental fees and salaries of some of his employees: Jay Peters, a Los Angeles radio dealer, sued him for $3,183 for the unpaid cost of the portable radio station, KGGM[2]; and five derby employees sued for almost $3,000 in unpaid back wages.[3] In addition, he was still hounded by creditors seeking to collect the remaining $16,626 balance owed to the Illinois Trust and Savings Bank. Paul Lowry of the *Los Angeles Times* wrote, "Between one thing and another C. C. seems to have had one devil of a time."[4]

Ten Pink Checks

As Friday night approached, rumors swirled that Pyle had failed to transfer the $48,500 from a California bank to New York as promised.[5] At 8 p.m. in the vast and almost empty Madison Square Garden, the prizewinners relaxed mightily as their director general marched out to present the prize money. Harry Berry, in his book *L.A. to New York, New York to L.A.*, claimed that one of Pyle's business associates advanced him $40,000 and F. F. Gunn made up the rest in celebration of his son's completion of the race.[6] However he did it, C. C. Pyle was all smiles as he exhibited ten pink checks drawn on the Bankers' Trust Company of New York, certified and dated May 31, 1928. A photographer snapped a picture of a relieved Andy Payne and beaming Charley Pyle holding the twenty-five-thousand-dollar first-place check.[7]

Almost no one witnessed the ceremony, however. Of the roughly four hundred watching, about half were runners, officials, and trainers associated with the upcoming twenty-four-hour race. The *Los Angeles Times* wrote that echoes of the brass band "rolled back like the voice of a small boy shouting in a tunnel."[8] Pyle had, once again, badly misjudged New Yorkers' interest in his bunioneers.

A Sad End

After the ceremony came the final contest. As the race started, the band played in three-minute spurts, and some of the fans yelled occasionally.[9] The race consisted of twenty two-man teams composed of forty of the best derby runners. The men ran in relays, with one team member relieving the other whenever he wanted to do so. Those men not running could rest on two rows of cots on the floor.[10] The race began at 9 p.m. and went until 11 p.m. the next night. For the entire twenty-six hours, the almost empty temple "resounded with the dull thud, thud, thud of plodding feet" of some the greatest ultramarathoners on the planet, including the dream team of Peter Gavuzzi and Arthur Newton.[11]

In the end, the team of Phillip Granville and Frank Von Flue took the $1,000 first-place prize, having covered 183 miles. Peter Gavuzzi and Arthur Newton collected $750 for second, finally earning a small monetary award for the thousands of combined miles they had logged across America. Third place went to the Richman brothers, Arthur and Sam, who put their $500 prize money toward a new carburetor for the car that had taken them to Los Angeles and back. Eddie Gardner, who teamed with the Finn Gunnar Nilson, failed to finish the race when Nilson was forced out of the contest with an injury.[12]

Results from 26-Hour Man Race[13]

9 p.m., June 1, 1928–11 p.m., June 2, 1928
Madison Square Garden

Team	Prize Money	Distance Covered
1 Phillip Granville / Frank Von Flue	$1,000	183 miles
2 Arthur Newton / Peter Gavuzzi	$750	182 miles

3	Arthur Richman / Sam Richman	$500	164 miles
4	Roy McMurtry / Johnny Salo	$400	162 miles
5	Andy Payne / August Fager	$350	161 miles
6	Arthur Killingsworth / John Vierra	$300	153 miles
7	Paolo Bruno / Joseph Conto	$255	151 miles
8	Mike Joyce / Richard Thomas	$200	150 miles
9	Morris Richman / George Rehayn	$150	145 miles
10	Tom Ellis / Fred Kamier	$100	142 miles
11	A. Constantinoff / George Jussick		138 miles
12	James Pollard / Allan Currier		136 miles
13	M. B. McNamara / Alfred Middlestate		118 miles
14	A. C. Dotty / W. A. Downing		114 miles
15	Teducio Rivera / Pat Harrison		108 miles
16	Guy Shields / Bill Thompson		108 miles

After the end of his two-man event, Charley retreated to the "seclusion of a speakeasy across the street from the garden, and admitted that for once he was beaten."[14] The sun had set on his bunion derby parade.[15] The following day, after sleeping on cots in the garden, the men hunted him up, collected their hundred-dollar deposits, and scattered to the winds, leaving the ex-director general deeply in debt.[16]

Andy Payne did in fact use his money to lift the mortgage off the family farm, as well as to speculate in land and go to college.[17] Johnny Salo returned to Passaic and bought a little house on Spring Street.[18] He settled down to a quiet life with his wife and two children, walking a beat as a $2,100-a-year police officer.[19] Phillip Granville ended the race in a dispute with his manager, W. J. Westcott, who took possession of Phillip's $5,000 derby check. Westcott claimed he was entitled to 40 percent of the winnings, plus reimbursement for the $1,300 he paid in expenses on the trip. The mayor of Hamilton, Ontario, settled the dispute, awarding Phillip $2,850 and Westcott $2,150—the sixty-forty split, plus another $150 for Westcott's expenses.[20]

Eddie Gardner took almost a month to make his way home, stopping at his alma mater, the Tuskegee Institute in Alabama.[21] He spoke at evening chapel and paced the Tuskegee track team in a two-mile run around the school's "Alumni Bowl," where the alumni association presented him with a loving cup.[22] Ed "the Sheik" Gardner was unquestionably the greatest runner of his age in Alabama, and for that matter, the whole of the Old South, but only the state's nine hundred thousand black citizens acknowledged his accomplishments. There was not one line of print about him in Alabama's white newspapers, reflecting their outrage that he had thumbed his nose at the reign of Jim Crow segregation.

Seattle, Washington, was a different story. Like Sammy Robinson in Atlantic City, his hometown fans embraced him for his epic run. The Sheik arrived home by train on June 25, 1928, to his family and a huge mixed-race crowd. A reporter asked what was toughest about his cross-country race, and he ticked off his trek across the desert, the blizzard in Texas, and the seventy-five-mile lap in New York. He shook his head as he remembered.[23] In a gesture of thanks for his efforts, the *Seattle Post Intelligencer* editors sponsored a fundraiser for the down payment on a four-thousand-dollar house for him.[24]

Appendix I

THEIR CONQUEST

The one listing of race finishers comes from a May 28, 1928, article in the *Los Angeles Times*. Guy Shields is listed twice, as finishing in fortieth and forty-sixth place. It appears Eugene Germaine's name was omitted with the double listing of Shields. When Germaine is included, we have a full list.[1] Beyond the first ten, some appeared occasionally in the press, but all but a handful have been forgotten. They are the silent heroes of the long trail. They survived in drafty tents, ate meager rations, ran on resoled shoes, and gutted out injuries that would have ousted lesser men, all for the honor of reaching Gotham City on their own two feet.

The heroic nature of their quest resonates from the heart of ancient myth. Joseph Campbell, in his book *The Hero of a Thousand Faces*, focused on the role of the mythological hero in ancient myths—that rare individual who follows a faint, often inaudible call from the gods for adventure that many hear but most ignore. Following this call takes the hero on a dangerous journey from the known into the unknown, and at the end the hero realizes, "The perilous passage was a labor not of attainment but of re-attainment, not of discovery but rediscovery. . . . The godly power sought and dangerously won was revealed to have been within the heart of the hero all the time."[2] And so it was with the men of the bunion derby.

Finishers in the Los Angeles to New York Transcontinental Race
March 4–May 26, 1928
As listed in the *Los Angeles Times*

Name	Home	Time
1 Andrew Payne	Claremore, Oklahoma	573:40:13
2 Johnny Salo	Passaic, New Jersey	588:40:13
3 Phillip Granville	Hamilton, Ontario, Canada	613:42:30
4 Mike Joyce	Cleveland, Ohio	636:43:08
5 Guisto Umek	Trieste, Italy	641:27:16
6 William Kerr	Minneapolis, Minnesota	641:37:47
7 Louis Perrella	Albany, New York	658:45:42
8 Eddie Gardner	Seattle, Washington	659:56:47
9 Frank Von Flue	Kerman, California	681:41:49
10 John Cronick	Saskatoon, Sask., Canada	681:42:38
11 Harry Abramowitz	New York, New York	
12 Roy McMurtry	Indianapolis, Indiana	
13 James Pollard	Reno, Nevada	
14 August Scherrer	Ulster, Switzerland	
15 Seth Gonzales	Denver, Colorado	
16 Allan Currier	Rouge River, Oregon	
17 A. Constantinoff	Montréal, Quebec, Canada	
18 Arthur Killingsworth	Soma, California	
19 George Rehayn	Daly City, California	
20 Fred Kamier	Miami Beach, Florida	
21 Paul Smith	Oregon (press reports)	
22 George Liebergall	Belleview, Alberta, Canada	
23 Roy Sandsberry	Beverly Hills, California	
24 John Vierra	Hawaii	
25 Hoke Norville	Los Angeles, California	
26 William Morady	Newark, New Jersey	
27 Norman Codeloppi	Pasadena, California	
28 Harry Gunn	Los Angeles, California	

29	Arthur Richman	New York, New York
30	George Jussick	Detroit, Michigan
31	Stan Steveno	Calgary, Canada
32	Karl Larson	Los Angeles, California
33	John Stone	Marion, Indiana
34	Teducio Rivera	Manila, Philippines
35	Toby Joseph Cotton	Los Angeles, California
36	Paul Simpson	Burlington, North Carolina
37	Wynn Roberts	Wallace, Idaho
38	Herbert Hedemann	New York, New York
39	Richard Thomas	Cornwall, England
40	Guy Shields	Los Angeles, California
41	Claude Brown	Home Garden, California
42	Thomas Ellis	Hamilton, Ontario, Canada
43	Alfred Middlestate	Paulsboro, New Jersey
44	Sam Richman	New York, New York
45	Sammy Robinson	Atlantic City, New Jersey
46	Eugene Germaine	Canada (based upon press report from finish)
47	John Pederson	Spokane, Washington
48	Morris Richman	New York
49	Pat Harrison	Sullivan, Missouri
50	Wildfire Thompson	Berryville, Arkansas
51	Sidney Morris	Los Angeles, California
52	Ernst Cooney	San Bernardino, California
53	Juri Lossman	Estonia
54	Mike Kelly	Goshen, Indiana
55	Anton Isle	Austria

Appendix II

THE STARTERS

Starters in the Los Angeles to New York Transcontinental Race[1]

March 4–May 26, 1928

As listed in the *Arizona Republican*

Name	Number		Town	State/ Province	Country
Abramowitz, Harry	1	121	Bronx NYC	New York	USA
Alfano, Louis	1	158			Italy
Allen, Paul	1	21	Monrovia	California	USA
Allenfort, P. C.	1	176	San Jacinto Valley	California	USA
Anderson, Lester H.	1	46	Eisinore	Utah	USA
Arax, Harry	1	51			Turkey
Barnes, A. J.	1	129	Middlefield	Ohio	USA
Bender, A. N.	1	131	Waterloo	Iowa	USA
Blaze, M. M.	1	63	Huntington Park	California	USA
Bratton, William H.	1	115	Hoisington	Kansas	USA
Brown, C. R.	1	193	Home Garden	California	USA
Brunson, Walter H.	1	133	Los Angeles	California	USA
Bruno, Paolo	1	249			Italy
Busch, William H.	1	78	Pittsburgh	Pennsylvania	USA
Butcher, O. L.	1	30	Rock Island	Illinois	USA

176

Name	Number	Town	State/ Province	Country
Campbell, Kenneth	1 160	Ranger	Texas	USA
Calkins, G. R.	1 49	Des Moines	Iowa	USA
Cardinale, Leonard	1 100	Newark	New Jersey	USA
Case, George	1 217	Reno	Nevada	USA
Cheetham, Harry	1 232	Los Angeles	California	USA
Chavez, Frank	1 184	Pasadena	California	USA
Clarizo, Guicomo	1 201			Italy
Clary, William C.	1 181	Amarillo	Texas	USA
Codeluppi, Norman	1 196		Pennsylvania	USA
Constantinoff, A.	1 71		Siberia	Russia
Conto, Joseph	1 128			Italy
Cooney, Ernest	1 187	San Bernardino	California	USA
Cotton, Joseph T.	1 117	Los Angeles	California	USA
Cronick, John	1 188	Saskatoon	Saskatchewan	Canada
Currier, Allan D.	1 97	Rouge River	Oregon	USA
Davies, David	1 124	Sandwich	Ontario	Canada
De Angelis, Angelo	1 154	Brattleboro	Vermont	USA
De Marr, Patrick	1 146	Los Angeles	California	USA
Dilks, Earle L.	1 177	Newcastle	Pennsylvania	USA
Doty, A. C.	1 198	San Pedro	California	USA
Downing, W. A.	1 205	Los Angeles	California	USA
Ellis, Thomas B.	1 206		Wales	UK
Elliot, W. T.	1 148	Coronado	California	USA
Ellsworth, Roderick	1 2	Monongahela	Pennsylvania	USA
Endrizzi, Billy	1 80	Hurley	Wisconsin	USA
Erickson, Nestor	1 125			Finland
Estoppy, Eugene	1 98			Switzerland
Fager, August	1 149			Finland
Fekete, Mike	1 242			Hungary
Ferguson, William J.	1 186			Canada
Fleming, James	1 161		Scotland	UK
Friason, William O.	1 19	Cincinnati	Ohio	USA
Freeman, Leroy	1 213	Oklahoma City	Oklahoma	USA
Frost, Lucien	1 220	Los Angeles	California	USA
Gardner, Eddie	1 165	Seattle	Washington	USA
Gatson, Milton	1 151			Greece
Gattis, Leonard	1 132	Fresno	California	USA
Gaughan, John E.	1 204	Miami	Florida	USA
Gauvin, "Young"	1 194	Dover	New Hampshire	USA
Gavuzzi, Peter	1 103	Southampton	England	UK
Gehmaier, Carl	1 218			Switzerland

Name	Number	Town	State/Province	Country
Gallena, C. M.	1 5	West Palm Beach	Florida	USA
Gemmell, Andrew D.	1 3		Scotland	UK
Germaine, Eugene	1 1	Montreal	Quebec	Canada
Gillespie, Frank J.	1 40	Chicago	Illinois	USA
Gleason, James F.	1 114	Los Angeles	California	USA
Gober, John A.	1 36	Moberly	Missouri	USA
Gonzales, Seth	1 17	Denver	Colorado	USA
Gordon, James D.	1 25	Los Angeles	California	USA
Granville, Phillip	1 84	Hamilton	Ontario	Canada
Grafsky, Walter J.	1 23	St. Paul	Minnesota	USA
Gunn, Harry	1 65	Los Angeles	California	USA
Haroholdt, Orville	1 245	Cleveland	Ohio	USA
Harrison, O. B. "Pat"	1 156	St. Louis	Missouri	USA
Hart, Charles M.	1 102	Southampton	England	UK
Haynes, Elton	1 48	Akron	Ohio	USA
Hedemann, H.	1 112			Australia
Hess, Carl	1 237	Grav		Austria
Holmes, Ellis	1 190	Burbank	California	USA
Houfstater, Dwight	1 223	Manistee	Michigan	USA
Isle, Anton	1 243			Austria
Jensen, C. H.	1 24	Oakland	California	USA
Jensen, F. Harvey	1 116	Portland	Oregon	USA
Joachim, Alex J.	1 199	Hollywood	California	USA
Johanson, Martin	1 9			Sweden
Johnson, Frank	1 155	Granite City	Illinois	USA
Johnson, Harry G.	1 172	Los Angeles	California	USA
Joyce, Mike	1 83	Cleveland	Ohio	USA
Jussick, George	1 234			Poland
Kamier, Fred	1 73			Germany
Kelley, James	1 75	Sandusky	Ohio	USA
Kelly, Mike	1 224	Goshen	Indiana	USA
Kennedy, Clifton	1 207	Los Angeles	California	USA
Kerr, H. W.	1 7	Minneapolis	Minnesota	USA
Kester, Herman	1 31	Riverside	California	USA
Killingsworth, Arthur	1 120	Loomis	California	USA
Kitto, William E.	1 164	Los Angeles	California	USA
Kolehmainen, Willie	1 134			Finland
Kraus, J. J.	1 247	Regina		Canada
Larson, Karl J.	1 174			Denmark

Name	Number		Town	State/ Province	Country
Le Sage, Dick	1	18	Montreal	Quebec	Canada
Lehto, Lauri	1	39			Finland
Liebergall, George	1	12	Bellevue	Alberta	Canada
Lossman, Juri	1	56	Tallina		Estonia
Madore, Joseph	1	173		Nova Scotia	Canada
Mahoney, Pat	1	66	Long Beach	California	USA
McMullen, Alexander	1	105			Ireland
McMurtry, Roy	1	45	Newhall	California	USA
McNamara, M. B.	1	143			Australia
McNutt, Harold A.	1	6		Alberta	Canada
Metcalf, Osmund	1	189	Toronto	Ontario	Canada
Meyers, William	1	127	Missoula	Montana	USA
Middlestate, Alfred	1	3			Germany
Miller, Charles V.	1	233	Walnut Park	California	USA
Minnick, Saylor H.	1	111	Detroit	Michigan	USA
Morady, William	1	167	Newark	New Jersey	USA
Morgan, D. R.	1	229	Empire	Oregon	USA
Morris, Sidney S.	1	182	Los Angeles	California	USA
Muller, Anthony	1	140	Los Angeles	California	USA
Murray, Morris	1	27	New York City	New York	USA
Nagoski, Frank	1	20			Germany
Newton, Arthur	1	135	London	England	UK
Nielson, Niels P.	1	126			Denmark
Nilson, Gunnar	1	110			Finland
Norville, Hoke	1	185	Los Angeles	California	USA
Otto, Francis T.	1	118	Chicago	Illinois	USA
Payne, Andrew	1	43	Claremore	Oklahoma	USA
Pearson, Laurie	1	191	Los Angeles	California	USA
Pederson, John E.	1	95			Norway
Perisick, Nick	1	214	Long Beach	California	USA
Perrella, Louis J.	1	74	Albany	New York	USA
Phillipson, Jack	1	33		England	USA
Pineo, Cecil	1	44	Dover	New Hampshire	USA
Poikonen, George	1	235			Finland
Pollard, James A.	1	169	Reno	Nevada	USA
Quamawahu, Nicholas	1	203	Oraibi	Arizona	USA
Rea, Harry	1	89		England	UK
Rehayn, George	1	208			Germany
Reese, Austin	1	34	Gordon	Nebraska	USA

Name	Number		Town	State/Province	Country
Richman, Arthur	1	244	Brooklyn	New York	USA
Richman, Morris	1	216	Mt. Vernon	New York	USA
Richman, Samuel	1	59	New York City	New York	USA
Ricketts, Walter	1	139			Canada
Rivera, T. C.	1	50			Philippines
Roberts, Wynn R.	1	212	Wallace	Idaho	USA
Robinson, Sammy	1	119	Atlantic City	New Jersey	USA
Rogers, Alfred N. A.	1	197	New York City	New York	USA
Rothschild A.	1	70			Germany
Salmi, Paul	1	42		Hawaii	USA
Salo, John	1	107	Passaic	New Jersey	USA
Sandsberry, Roy T.	1	76	Beverly Hills	California	USA
Saperstein, Morris	1	137	Newark	New Jersey	USA
Scherrer, August	1	209			Switzerland
Senkus, Louis	1	178			
Shaw, James	1	248	Fullerton	California	USA
Sheare, Harry	1	123	San Francisco	California	USA
Shields, Guy	1	87	Baxter Springs	Kansas	USA
Shipp, Homer H.	1	159	Ranger	Texas	USA
Simpson, Paul	1	37	Burlington	North Carolina	USA
Sims, Guy	1	13	Neosho	Missouri	USA
Skooglun, David N.	1	226	St. Paul	Minnesota	USA
Smallwood, Percy	1	145		Wales	UK
Smith, Paul A.	1	53	Gates	Oregon	USA
Souminen, Arne	1	141	Detroit	Michigan	USA
Stern, Joseph	1	192			South Africa
Steveno, S.	1	163	Calgary	Alberta	Canada
Stone, John, Jr.	1	28	Marion	Indiana	USA
Streeter, Van	1	195	Anamosa	Iowa	USA
Studenroth, Arthur A.	1	88	Philadelphia	Pennsylvania	USA
Swabey, Henry	1	104	York Township	Ontario	Canada
Swensen, Carl A.	1	175	Los Angeles	California	USA
Taylor, George D.	1	92	Calgary	Alberta	Canada
Thomas, Richard J.	1	106		England	UK
Thompson, Wildfire	1	219	Berryville	Arkansas	USA
Tiedoke, Herbert	1	227			Germany
Toste, Anton	1	90			Portugal
Trimble, Troy A.	1	215	Los Angeles	California	USA
Turley, Charles A.	1	108	Tulsa	Oklahoma	USA
Umek, Guisto	1	79	Trieste		Italy

Name	Number		Town	State/ Province	Country
Urgo, Frank	1	91			Italy
Valis, John	1	183	Los Angeles	California	USA
Vierra, Johnny	1	41	Alameda	California	USA
Von Flue, Frank R.	1	152	Kerman	California	USA
Walker, Duane	1	171	Casper	Wyoming	USA
Wanttinen, Olli	1	238			Finland
Weathers, Murdock	1	228	Los Angeles	California	USA
Weliz, Joe	1	86	Los Angeles	California	USA
White, James	1	157	Duluth	Michigan	USA
White, John C.	1	225	Clinton	Oklahoma	USA
Whitton, Chester J.	1	202	Santa Paula	California	USA
Willberg, Carl I.	1	62	New York City	New York	USA
Williams, Ned	1	69	Arden	Delaware	USA
Wilson, James L.	1	162	Oakland	California	USA
Wilson, Matt A.	1	240	Asheville	North Carolina	USA
Winkle, Max R.	1	109	Washington	New Jersey	USA
Wyckoff, Don	1	241	Benkleham	Nebraska	USA
Zimmer, Kurt	1	236	Breslau		Germany
Zioikowski, Adam	1	130			Poland
Zumwalt, Thomas J.	1	179	Los Angeles	California	USA

194

No
Number
Listed

Name	Number	Town	State/ Province	Country
Gauvin, Alfred	1	Boston	Mass	USA
Gudie, W. W.	1	Los Angeles	California	USA
Lenkus, Louis	1	St. Louis	Missouri	USA
Sanchez, Eli	1	Albuquerque	New Mexico	USA
Young, Calvin	1	Dover	Delaware	USA

5

Total Starters   199

Appendix III

AFTER THE DERBY, A DERBY

When the 1928 derby ended, Charley Pyle was broke, and he had taken Red Grange along with him. Grange returned to Illinois and officially announced a split with Pyle, but the director general could not give up the dream of profiting from transcontinental racing and vowed to try once more in 1929.[1] He tried other things, too, including "Pyle's Patented Foot Box," which contained fixes for all the three thousand foot aliments he had identified on his race across America.

He was a man of big ideas, a man who had consistently pulled off the impossible. He had started the American Football League and owned his own National Football League franchise. He had to give it one more try.

For his 1929 race, he put up $60,000 in prize money, keeping the first prize at $25,000 and the second at $10,000, but increasing the winnings for the lower finishers and extending the monetary awards to fifteenth place.[2] He changed the design, too. Pyle realized one of his biggest errors in 1928 was assuming the expense of feeding and housing the racers. To remedy this, he required contestants to pay a $300 entry fee and cover all their own expenses associated with the cross-country race—food, lodging, training, and medical care.[3] He also planned to bypass most of

Route 66 and the towns that spurned him in 1928, and send "the caravan through towns more susceptible to his spirit of uplift." He also tried to polish the image of his traveling caravan. He jettisoned the seedy sideshows and added a vaudeville act composed of "21 young ladies of gentle breeding and excellent social standing."[4]

He reversed directions for the 1929 edition, starting the men from New York City. The 1929 bunioneers would race down the eastern seaboard to Baltimore; then west on what would become Highway 70 to St. Louis; retrace Route 66 through Missouri; turn south in Oklahoma; head west through the Texas plains, New Mexico, and Arizona; and end with a final spurt up the coast from San Diego to Los Angeles.[5]

With these changes, the derby was no longer a race for dreamers—there was no room for a starry-eyed farm boy or a desperate shipyard worker taking long shots at glory. In 1929, each man was his own wagon in the long caravan heading west. Only men of wealth, or those who could convince investors to back them, would compete. As a result, it was a race of the old sweats—the battle-tested veterans of 1928—supplemented with a handful of the wealthy and those with international reputations as endurance athletes.[6]

Andy Payne declined to defend his title, joining instead as part of the race patrol and as an entertainer in the evening tent show, where he told jokes and performed rope tricks while the ladies of the vaudeville company changed costumes between acts. Peter Gavuzzi returned for another try at the title he had come so close to grasping in 1928.[7] Johnny Salo came with a new trainer, a car filled with equipment, and his wife as a cook and supporter until the troupe reached Ohio.[8] Phillip Granville had the backing of a syndicate of "rich Canadian sportsmen," for he arrived in New York with a fully equipped car with a portable "radio set, beds, fishing tackle and other bunion-derby luxuries."[9] Many other old hands returned as well, including Eddie Gardner, Guisto Umek, Sam Richman, Smiling Sammy Robinson, and Arthur Newton.

New York to Los Angeles in Seventy-Eight Days

Under a warm sun and a bright sky, eighty men milled about Columbus Circle in New York City on Easter Sunday, March 31, 1929, for what would be the final installment of Charley Pyle's transcontinental races.[10]

A crowd of fifty thousand thronged the circle, bringing traffic to a stand-still. Scores of people climbed on the Columbus Monument and on the stone pillars leading to Central Park for a better look at this year's bunioneers.[11] In the face of mounting police anger over the mob scene, Charley conducted an abbreviated ceremony and sent his men off on their first leg to Elizabeth, New Jersey. As the men ran, patrons of speak-easies rushed to the doors and held their beer glasses aloft in a prohibi-tion-era salute to the racers.[12]

The streets were packed with Johnny Salo fans who had to settle for watching the Sheik beat New Yorker Sam Richman by twenty-five yards.[13] For his efforts, Gardner had to endure a hail of insults every bit as vile as those he heard in Texas in 1928. Johnny and Peter finished far behind the leaders but eventually established themselves as the front-runners by the time the race reached Baltimore after six days of run-ning.[14] The bunioneers then headed west over the rolling foothills of the Appalachian Mountains as the temperature spiked into the nineties.[15]

Then it began to rain, turning the winding mountain roads to mud and forcing Pyle's men to slip and slosh their way west.[16] By the time the derby cleared the mountains, an epidemic of shin splints had reduced the field to thirty-four, with Johnny Salo struggling with a cold.[17] The toughest of the bunch proved to be tiny Peter Gavuzzi who, though just 118 pounds, won five stage races in a row and moved into first place in the cumulative standings, where he had spent so much time the year before. He celebrated by smoking a pipe of his favorite tobacco.[18]

By the sixteenth day of the race, Salo had fallen to third place behind Gavuzzi and Gardner. Then Johnny showed his competitive heart and rallied to take the next four stage races, which averaged forty-seven miles apiece. He pushed Eddie out of second and dogged Peter's heels across the thick cornfields of Indiana.[19] With Salo surging, Eddie fought to stay with them as the derby crossed the Mississippi River. Over muddy Missouri roads, Gardner pulled a tendon and began a desperate battle to stay in the race, ignoring the pleas of his trainer to drop out. He fought on to Muskogee, Oklahoma, before the pain overwhelmed him and he ended his contest with Peter Gavuzzi and Johnny Salo.[20]

With the Sheik's departure, the bunioneers raced south to Texas, where weather taunted the men with torrential rains one day and broiling sun the next. Salo charged Gavuzzi over a red-clay road on an eighty-mile run to Dallas, which he won in eleven hours and twenty-two minutes, slicing an hour off Peter's lead.[21] Johnny continued his assault on the leader across Texas, splashing through a rain-soaked course to win four of the next five stage races, and finally passing Gavuzzi at Big Springs, once a resting place for gold prospectors heading west to California.[22]

Peter Gavuzzi opened a campaign to overtake Johnny near the Texas-New Mexico border. In one amazing performance, the Englishman won a thirty-mile race to El Paso, Texas, and regained the lead two days later after winning a sixty-three-mile stage to Deming, New Mexico. The pace of their duel was much faster than anything seen in the 1928 derby, with Johnny and Peter pushing each other into the seven- and eight-minute-mile range for days on end and leaving the rest of the field behind.[23]

At Deming, only twenty racers remained.[24] The final thousand miles began with a victory by the oldest man in the derby, fifty-five-year-old Herbert Hedemann, who won a sixty-three-mile race to Lordsburg, New Mexico.[25] Then Salo and Gavuzzi resumed their battle, with the lead changing hands almost daily. Some days they called a temporary truce, allowing Guisto Umek and Sam Richman to trade stage victories in their fight for the six-thousand-dollar third-place prize.[26]

As the group entered the scorching Sonora Desert, Salo went on a final rampage to wrest the lead from Peter and won three consecutive stage races. He now had a one-and-a-half-hour lead—the biggest of the derby—only to suffer crippling stomach cramps and watch his cushion melt away in the desert heat.[27] By the time Pyle's nomads staggered to the California border after seventy-three days and 3,258 miles of running, Peter held almost an hour lead over his ailing New Jersey challenger.[28]

In California, Pyle cut the remaining stage races from seven to five, increasing the daily mileage to about sixty-four miles—twenty more than the average stage run. He imposed the new schedule to bring the race to Los Angeles on Sunday, June 20, the day after the *Los Angeles Times* held its inaugural marathon. Charley planned to offer Los Angeles a "weekend of racing excitement" by staging his own grand finale: a derby-ending marathon around a track in Wrigley Park.[29] Pyle hoped the race would attract a huge crowd to fill his derby coffers—almost empty, once again, as the race neared its end. If the men were to be paid, Charley needed gate receipts. He had no F. F. Gunn to bail him out this time.

On the first day of the extended races, Johnny shook off his stomach cramps to win a grueling fifty-eight miles that took him on a three-thousand-foot climb from the desert floor into the mountains. He cut Gavuzzi's lead to about twenty minutes.[30] The next day, the duo battled to a second-place tie after a seventy-eight-mile run to San Diego, where Guisto Umek took first place.[31] Johnny halved Peter's lead again after running the last legs to Los Angeles. A reporter thought Johnny was the fresher man of the two; Peter, he said, was "plainly tuckered out."[32]

Unlike 1928, the 1929 edition was a nail biter with only minutes separating first and second place. The *Los Angeles Times* put its money on the Englishman, calling him the faster and more graceful of the two. The newspaper proclaimed, "If Gavuzzi doesn't win tonight's wind-up marathon over the marathon distance, we'll be very much surprised."[33]

The Englishman got off to a rocky start. There was confusion over whether the four-mile run to the track from the prior day's finish counted in the official timing. He jogged to the park, believing it was a warm-up run and that the actual race would not begin until all the bunioneers had reached the track. Johnny Salo had a different understanding and sprinted to Wrigley Park. When Peter arrived, he saw Johnny tearing around the oval. By this time, Peter had lost half his lead and he watched the remainder melt away under Johnny's "killing pace."[34] At the twenty-mile mark in the marathon, Gavuzzi made a last-ditch effort to regain first with a powerful sprint, but fell short by two minutes and forty-seven seconds after seventy-eight days and 3,600 miles of running.[35]

Over the next week, the director general tried to assure the press that the "boys will get their money," but in the end, he was forced to issue promissory notes payable in six months.[36] As in 1928, he had run up huge debts from creditors and unpaid staff. He never made good on his notes, and his embittered winners were left with worthless pieces of paper for their efforts. During the depression years, Pyle recouped some of his fortune through promotional schemes, including his "Believe It or Not" concession at the 1933 Chicago World's Fair. The great promoter died of a stroke in 1939.[37]

The End of the Road

Peter Gavuzzi, of all the men, felt the most betrayed. Twice denied his fabulous prize, he wanted to protest the finish to the press, but his famous friend Arthur Newton (who ran the 1929 derby until he was hit by a car in Indiana) advised him against it, fearing he would "look like a poor loser." After the derby, Peter moved to Canada where he scratched out a living as a professional racer and a marathon coach. He was in France during the German invasion in 1940 and spent the war years interned by the Germans. He returned to England after the war and lived near his old friend Arthur Newton. In later years, he claimed that he had kept things close in the last days of the race to insure an exciting finish, since Charley had warned him that the prize money depended on a good gate at the finish. Until his death in 1980, Gavuzzi kept Pyle's worthless promissory note as a bitter reminder of his days as a bunioneer.[38]

Johnny Salo returned to Passaic, New Jersey, and continued to walk a beat as a city police officer. He occasionally ran in professional races and thought about quitting his police job after he won the 1929 race, but Pyle's bankruptcy ended his dreams of early retirement. And then things got worse.[39] On October 4, 1931, Passaic citizens were looking for a diversion from the Depression that had left so many looking for work. They found some relief from the hard times in a baseball game between two local teams, the Garfield Bergans and the Second Warders. Officer Salo was there as part of the police detail, stationed along the third-base line, where an overflow crowd milled about. In the seventh inning, the crowd surged across the line as a crack of the bat sent a ball screaming to left field. Johnny stepped out into the field to push the crowd back, and a player for the Second Warders fielded the ball and whipped it down the third-base line to catch an advancing runner. The throw was perfect, but Salo was in its path and it hit him squarely on the right temple. He refused to be taken to a hospital, and despite his dazed condition remained at his post, showing the legendary toughness that had twice taken him across the United States. "I am not a quitter. I can take it," he told concerned fans. After the game, he remained at the field directing traffic, moments before he collapsed. He was rushed to nearby St. Mary's Hospital where physicians battled to save his life from a brain hemorrhage.[40]

The next day a stunned town awoke to read that its hero had died. The local paper announced, "Lion-hearted, iron-legged Johnny Salo, who twice pounded his stocky frame across the United States to fame and fortune, is dead!"[41] Police pallbearers marched on either side of his coffin as thousands of schoolchildren, several judges, and a congressman gathered for his funeral. Two hours before the service, the church was already filled to capacity, and thousands stood outside.[42] In 1998, Johnny Salo's name was inscribed in the National Law Enforcement Officers' Memorial in Washington, D.C., through the efforts of the Passaic Police Department.[43]

After the 1929 race, Andy Payne remained in Los Angeles in a failed attempt to break into show business as the "Dancing Cowboy from Oklahoma," then returned home and married Vivian, his old high school teacher and sweetheart. He was elected Clerk of the Oklahoma Supreme Court in 1934 and held that position for the next thirty-eight years. He died in 1977, and the stretch of Route 66 through Foyil has been preserved and renamed Andy Payne Boulevard, with a marker commemorating his run.[44]

Eddie Gardner never gave up his love of endurance sports, and raced when he could on the professional circuit. In Seattle, his second marriage ended in divorce and he devoted his spare time to training for the annual fifty-two-mile walking race around Lake Washington.[45] The Sheik entered his first hike in 1933, and led the race throughout the night against an enormous blonde-haired contestant named Charlie Preferment before dropping out from exhaustion near the finish line.[46] The next year he was back, and again led most of the way but faded and had to settle for third place.[47] Finally, in 1938, Eddie Gardner set the course record at eight hours and forty-six minutes.[48]

Throughout the Great Depression, Eddie worked as a repairman at the Wilsonian Apartments in Seattle. Then he switched and became a steel worker, a pipe fitter, and finally, a janitor.[49] He also found the love of his life, Flossie Procter. A child of the South, she was born in Atlanta, Georgia, and like Eddie, left for the North, living in Monmouth, New Jersey, for many years. They married and remained together until her death in 1960.[50] Eddie died of a stroke six years later. He was childless and widowed, but not forgotten.[51] His friend, *Seattle Post Intelligencer* sports writer Royal Brougham, wrote, "Eddie Sheik Gardner went to his last long rest this week, but not until the popular negro globe-trotter had racked up more running mileage than any Northwest athlete in history during his 35 years as a competitor."[52] For the thousands of black children who saw him in his trademark outfit on the long trail to New York, he was a star of hope and pride in a time of despair. He was Eddie Gardner, the Sheik of Seattle, an iron man and bunioneer.

Appendix IV

NO GENTLEMAN'S GAME

Professional distance running had always been a sport of the lower classes, since the earliest days of the American Republic. No "gentleman" would race for money, but to a poor man in the nineteenth century, the idea of winning fifty or a hundred dollars was very attractive when the average daily wage for a working man ranged from fifty cents to a dollar. By the late 1830s, professional endurance racing was second only to horse racing as a spectator sport.[1]

The sport first grabbed national attention in the mid-1830s, when a wealthy horse owner sponsored a race to do what many thought impossible: to run ten miles in less than an hour. Thirty thousand people came to a Long Island horseracing track to see nine men attempt it. To wild applause, twenty-four-year-old Henry Stannard of Killingworth, Connecticut, broke the mythical one-hour barrier by twenty seconds. He took home a purse of $1,300, and used it to open a new restaurant called "The Pedestrian," a name that came to describe a runner or walker who raced in long distance events for money.[2]

Exhibitions of long-distance walking also drew large crowds. William Hughes, for example, attracted thousands of fans on both coasts in the

1850s when he walked back and forth on a long plank, without rest, for hours on end.[3]

In the early 1860s, a Seneca Indian named Louis Bennett brought public attention to endurance racing after he beat Europe's greatest distance runners during a tour of England. Better known by his Indian name, Deerfoot, he raced with a headband, a short loincloth decorated with bells, and a single eagle feather, symbolizing the Eagle tribe of the Senecas.[4] In England, the top racers typically ran together in a pack. They began quickly, then slowed for the bulk of the distance and sprinted at the finish. The man with the best sprint usually won. Deerfoot changed the rules by racing hard the entire way, leaving the "fat kickers" in the dust and forcing the Europeans to rethink their methods.[5]

In 1867, Edward Weston almost single-handedly set off a revival of pedestrianism that had faded during the Civil War. He walked 1,320 miles from Portland, Maine, to Chicago in twenty-six days. He walked every day of the week but Sunday and earned $10,000 for his efforts— perhaps twenty times the average man's annual wage. In 1871, Weston walked 400 miles in five days around a track in New York City. Three years later, he covered 420 miles in six days, and earned $6,100 in gate receipts. Weston's feats captured national attention and, by the end of the 1870s, almost every town in America was sponsoring endurance races ranging from one to six days, as well as twenty-, fifty-, and one-hundred-mile distance races.[6]

In 1866, Weston's nemesis, Irish-born Daniel O'Leary, immigrated to the United States. In 1875, O'Leary broke into the elite ranks of pedestrians when he completed a 500-mile walk in six days around a track at an ice rink in Chicago. He then challenged Weston to a six-day race, with each man putting up $5,000 of his own money. In an epic duel, O'Leary beat Weston, covering 501 miles to Weston's 450, and repeated his victory in a 1876 rematch. Weston's loss was much to the chagrin of a wealthy English Lord and British Member of Parliament, John Astley, who had backed Weston in the second race and lost 20,000 pounds on the venture.[7]

Never afraid of a challenge, Lord Astley sponsored his own "six-day-go as you please" world championships, which came to be known as the Astley Belt Race after the large silver and gold championship belt he awarded to the winner. Astley held the first race at the Agricultural

Hall in London in March 1878, giving the contestants six days to cover as many miles as possible on a track made of loam and sawdust. O'Leary continued to dominate the sport by covering 520 miles and surviving on less than three hours sleep each day. In the fall, he defended his belt in Madison Square Garden and won a fortune of $10,000 in prize money before losing the third installment of the race to Charles Rowell of England.[8]

The belt races generated huge interest on both sides of the Atlantic. As ownership of the belt shifted back and forth across the ocean, fan interest rose to fever pitch. In the fourth race, held in London, Edward Weston returned to reclaim the belt for America after beating Rowell. Then in a final match in 1879, Rowell recaptured the belt from Weston, reaping a windfall of $30,000.[9]

By the mid 1880s, the sport had reached the zenith of its popularity. Interest waned in the face of allegations of race fixing, the growth of amateur athletics, and the introduction of new sports like bicycle racing.

The rise of amateurism evolved in part as a way to keep professionals and other undesirables with "inferior social credentials—working class, ethnics and blacks" apart from middle- and upper-class runners. The movement began in America in 1876, when the New York Athletic Club (NYAC) established standard rules of amateurism, barring anyone who had ever competed for prize money. Amateur athletes could not receive monetary rewards for racing, nor could coaches, officials, or scorers be paid. The English went so far as to bar competition to "mechanics, artisans, and laborers."[10]

In that year, the NYAC built the first cinder track and sponsored the first national track and field championship. Those who ran as non-professionals were athletes, and the professionals retained the title of pedestrians. By 1880, there were at least ninety amateur clubs on the eastern seaboard, though few blue-collar workers competed in amateur events because they worked long hours for low wages and had little access to coaching or sponsors.[11]

Pedestrianism made a brief comeback after the 1908 Olympic marathon in London sparked new interest. At the end of the Olympic run, a race official had to help a disoriented Dorado Pietri of Italy cross the finish line in the muggy weather. Pietri was later disqualified because of the assistance, and the second-place finisher, American Johnny Hayes, was declared the winner. Hayes had finished second in the 1907 Boston marathon, behind the Canadian Indian running star Tom Longboat, who also ran the Olympic race.[12]

The bizarre finish generated so much publicity that American sports promoters staged a race between Pietri and Longboat in 1908 in Madison Square Garden. A rowdy crowd of twenty-five thousand Italians and Canadians cheered their national heroes. Longboat won after Pietri collapsed from exhaustion. Pietri lost to Longboat again in a 1909 rematch. Then in April 1909, thirty thousand New Yorkers gathered to see world's best distance runners including Pietri, Longboat, and Hayes, run a marathon distance for a $10,000 cash prize. An unknown French waiter named Frances Herni St. Yves took the prize.[13]

That same year, then seventy-year-old Edward Weston left the General Post Office in New York for a walk across America. With a police escort and thirty Civil War comrades, America's first iron man marched out of the city and arrived in San Francisco 107 days later. He then walked back to New York City in seventy-seven days, though his second trip was not closely supervised.[14] After that, interest in endurance racing began to wane again until C. C. Pyle and his transcontinental bunioneers briefly revived it in last years of the 1920s.

Notes

Introduction

1. "Newton Again Leads Field in Sixth Lap," *San Francisco Chronicle*, 10 Mar. 1928; Max Stiles, "Britisher Wins Sixth Lap in Pyle's Derby," *San Francisco Examiner*, 10 Mar. 1928.

2. Royal Brougham, "He Used 14 Pairs of Shoes," *Seattle Post Intelligencer*, Morning After, 24 Aug. 1966; John J. Reddin's Q & A, *Seattle Times*, Sunday Supplement, Charmed Land Magazine, 11 Aug. 1968.

3. *Official Program: C. C. Pyle's First Annual International-Trans-Continental Foot Race, Los Angeles to New York–1928* (1928).

4. 1928 Program.

5. Charles "Kid" Regan, "Pyling It On," *St. Louis Times*, 28 April 1928.

6. "Four Negroes in Transcontinental Race from Los Angeles to N.Y.," *Black Dispatch*, 19 Apr. 1928.

7. Susan Croce Kelly, *Route 66* (Norman: University of Oklahoma Press, 1990), 3.

8. Kelly, *Route 66*, 3; Michael Wallis, *Route 66: The Mother Road* (New York: St. Martin's Press, 1990), 9.

9. Kelly, *Route 66*, 22, 31; Wallis, *Route 66: The Mother Road*, 9.

10. "Threatened Lives of Gardner and Granville," *Afro-American*, 28 Apr. 1928; "George Curtis Tells How Colored Runners Threatened in Texas and New Mexico," *The Enterprise*, 3 May 1928.

11. William E. Leuchtenburg, *The Perils of Prosperity: 1914–1932*, 2nd ed. (Chicago: University of Chicago Press, 1993), 178–188.

Chapter 1

1. Leuchtenburg, *Perils of Prosperity*, 143, 243, 248.
2. Kelly, *Route 66*, 37; Michael E. Parrish, *Anxious Decades: America in Prosperity and Depression, 1920–1941* (New York: W. W. Norton and Company, 1992), 113.
3. Leuchtenburg, *Perils of Prosperity*, 195; Parrish, *Anxious Decades*, 159, 177.
4. Leuchtenburg, *Perils of Prosperity*, 196–197.
5. John M. Carroll, *Red Grange and the Rise of Modern Football* (Chicago: University of Illinois Press, 1999), 70.
6. Leuchtenburg, *Perils of Prosperity*, 179.
7. Ibid., 185.
8. Parrish, *Anxious Decades*, 39–40.
9. Leuchtenburg, *Perils of Prosperity*, 184.
10. Kelly, *Route 66*, 8, 9, 13.
11. Ibid., 3.
12. Leuchtenburg, *Perils of Prosperity*, 184.
13. Kelly, *Route 66*, 12–13.
14. Ibid., 13–17; Wallis, *Route 66: The Mother Road*, 1–2.
15. Kelly, *Route 66*, 22, 30–31.
16. Jill Schneider, *Route 66 across New Mexico: A Wanderer's Guide* (Albuquerque: University of New Mexico Press, 1991), 172.
17. Wallis, *Route 66: The Mother Road*, 1–2.
18. Ibid., 19.
19. Nida Martin, "Girl Writer Has New Hero after Interview with the Galloping Ghost," *Amarillo Globe*, 5 Apr. 1928.
20. Carroll, *Red Grange*, 83.
21. James H. Thomas, *The Bunion Derby: Andy Payne and the Transcontinental Footrace* (Oklahoma City: Southwestern Heritage Books, Inc., 1980), 8; Carroll, *Red Grange*, 82–83.
22. Robert W. Peterson, *Pigskin: The Early Years of Pro Football* (New York: Oxford University Press, 1997), 85.
23. Bus Ham, "Red Grange, Just a Regular Guy," *Oklahoma City Times*, 14 Apr. 1928.
24. "Pat La Marr Leads Derby into Amarillo," *Amarillo Globe*, 5 Apr. 1928.
25. Peterson, *Pigskin*, 86.
26. Ibid., 85–86.
27. Ibid., 86–87.
28. Ibid., 88–90.
29. William K. Klingaman, *1929: The Year of the Great Crash* (New York: Harper and Row, 1990), 11.
30. Peterson, *Pigskin*, 98–101.

Chapter 2

1. Kelly, *Route 66*, 23–24.
2. Wallis, *Route 66: The Mother Road*, 12–13; Westbrook Pegler, "Advance Agent of Pyle's Bunion Derby Arrives at Gotham to Steam up Race," *Los Angeles Times*, 18 May 1928.
3. Kelly, *Route 66*, 33.
4. Crawford, Bill, "History: The 1928 Bunion Derby," *Oklahoma Today* (May/June 1998): 38.
5. Westbrook Pegler, "Advance Agent of Pyle's Bunion Derby Arrives in Gotham to Steam Up Race," *Los Angeles Times*, 18 May 1928.
6. 1928 Program.
7. Ibid.; Crawford, "History," 39; Charles Kastner, "The Sheik of Seattle. Ed Gardner Had a Dream: To Win the 1928 Bunion Derby," *Marathon and Beyond Magazine* (July/August 2001): 42–43.
8. Pegler, "Advance Agent of Pyle's Bunion Derby," *Los Angeles Times*, 18 May 1928.
9. 1928 Program; "Pyle Race Stars Start Grind Today," *Seattle Post Intelligencer*, 4 Mar. 1928.
10. "Our Boy Andy Lags in Derby Lap," *Daily Oklahoman*, 11 Apr. 1928.
11. Edward S. Sears, *Running Through the Ages* (Jefferson, NC: McFarland and Company, 2001), 166–168; "Time to Relent," *St. Louis Post-Dispatch*, 28 Apr. 1928.
12. "Footnotes," *Miami News Record*, 19 Apr. 1928; Harry Berry, *From L.A. to New York, from New York to L.A.* (Self published, 1990), 45.
13. "Transcontinental Marathon Runners Due in Tucumcari Monday," *Tucumcari American*, 30 Mar. 1928; Barry Lewis, *Running the TransAmerica Footrace: Trials and Triumphs of Life on the Road* (Mechanicsburg, PA: Stackpole Books, 1994), 19.
14. Verne Mae Park, "Shoemaker for Bunion Derby," *Fremont Messenger*, 14 May 1928; Burgess Gordon and John C. Baker, "Observations on the Apparent Adaptability of the Body to Infections, Unusual Hardships, Changing Environment, and Prolonged Stress," *The American Journal of Medical Science*, July 1929, reprinted in Berry, *From L.A. to New York*, 159; "Granville and Gardner among Prize Winners," *Afro-American*, 2 Jun. 1928.
15. Lewis, *Running the TransAmerica Footrace*, 19; Jim Powers, "Newton Leads Bunion Boys in Pyle's Race," *Hamilton Spectator*, 10 Mar. 1928.
16. "Part of Pyle's Caravan," *Amarillo Globe*, 5 Apr. 1928; Thomas, *Bunion Derby*, 23; Berry, *From L.A. to New York*, 46.
17. "Pyle Will Be There to Pay Andy," *Oklahoma City Times*, 24 May 1928; "Favor Indians to Win Big Pyle Race," *New Mexico State Tribune*, 3 Mar. 1928; "Three Months Before Runners End Jaunt," *Amarillo Daily News*, 4 Mar. 1928.
18. Pegler, "Advance Agent of Pyle's Bunion Derby," *Los Angeles Times*, 18 May 1928; Thomas, *Bunion Derby*, 13; George Scherck, "What's This Bunion Derby All About?" *Seattle Post Intelligencer*, 9 Mar. 1928; The Pyle Runners and Their Motor Escort," *The Binghamton Press*, 21 May 1928.

19. Pegler, "Advance Agent of Pyle's Bunion Derby," *Los Angeles Times*, 18 May 1928; "Motor Coffee Pot with Pyle," *New Mexico State Tribune*, 28 Mar. 1928; "Maxwell House to Serve Coffee to Foot Racers," *Amarillo Daily News*, 4 Mar. 1928.

20. Westbrook Pegler, "Los Angeles is Runner's Goal," *Los Angeles Times*, 31 Mar. 1929; Robert A. French, "Bunion Plodders Skirt Toledo," *Toledo Blade*, 11 May 1928; Thomas, *Bunion Derby*, 112.

21. "C. C. Pyle's Auto Broadcasting Station Here," *Amarillo Daily News*, 3 Apr. 1928.

Chapter 3

1. Tim Noakes, *Lore of Running*, 4th ed. (Champaign, IL: Human Kinetics, 2003), 378; Bill Crawford, "History: the Bunion Derby," *Oklahoma Today*, May/June 1998; "Trans-Continental Runners Set for Getaway Sunday," *Seattle Post Intelligencer*, 3 Mar. 1928.

2. Berry, *From L.A. to New York*, 13; Noakes, *Lore of Running*, 378.

3. Sears, *Running through the Ages*, 228; Noakes, *Lore of Running*, 328–329.

4. Noakes, *Lore of Running*, 378; Thomas, *Bunion Derby*, 18–19.

5. Noakes, *Lore of Running*, 378–380; Braven Dyer, "Runners Leave on Long Jaunt," *Los Angeles Times*, 4 Mar. 1928.

6. Berry, *From L.A. to New York*, 11–12; Noakes, *Lore of Running*, 464; Sears, *Running through the Ages*, 225; Raymond Krise and Bill Squires, *Fast Tracks: The History of Distance Running* (Brattleboro, VT: Stephen Greene Press, 1982), 41–42.

7. Braven Dyer, "Runners Leave on Long Jaunt," *Los Angeles Times*, 4 Mar. 1928; Leland C. Lewis, "Dark Horse Cropping Out in Derby Run," *Fremont Messenger*, 11 May 1928.

8. Dyer, "Runners Leave on Long Jaunt," *Los Angeles Times*, 4 Mar. 1928.

9. Ibid.

10. Berry, *From L.A. to New York*, 40; Dyer, "Runners Leave on Long Jaunt," *Los Angeles Times*, 4 Mar. 1928; David W. Kellum, "Gardner, Josephs, Robinson, Other Bunion Derby Runners Reach Chicago En Route," *Chicago Defender*, 12 May 1928.

11. Berry, *From L.A. to New York*, 40; Dyer, *Los Angeles Times*, 4 Mar. 1928; Dyer, "Granville May Win Pyle's Run," *Los Angeles Times*, 1 Apr. 1928.

12. W. J. Westcott to Mayor Burton, Hamilton, Ontario, "Granville's Manager Claims Hamilton Man Could Be Near Front," *Hamilton Spectator*, 5 Apr. 1928; "Hearty Reception for Hamilton's Derby Hero," *Hamilton Spectator*, 29 May 1928.

13. George Scherck, "Sports Drift," *Seattle Post Intelligencer*, 26 May 1928; Henry Farrell, "More Running on for Pyle Troupe after Gotham Goal," *Seattle Star*, 17 May 1928.

14. "Pyle Race to Start Sunday, Rain or Shine," *San Francisco Chronicle*, 3 Mar. 1928; Dyer, "Finn Gets to Puente First," *Los Angeles Times*, 5 Mar. 1928.

Chapter 4

1. 1928 Program.
2. Gordon and Baker, "Observations," 161.
3. List of Starters, Appendix II.
4. United States Government, Thirteenth Census of the United States, 1910 Population Schedule, Twelfth Census.
5. Kathleen Eriksen, El Pueblo Historical Museum, Colorado Historical Society, "Re: Black Alabama Steel Workers in Pueblo," Letter to Author, 2 Jan. 2003.
6. Twelfth Census, 1900 Schedule.
7. Pueblo Library District, Early Black Residents of Pueblo, Colorado, in 1900, 1991; Eriksen to Kastner, 2 Jan. 2003; Thirteenth Census, Population Schedule, 1910.
8. Thirteenth Census, Population Schedule, 1910; Richard C. Berner, *Seattle 1900–1920: From Boomtown, to Urban Turbulence, to Restoration* (Seattle, WA: Charles Press, 1991), 60–63.
9. Washington, Department of Health, Certificated Copy of Death Certificate, Minnie Gardner, Num. 2216, 23 Nov. 1911.
10. Cathy Galbraith, The Bosco-Milligan Foundation; Cornerstones of Community: The Building of Portland's African American History, "Re: George and Susan Gardner in Portland." E-mail to author. 8 Mar. 2002.
11. Berner, *Seattle 1900–1920*, 63; Nard Jones, *Seattle* (New York: Doubleday and Company, Inc., 1972), 151, 315; Alfred O. Quinn, *Iron Rails to Alaskan Copper: The Epic Triumph of Erastus Corning Hawkins* (Whiteface, NY: D'Alouquin Publishing Co., 1995), 151, 170–171.
12. Tuskegee University, Office of the Registrar, Transcript, Biography of Student, Ed Gardner.
13. Transcript, Individual Records of Tuskegee Students, Edward Gardner; Washington, 58.
14. *Annual Catalog Bulletin*, Tuskegee Institute, Vol. 12, 1917–1918: 24; "Eddie Gardner Has Returned As Feature to Tuskegee," *Amsterdam News*, 20 Jun. 1928; Elton Garrett, "Gardner Talks Race; Sees Runner Victor," *Seattle Post Intelligencer*, 7 May 1928; "Colored Sheik Now Rates As Possible Race Winner," *San Bernardino Sun*, 8 Mar. 1928.
15. "Ed Gardner Makes Great Run in Winning Big P.-I. Event," *Seattle Post Intelligencer*, 5 Jul. 1924; Willard Coghlan, "Gob Surprise of Classic Takes Third," *Seattle Post Intelligencer*, 6 Jul. 1926; "Couch Takes Second, One Lap Behind, *Seattle Post Intelligencer*, 7 Jul. 1927.
16. Royal Brougham, "He Used 14 Pairs of Shoes," *Seattle Post Intelligencer*, Morning After, 24 Aug. 1966; John J. Reddin's Q & A, *Seattle Times*, Sunday Supplement, Charmed Land Magazine, 11 Aug. 1968.
17. "Couch Takes Second," *Seattle Post Intelligencer*, 7 Jul. 1927.
18. United States Government, National Archives and Records Administration, National Personnel Records Center, Official Personnel File, Edward Gardner; Fifteenth Census, Population Schedules, 1930.

19. "Ed Gardner's Wife Has Too Many Silver Loving Cups," *Black Dispatch*, 19 Apr. 1928.

20. Elton Garrett, "Gardner Talks Race, Sees Runner Victor," *Seattle Post Intelligencer*, 7 May 1928.

21. "Ed Gardner's Wife," *Black Dispatch*, 19 Apr. 1928; Fifteenth Census, Population Schedules, 1930.

22. "Gardner is Hampered by Too Many Backers," *Afro-American*, 21 Apr. 1928; "Inference May Cause Gardner's Losing Coast to Coast Marathon," *The Enterprise*, 26 Apr. 1928.

23. "First Eagle Runner Signs Up for L.A. to N.Y. Foot Race," *California Eagle*, 3 Feb. 1928.

24. "Other Colored Runners Enter Pyle's Patient Pedalogue," *California Eagle*, 17 Feb. 1928.

25. "Runner Selected by Eagle to Be Backed by Watson Burns," *California Eagle*, 10 Feb. 1928.

26. "Local Business Men Hang up Additional Prizes for Ed. Gardner," *California Eagle*, 9 Mar. 1928.

27. Fourteenth Census, Population Schedules, 1920.

28. "10,000 Roar Welcome to 'Smiling Sammy,'" *Afro-American*, 2 Jun. 1928.

29. National Archives and Records Administration, National Personnel Records Center, Military Service Records. Samuel Robinson; Lorenzo J. Greene, Gary R. Kremer, and Antonio F. Holland, *Missouri's Black Heritage* (Columbia: University of Missouri Press, 1993), 141.

30. Kellum, "Gardner, Josephs, Robinson, Other Bunion Derby Runners Reach Chicago En Route East," *Chicago Defender*, 12 May 1928.

31. "Other Colored Runners Enter Pyle's Patient Pedalogue," *California Eagle*, 17 Feb. 1928; Kellum, "Gardner, Josephs, Robinson," *Chicago Defender*, 12 May 1928.

32. "Four Negroes in Transcontinental Race from Los Angeles to N.Y.," *Black Dispatch*, 19 Apr. 1928; "Gardner, Josephs, Robinson," *Chicago Defender*, 12 May 1928; Fourteenth Census, Population Schedules, 1920; Westbrook Pegler, "Oklahoma High School Boy Cops $25,000 Plum," *Los Angeles Times*, 27 May 1928.

33. "Four Negroes in Transcontinental Race," *Black Dispatch*, 19 Apr. 1928.

34. Fourteenth Census, Population Schedules, 1920; 1928 Program; "Gardner, Josephs, Robinson," *Chicago Defender*, 12 May 1928.

35. 1928 Program; "Other Colored Runners Enter," *California Eagle*, 17 Feb. 1928; "New Dash in Oklahoma Air," *Black Dispatch*, 12 Apr. 1928.

36. "Granville and Gardner Taboo Long Standing Prejudiced Tradition," *Pittsburg Courier*, 12 May 1928.

37. Benjamin J. Rader, *American Sports: From the Age of Folk Games to the Age of Televised Sports*, 2nd ed. (Englewood Cliffs, NJ: Prentice-Hall, 1990), 61; Sears, *Running through the Ages*, 147–148; John Cumming, *Runners and Walkers:*

A Nineteenth Century Sports Chronicle (Chicago: Regnery Gateway, 1981), 102–103, 118–119, 124.

38. Rader, *American Sports*, 62.
39. "Boy Walks Across Country, Stops in Gary on His Trip," *The Gary American*, 13 Apr. 1928; "Lindy of the Ground to Hit the Trail Again the Coming Sunday Morning," *Amsterdam News*, 13 Jun. 1928; "Do You Remember?" *California Eagle*, 13 Apr. 1928.
40. Thomas, *Bunion Derby*, 1.
41. "Rogers County's Running Human is Making Best Marathoners in the World Step Fast in Shoe-Sole Derby," *Daily Oklahoman*, 13 Mar. 1928.
42. Thomas, *Bunion Derby*, 1–5.
43. Thomas, *Bunion Derby*, 5; Crawford, "History," 39.
44. "Pa Payne Joins Son to Stick Until Bunion Derby Finishes in New York," *Daily Oklahoman*, 6 Apr. 1928.
45. "Andrew Payne Permits Rival to Gain Time," *Daily Oklahoman*, 13 Mar. 1928.
46. "'Keep Hands Off Andrew,' Payne's Former Schoolmaster Urges," *Daily Oklahoman*, 11 Apr. 1928.
47. "'Andy' Payne Requires Much Food, Eats Big Portions after Each Lap," *Joplin Globe*, 20 Apr. 1928; Arthur A. Heywood, "Bunion Derby Winner Here, Has Fame, Seeks Fortune," *Washington Post*, 29 May 1928.
48. Wendell Merrill, "Given Another Great Ovation Last Night at School Stadium," *Passaic Daily News*, 26 May 1928.
49. Arthur G. McMahon, "Noted Runner-Policeman Felled While Pushing the Crowd from Ball Ground," *Passaic Daily News*, 5 Oct. 1931; Jouni Koskela, "Professional Runner John Salo Was Born 100 Years Ago," *Raivaaga* (Finland), 28 April 1993.
50. Merrill, "Given Another Great Ovation," *Passaic Daily News*, 26 May 1928; McMahon, "Noted Runner-Policeman Felled," *Passaic Daily News*, 5 Oct. 1931; *Raivaaga* (Finland), Koskela, "Professional Runner John Salo," 28 April 1993.
51. *Los Angeles Times*, 27 May 1928; Leland C. Lewis, "Salo Cutting into Lead of Andy Payne, Derby Leader," *Fremont Messenger*, 14 May 1928; "Finn is Midget of Pyle's Caravan," *Daily Oklahoman*, 13 Apr. 1928.
52. Berry, *From L.A. to New York*, 33.
53. "Cross-Country Derby Continues Eastward," *St. Louis Post Dispatch*, 28 Apr. 1928.
54. Tom Derderian, *Boston Marathon: The First Century of the World's Premier Running Event* (Champaign, IL: Human Kinetics, 1996), 156.
55. "Friday Race Ends in Fairgrounds Oval Shortly after Noon," *Daily Oklahoman*, 13 Apr. 1928; Berry, *From L.A. to New York*, 21–23.
56. Bruce Tulloh, *Four Million Steps: Los Angeles to New York—the Famous Runner's Account of His Record-breaking Marathon* (London: Mayflower Books, 1970), 19; "'Damon' Carries On as 'Pythias' Is Forced Out," *Daily Oklahoman*, 31 Mar. 1928; Berry, *From L.A. to New York*, 25; Walter McMullen, The Sports Trail, "Smokes Cigarettes," *Hamilton Spectator*, 4 Apr. 1928.
57. Berry, *From L.A. to New York*, 75.

58. Emmet Crozier, "Runners May Sue Pyle for Gate," *New York Sun*, 26 May 1928; "Huge Throng Is Expected in City to See Entrants," *Joplin Globe*, 4 Apr. 1928; Berry, *From L.A. to New York*, 48.

59. Berry, *From L.A. to New York*, 41; "Marathon Men Begin Weary Plodding Again; It's a Hard Life, Mates," *Albuquerque Journal*, 29 Mar. 1928; "Marathoner Tells Interesting Tale," *Custer County Chronicle*, 10 May 1928.

60. "Payne Increases Derby Lead over English," *Joplin Globe*, 20 Apr. 1928.

61. "Grueling Derby Lap Takes Toll," *South Bend News-Times*, 8 May 1928.

62. Berry, *From L.A. to New York*, 36.

63. Ibid., 37.

64. "Derby Runner Reported to Have Collapsed Near Kennedy This Forenoon," *Jamestown Evening Journal*, 17 May 1928.

65. 1928 Program; "Friday Race Ends in Fairgrounds Oval," *Daily Oklahoman*, 13 Apr. 1928.

66. "Marathon Men Begin Weary Plodding Again," *Albuquerque Journal*, 29 March 1928.

67. "Pyle's Runners in Lebanon," *Lebanon Rustic*, 26 Apr. 1928; "Huge Throng Is Expected," *Joplin Globe*, 20 Apr. 1928; "Charles 'Kid' Regan, 'Pyling It On,'" *St. Louis Times*, 28 Apr. 1928.

68. Thomas, *Bunion Derby*, 49; *Albuquerque Journal*, "Marathon Men Begin Weary Plodding Again," 29 Mar. 1928; "C. C. Pyle's Blister Brigade Here Today," *Jamestown Morning Post*, 16 May 1928; "Cross Country Derby Limping Through St. Louis," *St. Louis Post Dispatch*, 27 April 1928.

Chapter 5

1. Kevin Starr, *Material Dreams: Southern California Through the 1920's* (New York: Oxford University Press, 1990), 69, 85.

2. "Transcontinental Marathon Runners Due in Tucumcari Monday, April 2," *Tucumcari American*, 30 Mar. 1928.

3. Thomas, *Bunion Derby*, 16–18.

4. "Transcontinental Footrace Starts from Los Angeles Sunday," *Arizona Gazette*, 3 Mar. 1928.

5. George Beale, "Pyle-Inn Café Cook Meets with Grief at Meal Time," *San Bernardino Daily Sun*, 4 Mar. 1928.

6. "Transcontinental Marathon Runners Due," *Tucumcari American*, 30 Mar. 1928.

7. Berry, *From L.A. to New York*, 47.

8. Gordon and Baker, "Observations," 160; Noakes, *Lore of Running*, 464.

9. Thomas, *Bunion Derby*, 20–23.

Chapter 6

1. "Long Drought Broken by Rain Fall," *Arizona Republican*, 3 Mar. 1928.

2. *San Francisco Chronicle*, 3 Mar. 1928; Thomas, *Bunion Derby*, 25.

3. Paul Lowry, "Rabbit Punches," *Los Angeles Times*, 7 Mar. 1928.

4. Thomas, *Bunion Derby*, 26.

5. Sid Olin, "The Morning After," *San Bernardino Daily Sun*, 15 Mar. 1928.

6. "Hikes 1000 Miles; Misses Derby," *San Francisco Chronicle*, 6 Mar. 1928.

7. Berry, *From L.A. to New York*, 47; Thomas, *Bunion Derby*, 47; "Finn Heads Runners on Initial Lap," *Seattle Post Intelligencer*, 5 Mar. 1928.

8. Berry, *From L.A. to New York*, 47.

9. "Finn Gets to Puente," *Los Angeles Times*, 5 Mar. 1928.

10. "Finn Leads Coast to Coast Runners after First Sixteen Miles," *Washington Post*, 5 Mar. 1928.

11. "Villain Would Give Pyle's Derby the Setting of a Thriller," *Joplin Globe*, 19 Apr. 1928.

12. "Finn Gets to Puente," *Los Angeles Times*, 5 Mar. 1928.

13. Ibid.

14. "Second Lap of Cross Country Run Under Way," *Seattle Daily Times*, 5 Mar. 1928; "Arizona Indian Quamawahu Is Fourth to Finish," *Arizona Gazette*, 4 Mar. 1928.

15. "Finn Gets to Puente," *Los Angeles Times*, 5 Mar. 1928.

16. "Rogers County 'Runningest Human' Is Making Best Marathoners in World Fast Step in Shoe-Sole Derby," *Daily Oklahoman*, 13 Mar. 1928.

17. "Finn Gets to Puente," *Los Angeles Times*, 5 Mar. 1928.

18. Thomas, *Bunion Derby*, 29; Berry, *From L.A. to New York*, 50.

19. Braven Dyer, "Finn Leads by Forty Minutes," *Los Angeles Times*, 6 Mar. 1928.

20. Sid Olin, "Severe Grind over Cajon Road to Victorville," *San Bernardino Daily Sun*, 6 Mar. 1928.

21. "Finnish Star Outruns Filed in Fast Time," *San Francisco Chronicle*, 6 Mar. 1928.

22. "Control for Second Night Named," *San Bernardino Daily Sun*, 3 Mar. 1928.

23. "Severe Grind over Cajon Road to Victorville May Force Many to Quit Race," *San Bernardino Daily Sun*, 6 Mar. 1928.

24. "Finn Leads by Forty Minutes," *Los Angeles Times*, 6 Mar. 1928.

25. "Severe Grind over Cajon Road," *San Bernardino Daily Sun*, 6 Mar. 1928.

26. Ibid.

27. "Finn Leads by Forty Minutes," *Los Angeles Times*, 6 Mar. 1928.

28. Ibid.

29. "Finnish Star Outruns Field in Fast Time," *San Francisco Chronicle*, 6 Mar. 1928.

30. "Finnish Flash Still Leading on Long Grind," *San Bernardino Daily Sun*, 6 Mar 1928.

31. John C. Hudson, *Across This Land: A Regional Geography of the United States and Canada* (Baltimore: Johns Hopkins University Press, 2002), 342; Kelly, *Route 66*, 142.

32. "Indian Runner Best in Pack in Total Time," *San Francisco Chronicle*, 7 Mar. 1928.

33. Maxwell Stiles, "Finn Winner in Third Lap of Marathon," *San Francisco Examiner*, 7 Mar. 1928.

34. Sid Olin, "The Morning After," *San Bernardino Daily Sun*, 9 Mar. 1928.

35. Paul Lowry, "Kolehmainen Injured Limb," *Los Angeles Times*, 7 Mar. 1928.

36. Russell J. Newland, "Victorville's People Greet Huge Caravan," *San Bernardino Daily Sun*, 7 Mar. 1928.

37. "Finn Winner in Third Lap of Marathon," *San Francisco Examiner*, 7 Mar. 1928.

38. Sid Olin, "Pyle Shows No Worries as Entries Slump," *San Bernardino Daily Sun*, 7 Mar. 1928.

39. Ibid.

Chapter 7

1. Jack D. Rittenhouse, *A Guide Book to Highway 66* (Albuquerque: University of New Mexico Press [a facsimile of the 1946 edition], 2000), 119–121; Lewis, *Running the TransAmerica Footrace*, 14.

2. Russell J. Newland, "Negro Speeds into Barstow Ahead of Van," *San Bernardino Daily Sun*, 8 Mar. 1928.

3. James S. Powers, "Phillip Granville in Thirty Fourth Place," *Hamilton Spectator*, 8 Mar. 1928.

4. Russell J. Newland, "Kolehmainen Is Forced Out," *Los Angeles Times*, 8 Mar. 1928; "Local Business Men Hang up Additional Prizes for Ed Gardner," *California Eagle*, 16 Mar. 1928.

5. George Scherck, "What's This Bunion Derby All About? How Pyle Figures to Profit from Race," *Seattle Post Intelligencer*, 9 Mar. 1928.

6. Paul Lowry, "Rabbit Punches," *Los Angeles Times*, 8 Mar. 1928.

7. "Negro Speeds into Barstow Ahead of Van," *San Bernardino Daily Sun*, 8 Mar. 1928.

8. "Kolehmainen Is Forced Out," *Los Angeles Times*, 8 Mar. 1928.

9. Russell J. Newland, "Continental Marathoners Now in Mojave Desert," *Arizona Gazette*, 8 Mar. 1928.

10. "Shoemaker for Bunion Derby," *Fremont Messenger*, 14 May 1928.

11. "Coast to Coast Marathoners Devour Bread by the Loaf and Steaks by the Pound," *Arizona Gazette*, 8 Mar. 1928.

12. Westbrook Pegler, "Athletes Peeved Group," *Los Angeles Times*, 25 May 1928.

13. Kelly, *Route 66*, 31; "Continental Marathoners Now in Mojave; Hopi Back in Race," *Arizona Gazette*, 8 Mar. 1928.

14. "Continental Marathoners Now in Mojave," *Arizona Gazette*, 8 Mar. 1928.

15. Russell J. Newland, "Newton Hits Steady Pace Across Sand," *San Bernardino Daily Sun*, 9 Mar. 1928.

16. "Newton Again Leads Field in Sixth Lap," *San Francisco Chronicle*, 10 Mar. 1928.

17. "Hot Footin' Papa's Fourth in Derby," *Cleveland Plain Dealer*, 12 May 1928.

18. Berry, *From L.A. to New York*, 52–53.
19. "Veteran Shows Way to Rivals," *Los Angeles Times*, 9 Mar. 1928.
20. Thomas, *Bunion Derby*, 39.
21. Rittenhouse, *Guide Book*, 116–117.
22. "Newton Again Leads Field in Sixth Lap," *San Francisco Chronicle*, 10 Mar. 1928.
23. Max Stiles, "Britisher Wins Sixth Lap in Pyle's Derby," *San Francisco Examiner*, 10 Mar. 1928.
24. James Powers, "Racers Reach Baghdad under Blazing Sun," *Arizona Republican*, 10 Mar. 1928.
25. "Newton Again Leads Field," *San Francisco Chronicle*, 10 Mar. 1928; International News Service, "Arizona Indian Will Be in Shape for Long Run," *Arizona Gazette*, 1 Mar. 1928.
26. Canadian Press Service, "Cronick Still Fourth," *Montreal Gazette*, 3 Apr. 1928; Canadian Press Service, "How Canadians Are Faring," *Hamilton Spectator*, 10 Mar. 1928.
27. "De Marr Leads Derby to Amarillo," *Amarillo Globe*, 5 Apr. 1928; "33rd Lap of Bunion Derby Finished Here," *Amarillo Daily News*, 6 Apr. 1928.
28. Wallis, *Route 66: The Mother Road*, 211.
29. Rittenhouse, *Guide Book*, 113–114.
30. James S. Powers, "Canadian Wins Eighth Lap of Derby," *Arizona Republican*, 12 Mar. 1928.
31. "Only 2293 Miles to New York," *Oklahoma City Times*, 6 Apr. 1928; "Newton Takes Second Honors," *Los Angeles Times*, 12 Mar. 1928.
32. Russell J. Newland, "Great Briton Again Lowers Elapsed Time," *San Bernardino Daily Sun*, 13 Mar. 1928.
33. Berry, *From L.A. to New York*, 56.
34. Noakes, *Lore of Running*, 465–466.
35. Tulloh, *Four Million Steps*, 20.
36. "Newton Takes Second Honors," *Los Angeles Times*, 12 Mar. 1928.
37. Russell J. Newland, "Newton Again Leads," *Los Angeles Times*, 11 Mar. 1928.
38. "Arizona Indian Will Be in Shape for Long Run," *Arizona Gazette*, 1 Mar. 1928.
39. James Powers, "Granville Eleventh after Sunday Effort," *Hamilton Spectator*, 12 Mar. 1928.
40. Benjamin Franklin, *Poor Richard's Almanack* (Philadelphia: A Peter Pauper Press), 6.
41. Lewis, *Running the TransAmerica Footrace*, 19.
42. Thomas, *Bunion Derby*, 42.
43. "Athletes Are Peeved Group," *Los Angeles Times*, 25 May 1928.
44. "Marathoners Get into Springfield with Bad Temper," *Springfield Daily News*, 22 Apr. 1928.
45. "Hearty Reception for Hamilton's Derby Hero," *Hamilton Spectator*, 29 May 1928.

204 Notes to pages 51–55

Chapter 8

1. "Newton Wins Ninth Lap in Bunion Derby," *San Francisco Chronicle*, 13 Mar. 1928.
2. Kelly, *Route 66*, 21.
3. Berry, *From L.A. to New York*, 58.
4. "Facing Arizona's Mountains Marathoners Trudge Behind Nimble Arthur Newton," *Arizona Gazette*, 13 Mar. 1928.
5. Jamie Jensen, *Road Trip USA: Cross-Country Adventures on America's Two-Lane Highways*, 3rd ed. (Emeryville, CA: Avalon Travel Publishing, 2002), 289; Richard Mangum and Sherry Mangum, *Route 66 Across Arizona: A Comprehensive Two Way Guide for Touring Route 66* (Flagstaff, AZ: Hexagon Press, 2001), 108.
6. James Powers, "Marathon Runners Reach Arizona," *Arizona Republican*, 13 Mar. 1928.
7. "Facing Arizona's Mountains Marathon Runners Trudge Behind Nimble Art Newton," *Arizona Gazette*, 13 Mar. 1928.
8. "South African Maintains Lead," *New Mexico State Tribune*, 13 Mar. 1928; Russell J. Newland, "Imported Runners Are Between Oatman and Kingman," *Daily Silver Belt*, 13 Mar. 1928.
9. "Veteran Adds to Race Lead," *Los Angeles Times*, 14 Mar. 1928.
10. Mangum and Mangum, *Route 66 Across Arizona*, 56–59, 108.
11. "Newton Scores Another Victory in Pyle's Derby," *San Francisco Chronicle*, 14 Mar. 1928; "Veteran Adds to Race Lead," *Los Angeles Times*, 14 Mar. 1928.
12. "'Runningest Human,'" *Daily Oklahoman*, 13 Mar. 1928.
13. Associated Press, "English Star Wins Heat to Peach Springs," *Arizona Republican*, 15 Mar. 1928.
14. Mangum and Mangum, *Route 66 Across Arizona*, 108; Wallis, *Route 66: The Mother Road*, 201.
15. "Runners Strike Yavapai County," *Prescott Evening Courier*, 15 Mar. 1928.
16. "Veteran Star Swells Lead," *Los Angeles Times*, 15 Mar. 1928.
17. "40 Mile Lap Thursday," *New Mexico State Tribune*, 15 Mar. 1928.
18. Russell J. Newland, "Hopi Indian Drops Out of Long Marathon Race; Pace Tells on Newton," *Arizona Republican*, 17 Mar. 1928.
19. Walter McMullen, The Sports Trail, *Hamilton Spectator*, 4 Apr. 1928.
20. Russell J. Newland, "Newton's Lead Cut by Winner," *Los Angeles Times*, 16 Mar. 1928.
21. "Damon Carries On," *Daily Oklahoman*, 31 Mar. 1928.
22. Newland, "Newton's Lead Cut by Winner," *Los Angeles Times*, 16 Mar. 1928; Noakes, *Lore of Running*, 465.
23. Newland, "Newton's Lead Cut by Winner," *Los Angeles Times*, 16 Mar. 1928.
24. "Runners Reach Seligman in Route thru Arizona," *Arizona Gazette*, 15 Mar. 1928.
25. "Time Change Cheats Bunion Raisers Out of Some Sleep," *Daily Silver Belt*, 15 Mar. 1928; Newland, "Newton's Lead Cut by Winner," *Los Angeles Times*, 16 Mar 1928; 1928 Program; Appendix 1.
26. Newland, "Newton's Lead Cut by Winner," *Los Angeles Times*, 16 Mar. 1928.

27. "Ed Gardner Drops to Seventh Place in Marathon Race," *Enterprise*, 17 Mar. 1928.
28. "Payne Fights Stiff Gale to Win Day's Lap," *Daily Oklahoman*, 16 Mar. 1928.
29. "Runners Strike Yavapai County," *Prescott Evening Courier*, 15 Mar. 1928.
30. Westbrook Pegler, "Pyle Bunion Caravan Hits Trail Today," *Chicago Tribune*, 31 Mar. 1929.
31. "Rough Roads, Bad Weather for Runners," *New Mexico State Tribune*, 16 Mar. 1928.
32. "Marathoners Get into Springfield with Bad Temper," *Springfield Daily News*, 22 Apr. 1928.
33. "Rough Roads, Bad Weather for Runners," *New Mexico State Tribune*, 16 Mar. 1928; Rittenhouse, *Guide Book*, 102–106.
34. "Indian Runner Finally Quits," *Los Angeles Times*, 17 Mar. 1928.
35. "Coast to Coast Racers Completed 515.8 Miles; In Flagstaff Saturday," *Coconino Sun*, 23 Mar. 1928.
36. "Indian Runner Finally Quits," *Los Angeles Times*, 17 Mar. 1928.
37. "Pyle Runners See Jack Lewis Beat Turk on Mat at Williams Last Night," *Arizona Gazette*, 17 Mar. 1928.
38. Mangum and Mangum, *Route 66 Across Arizona*, 75.
39. Rittenhouse, *Guide Book*, 101.
40. Russell J. Newland, "Erickson Wins Marathon Lap," *Los Angeles Times*, 18 Mar. 1928.
41. "Coast to Coast Racers," *Coconino Sun*, 23 Mar. 1928.
42. Ibid.; Wallis, *Route 66: The Mother Road*, 191–193; Rittenhouse, *Guide Book*, 99–101.
43. Jim Powers, "Gardner and Dilks End Marathon Lap in Tie at North Arizona Camp," *Arizona Republican*, 19 Mar. 1928.
44. "Bunion Derby Winner Here, Has Fame, Seeks Fortune," *Washington Post*, 29 May 1928.
45. Emmet Crozier, "Bunion Runners Reach Passaic," *New York Sun*, 25 May 1928.
46. Rittenhouse, *Guide Book*, 97–98.
47. George Scherck, "Sports Drift," *Seattle Post Intelligencer*, 20 Mar. 1928.
48. Arthur F. H. Newton, "Highway '66' Race," *Sayre Headlight*, 12 Apr. 1928.
49. Paul Lowry, "Rabbit Punches," *Los Angeles Times*, 20 Mar. 1928.
50. Newton, "Highway '66' Race," *Sayre Headlight*, 12 Apr. 1928.
51. "Coast to Coast Racers," *Coconino Sun*, 23 Mar. 1928.
52. "State Boy is Derby Leader," *Daily Oklahoman*, 20 Mar. 1928; "Payne Now in Second Place," *Daily Oklahoman*, 21 Mar. 1928.
53. "Collapse of Newton Peps Up Entrants," *Seattle Post Intelligencer*, 21 Mar. 1928.
54. Berry, *From L.A. to New York*, 64; "Collapse of Newton Peps Up Entrants," *Seattle Post Intelligencer*, 21 Mar. 1928.
55. Jim Powers, "Bunion Derby Lead is Taken By Detroiter," *Arizona Republican*, 21 Mar. 1928.
56. "Seattle Boy Leads Field to Navajo," *Seattle Post Intelligencer*, 22 Mar. 1928.

57. "Payne Keeps Second Place," *Seattle Daily Times*, 22 Mar. 1928; "New Dash in Oklahoma Air," *Black Dispatch*, 12 Apr. 1928.
58. "Gardner Wins Lap to Navajo," *Los Angeles Times*, 22 Mar. 1928.
59. Rittenhouse, *Guide Book*, 93–94.
60. "Payne Keeps Second Place in Road Race as Runners Plod On," *Seattle Daily Times*, 22 Mar. 1928.
61. "Seattle Boy Leads Field to Navajo," *Seattle Post Intelligencer*, 22 Mar. 1928.
62. Wallis, *Route 66: The Mother Road*, 183; Rittenhouse, *Guide Book*, 92.
63. "Gardner and Gonzales Tie," *Los Angeles Times*, 23 Mar. 1928.
64. "Gardner Is Hampered by Too Many Backers," *Afro-American*, 21 Apr. 1928.
65. "Gardner Talks Race, Sees Runner Victor," *Seattle Post Intelligencer*, 7 May 1928.

Chapter 9

1. Rittenhouse, *Guide Book*, 69.
2. Department of Commerce, *Historical Statistics of the United States: Colonial Times to the Present* (Washington, DC: U.S. Government Printing Office, 1976).
3. Schneider, *Route 66 Across New Mexico*, 39.
4. Rittenhouse, *Guide Book*, 90; Wallis, *Route 66: The Mother Road*, 175.
5. "Cross Country Footrace Proved Unique Affair," *Gallup Independent*, 30 Mar. 1928.
6. "Bar Carnival with Pyle's Bunion Derby," *Albuquerque Journal*, 24 Mar. 1928.
7. Berry, *From L.A. to New York*, 65.
8. "Marathon Runners Arrive Today from Lupton, Arizona," *Gallup Independent*, 23 Mar. 1928.
9. "To Wire Granville," *Hamilton Spectator*, 16 Mar. 1928.
10. "Marathon Runners Arrive Today," *Gallup Independent*, 23 Mar. 1928.
11. James Doran, "Salo is Second in Lengthy Lap," *South Bend News Times*, 8 May 1928; Berry, *From L.A. to New York*, 65.
12. "Marathon Runners are Ascending Rocky Mountains to Continental Divide Crest," *Daily Silver Belt*, 20 Mar. 1928.
13. Schneider, *Route 66 Across New Mexico*, 101.
14. "Gavuzzi Wins Lap in Derby," *Los Angeles Times*, 25 Mar. 1928.
15. Rittenhouse, *Guide Book*, 86.
16. "Derby Lap Captures by Gavuzzi," *Los Angeles Times*, 26 Mar. 1928.
17. Rittenhouse, *Guide Book*, 86.
18. "Pyle Derby Lap Is Won by Gardner," *Los Angeles Times*, 27 Mar. 1928.
19. Thomas, *Bunion Derby*, 53.
20. "Gardner Talks Race, Sees Runner Victor," *Seattle Post Intelligencer*, 7 May 1928.
21. Associated Press, "Seven Springs Next Stop for Derby Runners," *Seattle Daily Times*, 28 Mar. 1928.
22. "Marathon Lap Is Won by Gavuzzi," *Los Angeles Times*, 28 Mar. 1928.

23. Schneider, *Route 66 Across New Mexico*, 7.
24. "Pyle Carnival Can't Set Up in Duke City," *New Mexico State Tribune*, 24 Mar. 1928.
25. "Bar Carnival with Pyle's Bunion Derby," *Albuquerque Journal*, 24 Mar. 1928.
26. "Advance Men of Carnival Outfit Held," *Albuquerque Journal*, 24 Mar. 1928.
27. Kelly, *Route 66*, 30.
28. Schneider, *Route 66 Across New Mexico*, 142.
29. "Poor Food and Lodging Cause Trouble," *New Mexico State Tribune*, 31 Mar. 1928.
30. "Two Runners in Dead Heat in Pyle Race," *Los Angeles Times*, 29 Mar. 1928.
31. Barbara Hawley, "Barbara Views Bunion Derby and Wishes All Could Win," *Erie Dispatch-Herald*, 16 May 1928.
32. "Great Runner Hit by Pellet During Third Ward Game," *Passaic Daily News*, 5 Oct. 1931.
33. Walter McMullen, The Sports Trail, *Hamilton Spectator*, 19 May 1928.
34. "Hearty Reception for Hamilton Hero," *Hamilton Spectator*, 29 May 1928.
35. "Durable Finn Keeps Lead in Derby," *New Mexico State Tribune*, 30 Mar. 1928.
36. "Marathon Men Begin Weary Plodding Again; It's a Hard Life, Mates," *Albuquerque Journal*, 29 Mar. 1928.
37. "The Public Forum: The Marathon Men," *New Mexico State Tribune*, 5 Apr. 1928.
38. Ibid.
39. "Gonzales Wins Lap of Derby," *Los Angeles Times*, 3 Apr. 1928.
40. "Marathon Men Begin Weary Plodding Again," *Albuquerque Journal*, 29 Mar. 1928.
41. Berry, *From L.A. to New York*, 42–43.
42. Fred Jay, "Gentle Jolts," *Daily Oklahoman*, 25 Mar. 1928.
43. Schneider, *Route 66 Across New Mexico*, 149.
44. "Detroit Man Arrives First in Moriarty," *Albuquerque Journal*, 29 Mar. 1928.
45. "Poor Food and Lodging Cause Trouble in Pyle Marathon Camp, Trainer Tells Tribune," *New Mexico State Tribune*, 31 Mar. 1928.
46. Rittenhouse, *Guide Book*, 74–75; "Souminen Is First in Run," *Los Angeles Times*, 31 Mar. 1928.
47. Rittenhouse, *Guide Book*, 73–74; Schneider, *Route 66 Across New Mexico*, 171; "Runners End Lap in Tie," *Seattle Daily Times*, 1 Apr. 1928.
48. "Granville May Win Pyle's Run," *Los Angeles Times*, 1 Apr. 1928.
49. Rittenhouse, *Guide Book*, 73.
50. "Gardner Cops Lap in Derby," *Los Angeles Times*, 2 Apr. 1928.
51. "Sheik Gardner Drops to Eighth in Marathon Run," *Enterprise*, 30 Mar. 1928.
52. Rittenhouse, *Guide Book*, 71–73.
53. Wallis, *Route 66: The Mother Road*, 148–149.
54. "In the Field of Sports," *Tucumcari American*, 6 Apr. 1928; "Gonzales Wins Lap of Derby," *Los Angeles Times*, 3 Apr. 1928.
55. "In the Field of Sports," *Tucumcari American*, 6 Apr. 1928.

56. Cal Farley, "Farley Views Pyle Runners As They Quit," *Amarillo Daily News*, 3 Apr. 1928.

57. "Gonzales Wins Lap of Derby," *Los Angeles Times*, 3 Apr. 1928.

58. "In the Field of Sport," *Tucumcari American*, 6 Apr. 1928.

59. "Oklahoma Boy Wins Hand from Roadside Crowd," *Amarillo Daily News*, 3 Apr. 1928.

60. "Cronick Still Fourth," *Montreal Gazette*, 3 Apr. 1928.

61. Rittenhouse, *Guide Book*, 68–70.

62. Wallis, *Route 66: The Mother Road*, 146.

63. "Baggage Truck Burns," *Tucumcari American*, 6 Apr. 1928.

64. "Gardner and Wantinnen Tie in Derby," *Los Angeles Times*, 4 Apr. 1928.

65. Ibid.

66. "George Curtis Tells How Colored Runners Threatened in Texas and New Mexico," *Enterprise*, 3 May 1928.

67. "Barney Oldfield, Car Race King, Visits Toney Chisum; Leaves for Eastern Tour," *Amarillo Daily News*, 2 Apr. 1928.

68. Leon C. Metz, *Roadside History of Texas* (Missoula, MT: Mountain Press Publishing Company, 1994), 391–392, 406; Rittenhouse, *Guide Book*, 64.

Chapter 10

1. *Historical Statistics*, Series A, 195–209, Population of States, by Sex, Race, Urban-Rural Residence, and Age: 1790–1970, 35.

2. Alwyn Barr, *Black Texans: A History of African Americans in Texas, 1528–1995*, 2nd ed. (Norman, OK: Red River Books, 1996), 17–20.

3. Barr, *Black Texans*, 49–51, 58.

4. Ibid., 141–142.

5. Ibid., 116, 142–144, 158–159; Leuchtenburg, *Perils of Prosperity*, 209.

6. "Why Jump on Granville?" *Amsterdam News*, 20 Jun. 1928.

7. "El Reno Welcomes Runners with Open Arms," *Black Dispatch*, 19 Apr. 1928.

8. "Pyle Racers Tell Oklahoma City They Will Finish in New York City," *Black Dispatch*, 19 Apr. 1928.

9. Thomas, *Bunion Derby*, 57; Rittenhouse, *Guide Book*, 64.

10. "Weather Range in Amarillo Is Wide," *Amarillo Daily News*, 5 Apr. 1928.

11. Thomas, *Bunion Derby*, 57.

12. Walter McMullen, The Sports Trail, "Gavuzzi Smokes Cigarettes," *Hamilton Spectator*, 4 Apr. 1928; "Gavuzzi Wins Race Lap," *Los Angeles Times*, 5 Apr. 1928.

13. "Granville and Gardner among Prize Winners," *Afro-American*, 28 Apr. 1928.

14. Thomas, *Bunion Derby*, 57.

15. "Bunion Derby Winner Here," *Washington Post*, 29 May 1928.

16. Arch Ward, "Pyle Caravan Straggles In, Shows Here; Off Today," *Chicago Tribune*, 6 May 1928.

17. "Gardner Talks Race, Sees Runner Victor," *Seattle Post Intelligencer*, 7 May 1928.
18. "Detroit Racer Is Six Hours Ahead of Oklahoma Boy," *Amarillo Globe*, 5 Apr. 1928.
19. "90 Runners in Bunion Derby," *Montreal Gazette*, 7 Apr. 1928.
20. "33rd Lap of Bunion Derby Finished Here," *Amarillo Daily News*, 6 Apr. 1928.
21. "Local Runner Captures Lap in Pyle's Race," *Los Angeles Times*, 6 Apr. 1928.
22. Ibid.
23. "33rd Lap of Derby Finished Here," *Amarillo Daily News*, 6 Apr. 1928.
24. Farley, "Farley Views Pyle Runners," *Amarillo Daily News*, 5 Apr. 1928.
25. "Pa Payne Joins Son to Stick Until Bunion Derby Field Finishes in New York," *Daily Oklahoman*, 6 Apr. 1928.
26. "Local Runner Captures Lap in Pyle's Race," *Los Angeles Times*, 6 Apr. 1928.
27. "Bunion Derby Encounters Great Weather," *Tucumcari American*, 13 Apr. 1928; "Granville Sets Derby Pace," *Los Angeles Times*, 8 Apr. 1928.
28. Wallis, *Route 66: The Mother Road*, 131.
29. "C. C. Pyle's Auto Broadcasting Station Is Here," *Amarillo Daily News*, 3 Apr. 1928.
30. "Runners Due Here Thursday During Game," *Amarillo Daily News*, 2 Apr. 1928; "Veterans Sponsor Big Dance Here for Cross-Country Men," *Amarillo Daily News*, 5 Apr. 1928.
31. "33rd Lap of Bunion Derby Finished Here," *Amarillo Daily News*, 6 Apr. 1928.
32. "Pat La Marr Leads Derby into Amarillo," *Amarillo Globe*, 5 Apr. 1928.
33. Lemmel F. Parton, "Bunion Boys Stick Close to Pyle," *Oklahoma City Times*, 28 May 1928.
34. "Pyle and Grange Form Contrasts as Marathon Pilots," *Amarillo Daily News*, 6 Apr. 1928.
35. "Pat La Marr Leads Derby into Amarillo," *Amarillo Globe*, 5 Apr. 1928.
36. Ibid.
37. "As I See It by J," *Sayre Headlight*, 12 Apr. 1928.
38. "Trainer of Paddock," *Amarillo Daily News*, 5 Apr. 1928.
39. "Ross Stealing Pyle's Stuff by Planning Marathon Swim," *Seattle Star*, 10 May 1928.
40. "State Runner Holds Own in Pyle's Derby," *Daily Oklahoman*, 7 Apr. 1928; Rittenhouse, *Guide Book*, 65.
41. Wallis, *Route 66: The Mother Road*, 130.
42. Rittenhouse, *Guide Book*, 64–65.
43. "Erickson New Leader Among Long Runners," *Daily Oklahoman*, 7 Apr. 1928.
44. "Finn Star Wins Lap in Derby," *Los Angeles Times*, 7 Apr. 1928.
45. "Bunion Derby Encounters Great Weather," *Tucumcari American*, 13 Apr. 1928.
46. "Erickson New Leader Among Long Runners," *Daily Oklahoman*, 7 Apr. 1928.
47. "Granville Nails Fifth Position in Long Journey," *Hamilton Spectator*, 7 Apr. 1928.
48. "Bunion Derby Encounters Great Weather," *Tucumcari American*, 13 Apr. 1928.
49. "Granville Sets Derby Pace," *Los Angeles Times*, 8 Apr. 1928.
50. "Pa Payne Joins Son," *Daily Oklahoman*, 6 Apr. 1928.
51. "Snow Rain, Hold Back Pacers," *Daily Oklahoman*, 8 Apr. 1928.

52. "Youngest Cross-Continent Runner Recipient of Great Praise," *Black Dispatch*, 14 Jun. 1928.

53. Thomas, *Bunion Derby*, 59.

54. "Pyle Racers Tell Oklahoma City They Will Finish in New York," *Black Dispatch*, 19 Apr. 1928.

55. "Inspects Man's Head to Determine Whether He Is a 'Dam Niggah,'" *Black Dispatch*, 19 Apr. 1928.

56. "Pyle Racers Tell Oklahoma City," *Black Dispatch*, 19 Apr. 1928.

57. Kelly, *Route 66*, 36.

58. "Granville Sets Derby Pace," *Los Angeles Times*, 8 Apr. 1928; "Sprained Tendon Disables Racer and Andrew Payne Moves Up from Second Place; Englishman Next," *Amarillo Globe*, 9 Apr. 1928.

59. "Runners Marked for Life," *Hamilton Spectator*, 19 Apr. 1928.

60. "Andrew Payne Wins Lap," *Los Angeles Times*, 9 Apr. 1928.

61. 1928 Program.

62. "Andy Payne Wins Lap in Pyle's Cross-Country Race," *Los Angeles Times*, 9 Apr. 1928; Thomas, *Bunion Derby*, 56.

63. "Pyle Racers Tell Oklahoma City," *Black Dispatch*, 19 Apr. 1928; "George Curtis Tells How Colored Runners Were Threatened in Texas and New Mexico," *Enterprise*, 3 May 1928.

64. "Attaboy, Eddie, Ol' Hoss! You Tell Em!" *California Eagle*, 25 May 1928.

65. "Andy Payne Wins Lap," *Los Angeles Times*, 9 Apr. 1928.

66. "Gavuzzi First in Derby Lap," *Los Angeles Times*, 10 Apr. 1928.

Chapter 11

1. Barbara Palmer, *Oklahoma: Off the Beaten Path*, 3rd ed. (Guilford, CT: Globe Pequot Press, 2001), xi.

2. Hudson, *Across This Land*, 251–253.

3. Palmer, *Oklahoma*, viii.

4. Ibid.

5. *Historical Statistics*, Population by Sex, Race, Urban Residence, and Age, Section A, 195–209, 1930: 33; Hudson, *Across This Land*, 253–255.

6. United Press, "Will Rogers to Greet Payne at Capital," *Amarillo Globe*, 9 Apr. 1928.

7. "Bunion Derby Boys Stick Close to Pyle, Ready to Endorse Anything—For Cash," *Oklahoma City Times*, 28 May 1928.

8. "Highway Racers Create Interest," *Sayre Headlight*, 12 Apr. 1928; "Gavuzzi First in Derby Lap," *Los Angeles Times*, 10 Apr. 1928.

9. "Oklahoma Has Two in Derby," *Daily Oklahoman*, 9 Apr. 1928.

10. "Highway Racers Create Interest," *Sayre Headlight*, 12 Apr. 1928.

11. "Payne Trails in State Lap," *Oklahoma City Times*, 10 Apr. 1928.

12. "Our Boy Andy Lags in Derby," *Daily Oklahoman*, 11 Apr. 1928.

13. "Gardner Wins Lap of Derby," *Los Angeles Times*, 11 Apr. 1928.

14. "Threatened Lives of Gardner, Granville," *Afro-American*, 28 Apr. 1928.

15. *Historical Statistics*, Population by Sex, Race, Urban Residence, and Age, Section A, 195–209, 1930: 33.

16. "Gardner Wins Lap of Derby," *Los Angeles Times*, 11 Apr. 1928; "'I'm Watching Phillip Granville,' Says Andy Payne," *Black Dispatch*, 12 Apr. 1928.

17. "Crowd Witnesses Marathon Start," *Custer County Chronicle*, 12 Apr. 1928.

18. See, for example, "Gardner and Granville Hold Pace," *Pittsburgh Courier*, 28 Apr. 1928; "Four Negroes in Transcontinental Race from Los Angeles to N.Y.," *Afro-American*, 28 Apr. 1928; and "Race Begins to Look Like Parade of Ethiopia," *California Eagle*, 27 Apr. 1928.

19. "Pyle's Mammoth Truck Crashes through Bridge," *Oklahoma City Times*, 12 Apr. 1928.

20. "Crowd Witnesses Marathon Start," *Custer County Chronicle*, 12 Apr. 1928.

21. "Our Boy Andy Finds Admirers Handicap," *Daily Oklahoman*, 12 Apr. 1928.

22. "Payne, Briton Finish in a Tie," *Oklahoma City Times*, 11 Apr. 1928.

23. Francis L. Fugate and Roberta B. Fugate, *Roadside History of Oklahoma* (Missoula, MT: Mountain Press Publishing Company, 1991), 337.

24. "Payne and Gavuzzi Tie for Marathon Lap," *Los Angeles Times*, 12 Apr. 1928.

25. Ibid.

26. Palmer, *Oklahoma*, 144.

27. "Friday's Race Ends in Fairgrounds Oval Shortly after Noon," *Daily Oklahoman*, 13 Apr. 1928.

28. "Nielson Cops Lap in Pyle's Marathon Race," *Los Angeles Times*, 13 Apr. 1928.

29. "Runners Fed Poorly," *Montreal Gazette*, 21 Apr. 1928.

30. "El Reno Welcomes Runners with Open Arms," *Black Dispatch*, 19 Apr. 1928.

31. "Granville's Race Depends upon Section in Which He Is Running," *Afro-American*, 13 Apr. 1929; "Why Jump on Phil Granville?" *Amsterdam News*, 20 Jun. 1928.

32. Fugate and Fugate, *Roadside History of Oklahoma*, 149.

33. "Entire Fruit Crop of State May Be Killed," *Daily Oklahoman*, 14 Apr. 1928.

34. "Friday's Race Ends in Fairground Oval Shortly After Noon," *Daily Oklahoman*, 13 Apr. 1928.

35. "Marathoners Arrive as Crowd Does Own Derby Trying to Locate Them," *Daily Oklahoman*, 14 Apr. 1928.

36. Meredith 'Hoppe' Williams, "Almost Everyone Lines Road to See Petal Pioneers Pound Pavement," *Daily Oklahoman*, 14 Apr. 1928.

37. Ibid.

38. "Almost Everyone Lines Road to See Pedal Pioneers Pound Pavement," *Daily Oklahoman*, 14 Apr. 1928.

39. "Mile Long Parade to Wind through City," *Oklahoma City Times*, 12 Apr. 1928.

40. "Sipes' Foods Wins in the Long Run," *Oklahoma City Times*, 13 Apr. 1928.

41. "Streets, Roads, Filled by Crowds Watching Race," *Oklahoma City Times*, 13 Apr. 1928.
42. Chamber of Commerce Advertisement, *Daily Oklahoman*, 13 Apr. 1928.
43. Charles I. Brill, "Pacing the Sport World," *Daily Oklahoman*, 14 Apr. 1928.
44. "Ralph Scott Sues Pyle for $4,000 in Back Pay," *Los Angeles Times*, 14 Apr. 1928; "State's Hope Holds Margin over Gavuzzi," *Daily Oklahoman*, 14 Apr. 1928.
45. "Cross Country Derby Runners Face Long Lap," *Seattle Daily Times*, 14 Apr. 1928.
46. "Little Excitement Seen in Marathon Race Show," *Daily Oklahoman*, 14 Apr. 1928.
47. "Athletes Are Peeved Group," *Los Angeles Times*, 25 May 1928.
48. Emmet Crozier, "Runners May Sue Pyle for Gate," *New York Sun*, 26 May 1928.
49. "Marathoners Arrive as Crowd Does Own Derby Trying to Locate Them," *Daily Oklahoman*, 14 Apr. 1928; "Ralph Scott Sues Pyle for $4,000 in Back Pay," *Los Angeles Times*, 14 Apr. 1928.
50. "Pyle Loses City Payment," *Oklahoma City Times*, 14 Apr. 1928.
51. Ibid.
52. "Threatened Lives of Gardner, Granville," *Afro-American*, 28 Apr. 1928.
53. "Pyle Racers Tell Oklahoma City," *Black Dispatch*, 19 Apr. 1928.
54. Ibid.
55. Ibid.
56. "Three Drop Out of Race to Gotham," *Los Angeles Times*, 15 Apr. 1928.
57. Ibid.
58. Rittenhouse, *Guide Book*, 50–52.
59. "Three Drop Out of Race to Gotham," *Los Angeles Times*, 15 Apr. 1928.
60. Ibid.
61. Ibid.
62. Crozier, "Runners May Sue," *New York Sun*, 26 May 1928.
63. "Bunion Racers Disrupt Lincoln County Track Meet," *Black Dispatch*, 19 Apr. 1928.
64. Ibid.
65. "Threatened Lives of Gardner, Granville," *Afro-American*, 28 Apr. 1928.
66. "Bunion Racers Disrupt Lincoln Co. Track Meet," *Black Dispatch*, 19 Apr. 1928.
67. Ibid.
68. "Olympic Club Sends Best Wishes to Granville at Tulsa," *Hamilton Spectator*, 16 Apr. 1928.
69. Rittenhouse, *Guide Book*, 49–51.
70. "Gavuzzi Is Winner of Derby," *Los Angeles Times*, 16 Apr. 1928; "Four Negroes in Transcontinental Race," *Black Dispatch*, 19 Apr. 1928.
71. "Andy Not Worried," *Miami News Record*, 17 Apr. 1928.
72. "Peter Gavuzzi, Winner of Bristow to Tulsa Gallop," *Los Angeles Times*, 17 Apr. 1928.
73. "Gavuzzi Increases Lead in Derby Lap to Tulsa," *Oklahoma City Times*, 17 Apr. 1928.
74. Editorial, "Tiny Times," *Oklahoma City Times*, 8 Apr. 1928.
75. Rittenhouse, *Guide Book*, 45–49; Palmer, *Oklahoma*, 23–24.
76. "I'm Watching Phillip Granville, Says Andy," *Black Dispatch*, 19 Apr. 1928.
77. Ibid.

78. "Englishman Finishes in City at 2:04; Andy at 3:37," *Miami News Record*, 18 Apr. 1928.
79. "Payne Paces Runners into Chelsea Stop," *Daily Oklahoman*, 18 Apr. 1928.
80. "Englishman Finishes in City," *Miami News Record*, 18 Apr. 1928.
81. Wallis, *Route 66: The Mother Road*, 17; "Payne Leads Pyle Stars through His Home Town," *Los Angeles Times*, 18 Apr. 1928.
82. "Payne Leads Derby Pace in Claremore; Gavuzzi Drops Out?" *Miami News Record*, 17 Apr. 1928.
83. "Payne Leads Pyle Stars Through His Home Town," *Los Angeles Times*, 18 Apr. 1928.
84. Palmer, *Oklahoma*, 33–34; Fugate and Fugate, *Roadside History of Oklahoma*, 324–325.
85. Crawford, "History," 39.
86. Ibid.; "Payne Paces Runners into Chelsea Stop," *Daily Oklahoman*, 18 Apr. 1928.
87. "Englishman Finishes in City," *Miami News Record*, 18 Apr. 1928.
88. Ibid.
89. "Payne Leads Pyle Stars," *Los Angeles Times*, 18 Apr. 1928.
90. "Payne Paces Runners into Chelsea Stop," *Daily Oklahoman*, 18 Apr. 1928.
91. "Bunioneers End Trek in New York," *Cleveland Plain Dealer*, 27 May 1928.
92. Rittenhouse, *Guide Book*, 41–42.
93. "Many Thousands in Miami Watch Pyle Runners," *Joplin Globe*, 19 Apr. 1928.
94. "All Runners Number 77 Finish Here," *Miami News Record*, 19 Apr. 1928.
95. "Missourian Taking Lead As He Nears Missouri Border," *Springfield Leader*, 19 Apr. 1928.
96. "Many Thousands in Miami Watch Pyle Runners," *Joplin Globe*, 19 Apr. 1928; "Payne Paces Runners into Chelsea Stop," *Daily Oklahoman*, 18 Apr. 1928.
97. "All Runners, Numbering 77, Finished Here," *Miami News Record*, 19 Apr. 1928; "Gavuzzi Wins Derby Lap," *Los Angeles Times*, 19 Apr. 1928.
98. "Notes on the Bunion Derby," *Joplin Globe*, 20 Apr. 1928.
99. "Dark Horses Forge Ahead in Day's Race," *Miami News Record*, 19 Apr. 1928.
100. "Missourian Taking Lead," *Springfield Leader*, 19 Apr. 1928.
101. "Mr. Pyle, the 'Idealist,'" *Carthage Evening Press*, 20 Apr. 1928.
102. "'Dark Horses' Forge Ahead in Day's Race," *Miami News Record*, 19 Apr. 1928; "'Andy' Payne Requires Much Food," *Joplin Globe*, 20 Apr. 1928.

Chapter 12

1. Phyllis Rossiter, *A Living History of the Ozarks* (Gretna, LA: Pelican Publishing Company, Inc., 2001), 27.
2. Ibid., 17, 19; Hudson, *Across This Land*, 131.
3. Rossiter, *A Living History of the Ozarks*, 45–48, 214.
4. Ibid., 92–96; Rittenhouse, *Guide Book*, 38–39; Hudson, *Across This Land*, 134–135.
5. "Convicted By Their Own Statements," *Carthage Evening Press*, 20 Apr. 1928.

6. "Huge Throng Is Expected in City to See Entrants," *Joplin Globe*, 19 Apr. 1928.
7. "Runners Due in City by Noon; $1,500 Posted to Protect Pyle," *Springfield Daily News*, 21 Apr. 1928.
8. "'Dark Horses' Forge Ahead," *Miami News Record*, 19 Apr. 1928.
9. "Payne Increases Derby Lead over English Entrant," *Joplin Globe*, 20 Apr. 1928.
10. Work Sheet A, Individual Time Sheet, John Gober.
11. "Gober Who Led Pack into City, Undaunted by Position in Race," *Joplin Globe*, 20 Apr. 1928.
12. "'Andy' Payne Requires Much Food," *Joplin Globe*, 20 Apr. 1928.
13. "Andy Payne Increases Derby Lead," *Los Angeles Times*, 20 Apr. 1928.
14. "Payne Increases Derby Lead over English Entrant," *Joplin Globe*, 20 Apr. 1928.
15. D. D. Rayfield, "Throngs Surround Football Star with Pyle's Race," *Springfield Leader*, 19 Apr. 1928.
16. "Mr. Pyle, the 'Idealist,'" *Carthage Evening Press*, 20 Apr. 1928.
17. "Notes on Bunion Derby," *Joplin Globe*, 20 Apr. 1928.
18. "Andy Payne Requires Much Food," *Joplin Globe*, 20 Apr. 1928.
19. Rossiter, *A Living History of the Ozarks*, 126–127.
20. "Runners Due in City By Noon, $1500 Posted to Protect Pyle," *Springfield Daily News*, 21 Apr. 1928.
21. "Eggs Tossed at Derby Auto; and They Weren't So Fresh Either," *Daily Oklahoman*, 21 Apr. 1928.
22. Charles I. Brill, "Pacing the Sporting World," *Daily Oklahoman*, 21 Apr. 1928.
23. "Missouri Marathon Man Wins," *Los Angeles Times*, 21 Apr. 1928.
24. "Runners Due in City By Noon," *Springfield Daily News*, 21 Apr. 1928.
25. Ibid.
26. "Payne Is Still Hour Ahead for Marathon Cash," *Seattle Daily Times*, 21 Apr. 1928.
27. "'Dark Horse' Leads Runners into City; It's a Strange Gang," *Springfield Daily News*, 22 Apr. 1928.
28. Rossiter, *A Living History of the Ozarks*, 117.
29. Wallis, *Route 66: The Mother Road*, 57.
30. "Throngs Surround Football Star with Pyle Race Party," *Springfield Leader*, 19 Apr. 1928.
31. "Race Will End at Convention Center," *Springfield Leader*, 20 Apr. 1928.
32. "Payne Tenth Saturday but Still Leading," *Daily Oklahoman*, 22 Apr. 1928; "De Marr is Barred in Pyle Run," *Los Angeles Times*, 22 Apr. 1928.
33. "Motorists Drive Out to Meet Sturdy Athletes in Long Grind," *Springfield Leader*, 21 Apr. 1928.
34. "Threatened Lives of Gardner, Granville," *Afro-American*, 28 Apr. 1928.
35. "Marathoners Get into Springfield in Bad Temper," *Springfield Daily News*, 22 Apr. 1928.
36. *Historical Statistics*, Population by Sex, Race, Urban Residence, and Age, Section A, 195–209, 1930: 30.

37. "Highway 66 Race Is Won by Italian Champ," *Springfield Daily News*, 23 Apr. 1928; "Runners Visit Conway," *Conway Weekly Record*, 26 Apr. 1928.
38. "Walker Is Winner of Derby Lap," *Los Angeles Times*, 23 Apr. 1928.
39. Rossiter, *A Living History of the Ozarks*, 76.
40. "Runners Will Be Here Next Sunday," *Lebanon Rustic*, 19 Apr. 1928.
41. "Pyle Runners in Lebanon Monday," *Lebanon Rustic*, 26 Apr. 1928.
42. "Granville and Gardner Tie to Win Derby," *Los Angeles Times*, 24 Apr. 1928.
43. "Racers Trudge Through Mud," *Illinois State Register*, 23 Apr. 1928.
44. "Trans-Continental Runners Stop at Rolla," *Rolla Herald*, 26 Apr. 1928; Rittenhouse, *Guide Book*, 25–27.
45. "Granville and Gardner Hold 4th and 5th Place," *Black Dispatch*, 26 Apr. 1928.
46. Canadian Press Service, "Philip Granville in Tie for First Again," *Hamilton Spectator*, 25 Apr. 1928.
47. "Trans Continental Racers," *Rolla Herald*, 26 Apr. 1928.
48. "The Foot Racer," *New Era*, 28 Apr. 1928.
49. Crozier, "Runners May Sue Pyle," *New York Sun*, 26 May 1928.
50. Rittenhouse, *Guide Book*, 23–25.
51. Bill Witt, "He Rides While Runners Pick 'Em Up and Lay 'Em Down," *Seattle Star*, 26 Apr. 1928.
52. "Payne Loses Bunion Lead to Britisher," *Seattle Post Intelligencer*, 26 Apr. 1928.
53. "Ed Gardner Sixth in Marathon Race," *Enterprise*, 26 Apr. 1928.
54. "Payne Relinquishes Lead in Marathon to Gavuzzi; Granville Cops Pyle Lap," *Los Angeles Times*, 26 Apr. 1928.
55. "The Cross Country Runners Are Coming," *Sullivan News*, 26 Apr. 1928.
56. "Pyle's Runners Pace through Here Today," *St. Louis Daily Globe Democrat*, 27 Apr. 1928.
57. "Pyle Painful Procession in Here Today," *St. Louis Star*, 27 Apr. 1928.
58. "Cross-Country Derby Limping Through St. Louis," *St. Louis Post Dispatch*, 27 Apr. 1928.
59. Charles (Kid) Regan, "Pyle Blushed at Idea of Bunion Derby But It Proved Great Racket," *St. Louis Times*, 27 Apr. 1928.
60. "Gavuzzi Leads Cross Country Field in Hike," *Seattle Daily Times*, 27 Apr. 1928.
61. "Gavuzzi Victor in Derby Lap," *Los Angeles Times*, 27 Apr. 1928.
62. "Gavuzzi Leads," *Seattle Daily Times*, 27 Apr. 1928.
63. "Granville Starts in to Run Leaders Down," *Hamilton Spectator*, 26 Apr. 1928.
64. "Ed Gardner Sixth in Marathon Race," *Enterprise*, 26 Apr. 1928.
65. "Briton Takes Lead Over Sooner," *Daily Oklahoman*, 27 Apr. 1928.
66. Ibid.
67. Picture Caption, "Alan Currier," *St. Louis Post Dispatch*, 27 Apr. 1928.
68. Wallis, *Route 66: The Mother Road*, 52.
69. "Cross-Country Derby Limping Through St. Louis," *St. Louis Post Dispatch*, 27 Apr. 1928.
70. Ibid.

71. "Gardner Takes Pyle Race Lap," *Los Angeles Times*, 28 Apr. 1928.
72. "'I Haven't Begun to Run Yet,' Says Gavuzzi, Ahead in Pyle's Marathon," *St. Louis Star*, 28 Apr. 1928.
73. Walter McMullen, The Sports Trail, *Hamilton Spectator*, 7 Jun. 1928.
74. Gerald Holland, "Race Leaders Could Run Away from De Mar at Marathon Distance, Referee Duffy Says," *St. Louis Post Dispatch*, 27 Apr. 1928.

Chapter 13

1. Hudson, *Across This Land*, 204.
2. Elliott Rudwick, *Race Riots at East St. Louis, July 2, 1917* (Chicago: University of Illinois Press, 1964), 47, 58–59.
3. "Cross Country Derby Continues Eastward," *St. Louis Post Dispatch*, 28 Apr. 1928.
4. "'I Haven't Begun to Run Yet,'" *St. Louis Star*, 28 Apr. 1928.
5. "Peter Gavuzzi Victor in Lap of Pyle's Marathon," *Los Angeles Times*, 29 Apr. 1928.
6. Edward Burns, "Psychiatrist Needed; Pyle's Hoofers Near," *Chicago Tribune*, 2 May 1928.
7. "Marathoner Tells Interesting Story," *Custer County Chronicle*, 10 May 1928.
8. "Englishman Is Still Fastest of Race Field," *Seattle Daily Times*, 30 Apr. 1928.
9. "Gavuzzi Wins Another Lap in Derby," *Chicago Tribune*, 30 Apr. 1928.
10. "Cross Country Runners Reach Virden," *Virden Recorder*, 3 May 1928.
11. Ibid.
12. Jensen, *Road Trip USA*, 892.
13. "Bunion Derby Runners Led into City by Eastern Man," *Illinois State Register*, 30 Apr. 1928.
14. "John Salo Wins Lap in Pyle's Marathon," *Los Angeles Times*, 1 May 1928.
15. "Briton First into Lincoln on U.S. Race," *Lincoln Evening Courier*, 1 May 1928.
16. "Plans Concluded for Local Night Stop," *Lincoln Evening Courier*, 30 Apr. 1928.
17. "New York Newspapers Make Attack on Pyle," *Passaic Daily Herald*, 25 May 1928.
18. "Pyle Runners Stage a Tie in Lincoln Race," *Illinois State Register*, 1 May 1928; "Grange Denies Claim of Bank at Champaign," *Pontiac Daily Leader*, 1 May 1928.
19. Jensen, *Road Trip USA*, 894.
20. "Gavuzzi Increases Lead," *Los Angeles Times*, 2 May 1928.
21. Ibid.
22. Edward Burns, "Psychiatrist Needed; Pyle's Hoofers Near," *Chicago Tribune*, 2 May 1928.
23. Ibid.; "Pyle, Grange, Here Today, Arrange Stop," *Lincoln Evening Courier*, 28 Apr. 1928.
24. Rittenhouse, *Guide Book*, 13; "Barber and Law Spoil Pyle's Day," *Los Angeles Times*, 3 May 1928.
25. "Barber and Law Spoil Pyle's Day," *Los Angeles Times*, 3 May 1928.
26. Ibid.

27. Ibid.
28. "Gardner and Granville Keep Pace in Race," *Enterprise*, 3 May 1928.
29. Edward Burns, "Mr. Pyle, Like Coxey, Will Lead His Army on Foot," *Chicago Tribune*, 3 May 1928.
30. "Barber and Law Spoil Pyle's Day," *Los Angeles Times*, 3 May 1928.
31. Thomas, *Bunion Derby*, 87.
32. Edward Burns, "Take It or Leave It, but Even a Marathoner Has His Worries," *Chicago Tribune*, 5 May 1928.
33. Rittenhouse, *Guide Book*, 12.
34. "Bunion Derby Runners Reach Pontiac Today," *Pontiac Daily Leader*, 3 May 1928.
35. "Local Boy Cops Pyle Derby Lap," *Los Angeles Times*, 4 May 1928.
36. "P. J. Jones Says—," *Hamilton Spectator*, 4 May 1928.
37. "Pyle Loses Palace of Wheels As Sheriff Serves Attachment," *Washington Post*, 3 May 1928.
38. "Footsore and Weary Bunion Derby Arrives," *Joliet Evening Herald News*, 4 May 1928.
39. Jensen, *Road Trip USA*, 896.
40. "Gardner Wins Pyle Lap, Runners in Chicago," *Los Angeles Times*, 5 May 1928.
41. "Runners Leave Pontiac for Joliet," *Pontiac Daily Leader*, 4 May 1928.
42. "Footsore and Weary Bunion Derby Arrives," *Joliet Evening Herald News*, 4 May 1928; "This Racket Has Bunion Derby Beaten," *Joliet Evening Herald News*, 6 May 1928.
43. "Footsore and Weary Bunion Derby Arrives," *Joliet Evening Herald News*, 4 May 1928.
44. "Runners Leave Pontiac for Joliet," *Pontiac Daily Leader*, 4 May 1928; "Gardner Wins Pyle Lap," *Los Angeles Times*, 5 May 1928.
45. "Pyle Puts Us on Main Street," *Joliet Evening Herald News*, 5 May 1928.
46. "Footsore and Weary Bunion Derby Arrives," *Joliet Evening Herald News*, 4 May 1928.
47. "Gardner Wins Pyle Lap," *Los Angeles Times*, 5 May 1928.
48. Hudson, *Across This Land*, 219.
49. Jack Schnedler, *Chicago*, 3rd ed. (Oakland, CA: Compass American Guides, 2001), 45–47.
50. Arch Ward, "Pyle's Caravan Straggles In, Show Here, Off Today," *Chicago Tribune*, 6 May 1928; Kellum, "Gardner, Josephs, Robinson," *Chicago Defender*, 12 May 1928.
51. Ward, "Pyle's Caravan Straggles In," *Chicago Tribune*, 6 May 1928.
52. "Salo Leads Pyle Runners into Chicago," *Los Angeles Times*, 6 May 1928.
53. Sam Otis, "Hard Roads and Automobiles," *Cleveland Plain Dealer*, 7 May 1928.
54. "Salo Leads Pyle Runners into Chicago," *Los Angeles Times*, 6 May 1928.
55. Schnelder, *Chicago*, 22, 41; Hudson, *Across This Land*, 207.
56. Steven Watson, *The Harlem Renaissance: The Hub of African American Culture, 1920–1930* (New York: Pantheon Books, 1995), 119; Jim Haskins and

N. R. Mitgang, *Mr. Bojangles: The Biography of Bill Robinson* (New York: Welcome
Rain Publishers, 1988), 170–171; "Bunion Derby Runners in Chicago," *Indianapolis
Recorder*, 12 May 1928; Kellum, "Gardner, Josephs, Robinson," *Chicago Defender*,
12 May 1928.

57. "Granville and Gardner Taboo Long Standing Prejudiced Tradition," *Pittsburg
Courier*, 12 May 1928.
58. Bill Gibson, "Gardner, Granville Both Confident of $25,000 Plum," *Afro-
American*, 13 Apr. 1928.
59. Edward Burns, "Take It or Leave It, but Even a Marathoner Has His Worries,"
Chicago Tribune, 5 May 1928.
60. Carroll, *Red Grange*, 150.
61. Ward, "Pyle's Caravan Straggles In," *Chicago Tribune*, 6 May 1928.
62. Ibid.
63. Canadian Press, "Granville Keeps Place," *Montreal Gazette*, 7 May 1928.
64. "Runners Face 64 Mile Trek," *Goshen Daily Democrat*, 7 May 1928.

Chapter 14

1. "Runners Face 64 Mile Trek," *Goshen Daily Democrat*, 7 May 1928.
2. "Hoosiers Tie for Lead Over 28.4 Mile Lap," *Cleveland Plain Dealer*, 7 May 1928.
3. "Ed Gardner Back Home; He's Happy," *Seattle Post Intelligencer*, 6 Jun. 1928;
Noakes, *Lore of Running*, 465.
4. Robert A. French, "Bunion Plodders Skirt Toledo On Trek Across Ohio," *Toledo
Blade*, 11 May 1928.
5. Scherck, Sports Drift, *Seattle Post Intelligencer*, 11 May 1928.
6. "Bunion Sauce," *Miami News Record*, 20 May 1928.
7. Appendix B.
8. James Doran, "Salo Is Second in Lengthy Lap of Pyle Gallop," *South Bend News
Times*, 8 May 1928.
9. "Perrella Paces Derby into Mishawaka," *Los Angeles Times*, 8 May 1928.
10. James Doran, "Mishawaka Gets Derby Stopover," *South Bend News Times*, 6 May
1928.
11. Doran, "Salo Is Second in Lengthy Lap," *South Bend News Times*, 8 May 1928.
12. "Grueling Derby Lap Takes Toll," *South Bend Tribune*, 8 May 1928.
13. "Perrella Wins Longest Lap in Derby," *Cleveland Plain Dealer*, 8 May 1928.
14. "Grueling Derby Lap Takes Toll," *South Bend Tribune*, 8 May 1928; 1928 Program.
15. "Italian Wins Lap of Derby," *Los Angeles Times*, 9 May 1928; "Gardner Slips into
Eighth," *Seattle Post Intelligencer*, 9 May 1928.
16. "Canadian Leads Pyle's Pack on 41.8 Mile Trek," *Cleveland Plain Dealer*, 10 May
1928; Individual Time Sheet, Gardner.
17. Mabel V. Pollock, *Our State, Ohio 1823–2003: A Bicentennial History*
(Newcomerstown, OH: 1st Books, 2001), 83.

18. Robert A. French, "Bunion Plodders Skirt Toledo on Trek Across Ohio," *Toledo Blade*, 11 May 1928.

19. Ibid.

20. "Salo Alleges Mistreatment," *Montreal Gazette*, 11 May 1928.

21. French, "Bunion Plodders Skirt Toledo," *Toledo Blade*, 11 May 1928.

22. Ibid.

23. Ibid.

24. "Gavuzzi Quits Bunion Derby; Payne Leads," *Toledo Blade*, 11 May 1928.

25. "Salo Winner of Derby Lap," *Los Angeles Times*, 11 May 1928.

26. *Cleveland Plain Dealer*, 12 May 1928; French, "Bunion Plodders Skirt Toledo," *Toledo Blade*, 11 May 1928.

27. "Gavuzzi Quits Bunion Derby; Payne Leads," *Toledo Blade*, 11 May 1928.

28. "Hot Footin' Papa's Fourth in Derby," *Cleveland Plain Dealer*, 12 May 1928.

29. "Oklahoma Kid Leading Grind in Terrific Bunion Derby," *Fremont Messenger*, 12 May 1928.

30. "Gavuzzi Quits Bunion Derby," *Toledo Blade*, 12 May 1928; "Hot Footin' Papa's Fourth in Derby," *Cleveland Plain Dealer*, 12 May 1928.

31. "Oklahoma Kid Leading Grind," *Fremont Messenger*, 12 May 1928.

32. "Gavuzzi Quits Bunion Derby," *Toledo Blade*, 11 May 1928.

33. Jensen, *Road Trip USA*, 621–623.

34. "Random Shots," *Fremont Messenger*, 14 May 1928.

35. "Gavuzzi Quits Bunion Derby," *Toledo Blade*, 11 May 1928.

36. "Umek Carried Out Boast of His Handlers," *Fremont Messenger*, 14 May 1928.

37. "Hot Footin' Papa's Fourth in Derby," *Cleveland Plain Dealer*, 12 May 1928.

38. "Oklahoma Kid Leading Grind in Terrific Bunion Derby," *Fremont Messenger*, 12 May 1928.

39. "Ed Gardner Now Fights Shin Splints," *Seattle Post Intelligencer*, 12 May 1928.

40. Leland C. Lewis, "Dark Hours Cropping Out in Derby Run," *Fremont Messenger*, 11 May 1928.

41. Phillip W. Porter, "Homing Mike Beats Hoofers to Hug Kids," *Cleveland Plain Dealer*, 13 May 1928.

42. "Payne Is Winner of Derby Lap," *Los Angeles Times*, 13 May 1928.

43. Carol Poh Miller and Robert A. Wheeler, *Cleveland: A Concise History, 1796–1996*, 2nd ed. (Bloomington: Indiana University Press, 1997), 115–118.

44. Phillip W. Porter, "Dollars Rain as Hero Mike Jogs in City," *Cleveland Plain Dealer*, 14 May 1928.

45. "Young Joyces Just Can't See Papa for Tan," *Cleveland Plain Dealer*, 13 May 1928.

46. Ibid.

47. Porter, "Homing Mike Beats Hoofers," *Cleveland Plain Dealer*, 13 May 1928.

48. Phillip W. Porter, "Dollars Rain As Hero Mike Jogs in City," *Cleveland Plain Dealer*, 14 May 1928.

49. James E. Doyle, "The Sports Trail," *Cleveland Plain Dealer*, 11 May 1928.

50. Porter, "Dollars Rain As Hero Mike Jogs in City," *Cleveland Plain Dealer*, 14 May 1928; "Salo Wins Lap in Derby," *Los Angeles Times*, 14 May 1928.

51. Porter, "Dollars Rain As Hero Mike Jogs in City," *Cleveland Plain Dealer*, 14 May 1928.

52. Porter, "Homing Mike Beats Hoofers," *Cleveland Plain Dealer*, 13 May 1928.

53. Ibid.

54. Porter, "Dollars Rain As Hero Mike Jogs in City," *Cleveland Plain Dealer*, 14 May 1928.

55. Picture Caption, "Big and Little Joyces Hold Reunion," *Cleveland Plain Dealer*, 14 May 1928.

56. Porter, "Dollars Rain As Hero Mike Jogs in City," *Cleveland Plain Dealer*, 14 May 1928.

57. Ibid.

58. "Pays Pyle $1,000 to Be Host," *Cleveland Plain Dealer*, 12 May 1928.

59. Ibid.

60. "Oklahoma Kid Leading Grind," *Fremont Messenger*, 14 May 1928.

61. "Ed Gardner Second in Lap," *Seattle Post Intelligencer*, 14 May 1928; "Granville and Gardner Taboo Long Standing Prejudiced Tradition," *Pittsburgh Courier*, 19 May 1928.

62. Porter, "Dollars Rain As Hero Mike Jogs in City," *Cleveland Plain Dealer*, 14 May 1928.

63. Porter, "Homing Mike Beats Hoofers," *Cleveland Plain Dealer*, 13 May 1928.

64. "Here's the Lineup of Pyle's Pet Pike Pounders," *Cleveland Plain Dealer*, 13 May 1928.

65. Pollock, *Our State*, 58.

66. Jensen, *Road Trip USA*, 628; George Zimmermann and Carol Zimmermann, *Ohio: Off the Beaten Path*, 9th ed. (Guilford, CT: Globe Pequot Press, 2000), 27.

67. "Joyce Fourth in Lap, in Pink Condition," *Cleveland Plain Dealer*, 15 May 1928.

68. Ibid.

69. "Payne, Salo Lead Men to Ohio Town," *Seattle Post Intelligencer*, 15 May 1928.

70. "40 More Miles and Andy Payne's Race Is Ended," *Oklahoma City Times*, 26 May 1928.

71. Will Rogers, "Rogers Forsakes Joking to Praise the Bunion Derby," *Cleveland Plain Dealer*, 15 May 1928.

Chapter 15

1. Jensen, *Road Trip USA*, 629; Douglass Root, *Pennsylvania* (New York: Compass American Guides, 2003) 266–267.

2. Barbara Hawley, "Hundreds See Runners as They End 45-Mile Jump; 'Red' Grange With Them," *Erie Dispatch-Herald*, 15 May 1928.

3. "Barbara Views Bunion Derby and Wishes All Could Win," *Erie Dispatch-Herald*, 16 May 1928.

4. Ibid.

5. Leland C. Lewis, "Seattle Boy Gallops to Ninth Spot," *Seattle Post Intelligencer*, 16 May 1928; "Gardner Wins Derby Lap," *Los Angeles Times*, 16 May 1928.

6. Lewis, "Seattle Boy Gallops to Ninth Spot," *Seattle Post Intelligencer*, 16 May 1928.

7. "Throngs Witness Race Here," *Erie Daily Times*, 16 May 1928.

8. Charles J. Brill, "Andy Should Worry," *Daily Oklahoman*, 16 May 1928.

9. "Throngs Witness Race Here," *Erie Daily Times*, 16 May 1928.

10. "Salo Saving," *Passaic Daily Herald*, 16 May 1928.

11. "Barbara Views Bunion Derby and Wishes All Could Win," *Erie Dispatch-Herald*, 16 May 1928; John F. McCarthy, "Salo Saving Self for Finish in Pyle's Marathon," *Passaic Daily Herald*, 16 May 1928.

12. "Pyle Asked to Bring Marathon to Passaic," *Passaic Daily Herald*, 16 May 1928; "Legion Raises $1,000 Guarantee for Friday's Run to End at Stadium," *Passaic Daily Herald*, 22 May 1928.

13. "Comedy Crops Out in Pyle's Bunion Derby," *Fremont Messenger*, 16 May 1928.

14. Ibid.

15. "Barbara Views Bunion Derby," *Erie Dispatch-Herald*, 16 May 1928.

16. "Salo Gaining on Andy Payne," *Toledo Blade*, 17 May 1928.

17. Arthur G. McMahon, "Passaic Runner First into Jamestown," *Passaic Daily Herald*, 17 May 1928.

18. James F. McCarthy, "Picks Up an Hour and a Half from Erie to Jamestown; Running in Blind Dust," *Passaic Daily Herald*, 17 May 1928.

19. "John Salo Winner in Derby Lap," *Los Angeles Times*, 17 May 1928; "Derby Runner Reported to Have Collapsed Near Kennedy This Afternoon," *Jamestown Evening Journal*, 17 May 1928.

20. Westbrook Pegler, "Has Pyle Got It?" *Seattle Daily Times*, 25 May 1928.

21. "Derby Runner Reported to Have Collapsed," *Jamestown Evening Journal*, 17 May 1928.

22. S. C. M.'s Sportsorials: Comments on Local and General Affairs in the Sports Realm, *Jamestown Evening Journal*, 17 May 1928.

23. Ibid.

24. "Newton Says Runners Are in Fine Condition," *Jamestown Evening Journal*, 17 May 1928.

25. S. C. M.'s Sportsorials, *Jamestown Evening Journal*, 17 May 1928.

26. "Tootsie Trotters Will Stop Here Tomorrow," *Jamestown Evening Journal*, 15 May 1928.

27. "Salo Takes Hour Away from Andy," *Seattle Daily Times*, 17 May 1928.

28. "Cross Country Harriers to Be Here Thursday," *Bradford Era*, 15 May 1928.

29. Alan J. Gould, "Pyle Plans to Hold Bigger and Better Bunion Derby Show," *Bradford Era*, 19 May 1928.

30. "Seattle Boy Gallops to Ninth Spot," *Seattle Post Intelligencer*, 16 May 1928.

31. "Payne Lead in Derby Cut by John Salo," *Los Angeles Times*, 18 May 1928.
32. "Payne Nears Prize Money," *Toledo Blade*, 18 May 1928.
33. John F. McCarthy, "58 Minutes More Clipped by Salo from Payne Lead," *Passaic Daily Herald*, 19 May 1928.
34. "Salo Again Wins Lap in Pyle's Race," *Seattle Daily Times*, 20 May 1928.
35. "Salo Reaches Bath First in Lap of Pyle Marathon," *Los Angeles Times*, 20 May 1928.
36. Walter McMullen, The Sports Trail, *Hamilton Spectator*, 19 May 1928.
37. "Salo, Gardner Lead Callous Derby for Day," *Jamestown Morning Post*, 19 May 1928.
38. "Expect Cross Country Runners in Waverly Sometime on Sunday," *Sunday Telegram*, 20 May 1928.
39. "Andy Payne Holds Lead in Marathon Race across Country," *Los Angeles Times*, 21 May 1928.
40. Ibid.
41. McMullen, The Sports Trail, *Hamilton Spectator*, 21 May 1928.
42. "Marathoners on Longest Jaunt of Pyle Classic," *Seattle Daily Times*, 21 May 1928.
43. "Pyle Race Not to Stop in Binghamton," *Binghamton Press*, 18 May 1928.
44. "Salo Wins Lap of Derby," *Los Angeles Times*, 22 May 1928.
45. "Salo Leads Runners Into City; Records Expected to Fall Today," *Binghamton Press*, 21 May 1928.
46. "Pyle Runners Continue on to Liberty Today," *Binghamton Press*, 22 May 1928.
47. "Salo Captures Derby Lap," *Los Angeles Times*, 22 May 1928.
48. "Pyle Runners Continue on to Liberty Today," *Binghamton Press*, 22 May 1928.
49. "Derbyists Start for Middletown," *New York Post*, 23 May 1928.
50. "Town in Holiday Mood as Racers Struggle Through," *Liberty Register*, 23 May 1928.
51. "Payne's Lead Cut by Salo in Derby Lap," *Los Angeles Times*, 23 May 1928.
52. "Payne Fourth in 59 Mile Lap," *Washington Post*, 23 May 1928.
53. John F. McCarthy, "Bad Ankle Slows Salo's Speed," *Passaic Daily Herald*, 24 May 1928; Harry D. Nash, "Payne Far Ahead in Bunion Derby," *New York Post*, 24 May 1928.
54. Nash, "Payne Far Ahead in Bunion Derby," *New York Post*, 24 May 1928.
55. Ibid.; "Gardner Leads Pyle Athletes in Bunion Lap," *Los Angeles Times*, 24 May 1928.
56. Nash, "Payne Far Ahead in Bunion Derby," *New York Post*, 24 May 1928.
57. "Pot of Gold at the Finish of His 3,400 Mile Trek Glimpsed by Andy Payne," *Oklahoma City Times*, 24 May 1928.
58. "Airplane Start to Andy Payne," *Oklahoma City Times*, 24 May 1928.
59. Bernard Borneman, "Along the Way with John Salo," *Passaic Daily Herald*, 24 May 1928.
60. "Athletes Are Peeved Group," *Los Angeles Times*, 25 May 1928.
61. John F. McCarthy, "Salo Rests Ankle Going to Suffern," *Passaic Daily News*, 25 May 1928.
62. Crozier, "Bunion Runners Reach Passaic," *New York Sun*, 25 May 1928.
63. McCarthy, "Salo Rests Ankle Going to Suffern, Taking It Easy," *Passaic Daily News*,

25 May 1928; "Lesser Lights Cop Honors in Latest Marathon Jaunt," *Los Angeles Times*, 25 May 1928.

64. "Bad Ankle Slows Salo's Speed But He Remains Game," *Passaic Daily Herald*, 24 May 1928.
65. "Gotham's Eyes to Be on Andy Payne at Finish," *Los Angeles Times*, 25 May 1928.
66. Crozier, "Bunion Runners Reach Passaic," *New York Sun*, 25 May 1928.
67. "Turner Promises Police Guard for Marathon Leader," *Passaic Daily Herald*, 24 May 1928; "Passaic Bedecked, Greets Salo Today," *New York Times*, 25 May 1928.
68. George Scherck, Sports Drift, *Seattle Post Intelligencer*, 26 May 1928.
69. Raymond Daniell, "Passaic Out to Welcome Home Town Pyle Harrier," *New York Post*, 25 May 1928.
70. Emmett Crozier, "Bunion Runners Reach Passaic," *New York Sun*, 25 May 1928.
71. "Bunion Revolt Collapses; Salo Leads Pack into Hometown," *Miami News Record*, 25 May 1928.
72. "Plucky Legionnaire Runs Great Race with Andy Payne Far Behind on Way to Stadium," *Passaic Daily Herald*, 25 May 1928.
73. Wendell Merrill, "Given Great Ovation Last Night at School Stadium," *Passaic Daily News*, 26 May 1928.
74. "Turner Appoints Salo Patrolman on Birthday Eve," *Passaic Daily Herald*, 25 May 1928.
75. Dudley Nicholas, "Mr. Pyle Thinks It's Fine the Way Sights of Home Spur His Boy's Effort," *Daily Oklahoman*, 26 May 1928.
76. Edward J. Nash, "Bunion Derbyist 1 Day Out of Goal After 3,390 Miles," *Washington Post*, 26 May 1928.
77. Merrill, "Given Great Ovation," *Passaic Daily News*, 26 May 1928.
78. "Gotham's Eyes to Be on Andy at Finish Line," *Oklahoma City Times*, 25 May 1928.
79. Merrill, "Given Great Ovation," *Passaic Daily News*, 26 May 1928.
80. Ibid.
81. Dudley Nichols, "Mr. Pyle Thinks It's Fine the Way Sights of Home Spur His Boys to Effort," *Daily Oklahoman*, 26 May 1928.
82. Daniell, "Passaic Out to Welcome Home Town Pyle Harrier," *New York Post*, 25 May 1928.
83. "Exhibition Run in New York Is Cause of Fight," *Seattle Daily Times*, 25 May 1928.
84. "Bunion Runners Reach Passaic," *New York Sun*, 25 May 1928.
85. "Payne Appears Certain First Prize Winner," *Seattle Daily Times*, 26 May 1928.

Chapter 16

1. "Runners May Sue Pyle for Gate," *New York Sun*, 26 May 1928.
2. "55 Reach Goal Here in Coast Marathon," *New York Times*, 27 May 1928.
3. "10,000 Roar Welcome to 'Smiling Sammy,'" *Afro-American*, 2 June 1928.
4. "55 Reach Goal Here in Coast Marathon," *New York Times*, 27 May 1928;

"Oklahoma's Andy Payne Drags Down First Prize in Coast-to-Coast Run," *Daily Oklahoman*, 27 May 1928.

5. Thomas, *Bunion Derby*, 114; "Oklahoma's Andy Payne Drags Down First Prize," *Daily Oklahoman*, 27 May 1928.

6. Thomas, *Bunion Derby*, 114–115; "Oklahoma's Andy Payne Drags Down First Prize," *Daily Oklahoman*, 27 May 1928.

7. "Gardner and Granville Finish in Money," *Enterprise*, 31 May 1928.

8. "Oklahoma's Andy Payne Drags Down First Prize," *Daily Oklahoman*, 27 May 1928.

9. "1,000 See Bunion Derby End in New York," *Washington Post*, 27 May 1928.

10. "Our Boy Andy Asked to Pay Coolidge Visit," *Daily Oklahoman*, 28 May 1928; "55 Reach Goal Here in Coast Marathon," *New York Times*, 27 May 1928.

11. "55 Reach Goal Here in Coast Marathon," *New York Times*, 27 May 1928.

12. "1,000 See Bunion Derby End in New York," *Washington Post*, 27 May 1928.

13. Westbrook Pegler, "Oklahoma High School Boy Cops $25,000 Plum," *Los Angeles Times*, 27 May 1928.

14. "Bunioneers End Trek in New York," *Cleveland Plain Dealer*, 27 May 1928.

15. Parker Lamoore, "Our Boy Andy Asked to Pay Coolidge Visit," *Daily Oklahoman*, 28 May 1928.

16. Thomas, *Bunion Derby*, 118.

17. Crawford, "History," 40.

18. Pegler, "Oklahoma High School Boy," *Los Angeles Times*, 27 May 1928.

19. "Bunion Derby Winner Here," *Washington Post*, 29 May 1928.

20. "Hearty Reception for Hamilton's Derby Hero," *Hamilton Spectator*, 29 May 1928.

21. "Oklahoma Boy Winner of Transcontinental Race is Born Runner," *Daily Oklahoman*, 27 May 1928.

22. Sears, *Running through the Ages*, 230.

23. Walter McMullen, The Sports Trail, *Hamilton Spectator*, 28 May 1928.

24. "55 Reach Goal Here in Coast Marathon," *Afro-American*, 2 June 1928.

25. "Why Jump on Phil Granville," *Amsterdam News*, 20 June 1928.

26. "Bunioneers End Trek in New York," *Cleveland Plain Dealer*, 27 May 1928.

27. Crozier, "Runners May Sue Pyle for Gate," *New York Sun*, 26 May 1928.

28. Worksheet A, Individual Time Sheet, Gardner.

29. Pegler, "Oklahoma High School Boy," *Los Angeles Times*, 27 May 1928.

30. "Pyle Pacers Set to Drag into the Garden Tonight," *New York Post*, 26 May 1928.

31. Ibid.

Chapter 17

1. Westbrook Pegler, "Pyle's Heart Located on His Right Hip Following Frantic Search by Doctors," *Los Angeles Times*, 29 May 1928; Gordon and Baker,

"Observations," 163; "Pyle's Athletes Show Little Effect of Grind," *Washington Post*, 30 May 1928.

2. "Radio Company Sues Pyle for Derby Set," *Washington Post*, 30 May 1928.
3. "Pay Day in Pyle's Camp Tomorrow," *Los Angeles Times*, 31 May 1928.
4. Paul Lowry, "Rabbit Punches," *Los Angeles Times*, 29 May 1928.
5. "Pyle May or May Not Pay Off Cross Country Runners Tonight," *Amarillo Globe*, 1 Jun. 1928.
6. Berry, *From L.A. to New York*, 81.
7. "Bunion Pain at Climax; Pyle Parts with $48,500," *New York Post*, 1 Jun. 1928; "Payne Is Paid, 26 Hour Race Is Under Way," *Washington Post*, 2 Jun. 1928.
8. "Pyle Pays; Is Poorer by $48,500," *Los Angeles Times*, 2 Jun. 1928.
9. Westbrook Pegler, "C. C. Pyle Admits that for Once He Played Sucker Role," *Los Angeles Times*, 3 Jun. 1928.
10. "Pyle Pays; Is Poorer by $48,500," *Los Angeles Times*, 2 Jun. 1928; "Payne Is Paid," *Washington Post*, 2 Jun. 1928.
11. W. O. McGeeahn, "Down the Line," *Los Angeles Times*, 3 Jun. 1928.
12. Pegler, "C. C. Pyle Admits," *Los Angeles Times*, 3 Jun. 1928; "Phil Granville Again Cuts into Pyle's Prize Money," *Amsterdam News*, 6 Jun. 1928.
13. "Granville Splits First Prize for Race at New York," *Hamilton Spectator*, 4 Jun. 1928.
14. Pegler, "C. C. Pyle Admits," *Los Angeles Times*, 3 Jun. 1928.
15. Henry L. Farrell, "More Running on for Pyle Troupe after Gotham Goal," *Seattle Star*, 17 May 1928; Walter McMullen, The Sports Trail, *Hamilton Spectator*, 28 May 1928.
16. "Bunion Derbyists Reaping Rewards," *Fremont Messenger*, 29 May 1928.
17. "Home Folks Await Andy, Bringing $25,000 Bacon Home," *Miami News Record*, 3 Jun. 1928.
18. Peter Eichenbaum, "Passaic Hero to Get Long Over Due Police Honor," *Herald and News*, 11 May 1998.
19. "Great Runner Hit by Pellet during Third Ward Game," *Passaic Daily News*, 5 Oct. 1931.
20. "Granville Irons Out Trouble with Manager," *Hamilton Spectator*, 7 Jun. 1928.
21. "Ed Gardner Back Home; He's Happy," *Seattle Post Intelligencer*, 26 Jun. 1928.
22. "Eddie Visits Alma Mater," *Pittsburgh Courier*, 7 Jul. 1928.
23. "Ed Gardner Back Home," *Seattle Post Intelligencer*, 26 Jun. 1928.
24. "House Fund Planned for Ed 'Sheik' Gardner," *Enterprise*, 31 May 1928.

Appendix I

1. "Here's How They Finished," *LA Times*, 28 May 1928.
2. Joseph Campbell, *The Hero with a Thousand Faces*, 2nd ed. (Princeton, NJ: Princeton University Press, 1973), 39.

Appendix II

1. "Arizona Hopi in Fourth Place As Lap Closes," *Arizona Republican*, 5 March 1928.

Appendix III

1. Carroll, *Red Grange*, 151; "Grange-Pyle Company Goes Out of Business," *Los Angeles Times*, 6 Jun. 1928.
2. "Run to Coast Will Start Today," *New York Times*, 31 Mar. 1929.
3. Ibid.
4. "Pyle Bunion Caravan Hits Trail Today," *Chicago Tribune*, 31 Mar. 1929.
5. Westbrook Pegler, "Laydees and Gentulmen! Mr. Pyle's Big Derby Is On," *Chicago Tribune*, 1 Apr. 1929.
6. Charles Kastner, "Courage and Endurance: John Salo and Peter Gavuzzi's Epic Duel Across 1929 America." *Marathon and Beyond Magazine* (Jul./Aug. 2002): 80.
7. Westbrook Pegler, "Pyle Bunion Caravan Hits Trail Today," *Chicago Tribune*, 31 Mar. 1929.
8. Arthur G. McMahon, "Noted Runner-Policeman Felled while Pushing the Crowd from Ball Ground," *Passaic Daily News*, 5 Oct. 1931.
9. "Gardner and Granville, Both Confident of $25,000 Plum," *Afro-American* 13 Apr. 1929.
10. Edward J. Neil, "Gardner Wins Opening Dash," *Los Angeles Times*, 1 Apr. 1929.
11. Arthur J. Daley, "76 Start Long Run; 500,000 Line Course," *New York Times*, 1 Apr. 1929.
12. Westbrook Pegler, "Laydees and Gentulmen! Mr. Pyle's Big Derby Is On," *Chicago Tribune*, 1 Apr. 1929.
13. Edward J. Neil, "Gardner Wins Opening Dash," *Los Angeles Times*, 1 Apr. 1929; Daley, "76 Start Long Run," *New York Times*, 1 Apr. 1929.
14. "Salo Keeps Lead in Cross Country Run," *New York Times*, 7 Apr. 1929.
15. "Cross Country Field is Led by Gardner," *New York Times*, 8 Apr. 1929.
16. "Gavuzzi Cops Lap in Derby," *Los Angeles Times*, 12 Apr. 1929.
17. "Salo First Runner to Reach Richmond from Springfield," *Richmond Palladium*, 16 Apr. 1929.
18. "Gavuzzi Cops Lap in Derby," *Los Angeles Times*, 14 Apr. 1929.
19. "Salo Naps Another Lap," *Los Angeles Times*, 20 Apr. 1929.
20. "Gardner is Third; Leg Gives Trouble," *Afro-American*, 4 May 1929; Bill Gibson, "The Passing Review," *Afro-American*, 11 May 1929; "Ed Gardner Out of Pyle Marathon with Tendon Injury," *Seattle Post Intelligencer*, 5 May 1929.
21. "Salo First," *Los Angeles Times*, 11 May 1929.
22. "Salo Annexes Lead in Derby," *Los Angeles Times*, 19 May 1929; Leon C. Metz, *Roadside History of Texas* (Missoula, MT: Mountain Press Publishing Company, 1994), 426.
23. "Gavuzzi Again Tops Runners," *Los Angeles Times*, 30 May 1929.

24. "Pyle Harriers," *Los Angeles Times*, 2 Jun. 1929; "Simpson Wins Derby Lap," *Los Angeles Times*, 1 Jun. 1929.

25. "Hedemann Sets Derby Record," *Los Angeles Times*, 31 May 1929.

26. "Lead Changes Again in Pyle's Bunion Derby," *Globe and Mail*, 5 Jun. 1929.

27. "Pyle Expects Great Finish," *Los Angeles Times*, 10 Jun. 1929.

28. 1929 Time Sheets, Gavuzzi/Salo.

29. "Pyle's Grind Ends Sunday," *Los Angeles Times*, 9 Jun. 1929.

30. "Salo Gains on Foe in Derby Lap," *Los Angeles Times*, 13 Jun. 1929.

31. Braven Dyer, "Gavuzzi Holds Lead in Derby," *Los Angeles Times*, 14 Jun. 1929.

32. Braven Dyer, "Derby Lap Won by Abramowitz," *Los Angeles Times*, 15 Jun. 1929.

33. Braven Dyer, "Gavuzzi and Salo Battle for First Prize," *Los Angeles Times*, 16 Jun. 1929.

34. "John Salo Wins," *Seattle Post Intelligencer*, 17 Jun. 1929.

35. "Salo Final Spurt," *Chicago Tribune*, 18 Jun. 1929.

36. McMahon, "Noted Runner-Policeman Felled," *Passaic Daily News*, 5 Oct. 1931; Kastner, "Courage and Endurance," 84.

37. Carroll, *Red Grange*, 207; Obituary, "C. C. Pyle, Promoter of Sports Events," *New York Times*, 4 Feb. 1939.

38. Kastner, "Courage and Endurance," 86–87.

39. McMahon, "Noted Runner-Policeman Felled," *Passaic Daily News*, 5 Oct. 1931; Kastner, "Courage and Endurance," 86.

40. McMahon, "Noted Runner-Policeman Felled," *Passaic Daily News*, 5 Oct. 1931.

41. Ibid.

42. "Passaic Pays Tribute to Iron-Hearted Johnny Salo," *Passaic Daily Herald*, 8 Oct. 1931.

43. Peter Eichenbaum, "Passaic Hero to Get Long Over-Due Police Honors," *Herald and News*, 11 May 1998.

44. Crawford, "History," 39; Berry, *From L.A. to New York*, 82.

45. Charles Kastner, "Awakening the Spirit of the Lake Hike," *Northwest Runner Magazine* (March 2001): 28–32.

46. Paul O'Neil, "Thousands Wait All Night to Watch Hike Round Lake," *Seattle Star*, 7 May 1933.

47. "Perfrement Again Winner in Annual Washington Classic," *Seattle Star*, 28 July 1934.

48. Chick Garrett, "Woman Champ in Again; Ed Gardner Repeats for Men," *Seattle Star*, 13 Aug. 1938.

49. Official Personnel Folder, Edward Gardner.

50. Washington, Certified Copy of Death Certificate, Fossie R. Gardner, Num. 3298, June 7, 1960.

51. Washington, Certified Copy of Death Certificate, Edward Gardner, Num. 6454, Aug. 21, 1966.

52. Royal Brougham, "The Morning After," *Seattle Post Intelligencer*, 24 Aug. 1966.

Appendix IV

1. Cumming, *Runners and Walkers*, 38; Rader, *American Sports*, 40.
2. Sears, *Running through the Ages*, 68; Cumming, *Runners and Walkers*, 9, 10.
3. Cumming, *Runners and Walkers*, 48.
4. Krise and Squires, *Fast Tracks*, 9–11.
5. Ibid., 9.
6. Cumming, *Runners and Walkers*, 85; Rader, *American Sports*, 40; Krise and Squires, *Fast Tracks*, 6.
7. Sears, *Running through the Ages*, 140.
8. Krise and Squires, *Fast Tracks*, 16, 17; Noakes, *Lore of Running*, 464.
9. Krise and Squires, *Fast Tracks*, 16, 17.
10. Cumming, *Runners and Walkers*, 128–29; Rader, *American Sports*, 51; Sears, *Running through the Ages*, 70, 71.
11. Cumming, *Runners and Walkers*, 129.
12. Sears, *Running through the Ages*, 221–23.
13. Ibid., 224–25.
14. Cumming, *Runners and Walkers*, 98–99.

PLEASE INSPECT: Your Personalization, Your Financial Institution Name, and Your Account Number.

DM B 21 190712 137325 07 01 of 1

Do not use this notice as an order form!
W-SFGW

JOSEPH F BATTEER
276 OAKDALE AVE.
MILL VALLEY, CA 94941-1316

PLEASE INSPECT: Your Personalization,
Your Financial Institution Name, and
Your Account Number.

Our liability is limited to the replacement
of documents incorrectly printed.

Wells Fargo Bank, N.A.
California
wellsfargo.com

Your Satisfaction Is Important to Us
If you find an error, please call 1-800-TO-WELLS (1-800-869-3557)
immediately. Our liability is limited to the replacement of those
documents printed.

This pkg contains ___4___ book(s). Orders of more than one item
will ship separately and may not arrive at the same time.

⑆⑈2⑈04⑈288⑉2⑆ 5765⑈⑈⑈⑊34⑈8⑈⑉ 00731

Against Forgery and Fraud!

Your checks are negotiable documents printed with high-quality security features that prevent altering or counterfeiting and discourage theft. You can enhance the security surrounding your checks by taking these precautions:

- Examine new check packages carefully for evidence of tampering.
- Store your checks, deposit slips, monthly and quarterly statements and cancelled checks in a secure location.
- Reconcile your checking statement within 30 days of receiving to detect any irregularities
- Never give your checking account number to someone you don't know, especially over the telephone. Be particularly aware of unsolicited calls.
- Contact your financial institution immediately if your discover your checks have been lost or stolen
- To help guard against identity theft, we recommend not printing your Social Security number on checks

Bibliography

Books and Periodicals

Barr, Alwyn. *Black Texans: A History of African Americans in Texas, 1528–1995*. 2nd ed. Norman, OK: Red River Books, 1996.

Berner, Richard C. *Seattle 1900–1920: From Boomtown, to Urban Turbulence, to Restoration*. Seattle, WA: Charles Press, 1991.

Berry, Harry. *From L.A. to New York, from New York to L.A.* Self Published, 1990.

Campbell, Joseph. *The Hero with a Thousand Faces*. 2nd ed. Princeton, NJ: Princeton University Press, 1973.

Carroll, John M. *Red Grange and the Rise of Modern Football*. Chicago: University of Illinois Press, 1999.

Crawford, Bill. "History: The 1928 Bunion Derby." *Oklahoma Today* (May/June 1998): 38–45.

Cumming, John. *Runners and Walkers: A Nineteenth Century Sports Chronicle*. Chicago: Regnery Gateway, 1981.

Department of Commerce. *Historical Statistics of the United States: Colonial Times to the Present*. Washington, DC: U.S. Government Printing Office, 1976.

Derderian, Tom. *Boston Marathon: The First Century of the World's Premier Running Event*. Champaign, IL: Human Kinetics, 1996.

Franklin, Benjamin. *Poor Richard's Almanack*. Philadelphia: A Peter Pauper Press.

Fugate, Francis L., and Roberta B. Fugate. *Roadside History of Oklahoma*. Missoula, MT: Mountain Press Publishing Company, 1991.

Gordon, Burgess, and John C. Baker. "Observations on the Apparent Adaptability
    of the Body to Infections, Unusual Hardships, Changing Environment and
    Prolonged Strenuous Exertion." *The American Journal of the Medical Sciences* (July
    1929).
Greene, Lorenzo J., Gary R. Kremer, and Antonio F. Holland. *Missouri's Black Heritage.*
    Revised Edition. Columbia: University of Missouri Press, 1993.
Haskins, Jim, and N. R. Mitgang. *Mr. Bojangles: The Biography of Bill Robinson.* New
    York: Welcome Rain Publishers, 1988.
Hudson, John C. *Across This Land: A Regional Geography of the United States and
    Canada.* Baltimore: Johns Hopkins University Press, 2002.
Jensen, Jamie. *Road Trip USA: Cross-Country Adventures on America's Two-Lane
    Highways.* 3rd ed. Emeryville, CA: Avalon Travel Publishing, 2002.
Jones, Nard. *Seattle.* New York: Doubleday and Company, Inc., 1972.
Kastner, Charles. "Awakening the Spirit of the Lake Hike." *Northwest Runner Magazine*
    (March 2001): 28–32.
———. "Courage and Endurance: John Salo and Peter Gavuzzi's Epic Duel Across 1929
    America." *Marathon and Beyond Magazine* (July/August 2002): 77–90.
———. "The Sheik of Seattle. Ed Gardner Had a Dream: To Win the 1928 Bunion
    Derby." *Marathon and Beyond Magazine* (July/August 2001): 41–55.
Klingaman, William K. *1929: The Year of the Great Crash.* New York: Harper and Row,
    1990.
Kelly, Susan Croce. *Route 66.* Norman: University of Oklahoma Press, 1990.
Krise, Raymond, and Bill Squires. *Fast Tracks: The History of Distance Running.*
    Brattleboro, VT: Stephen Greene Press, 1982.
Leuchtenburg, William E. *The Perils of Prosperity, 1914–1932.* 2nd ed. Chicago:
    University of Chicago Press, 1993.
Lewis, Barry. *Running the TransAmerica Footrace: Trials and Triumphs of Life on the
    Road.* Mechanicsburg, PA: Stackpole Books, 1994.
Mangum, Richard, and Sherry Mangum. *Route 66 Across Arizona: A Comprehensive
    Two-Way Guide for Touring Route 66, Traveling East or West. One or Multiple-Day
    Tours.* Flagstaff, AZ: Hexagon Press, 2001.
Metz, Leon C. *Roadside History of Texas.* Missoula, MT: Mountain Press Publishing
    Company, 1994.
Miller, Carol Poh, and Robert A. Wheeler. *Cleveland: A Concise History, 1796–1996.* 2nd
    ed. Bloomington: Indiana University Press, 1997.
Noakes, Tim. *Lore of Running.* 4th ed. Champaign, IL: Human Kinetics, 2003.
Osofsky, Gilbert. *Harlem: The Making of a Ghetto: Negro New York, 1890–1930.* 2nd ed.
    New York: Harper Torchbooks, 1971.
Palmer, Barbara. *Oklahoma: Off the Beaten Path.* 3rd ed. Guilford, CT: Globe Pequot
    Press, 2001.
Parrish, Michael E. *Anxious Decades: America in Prosperity and Depression, 1920–1941.*
    New York: W. W. Norton and Company, 1992.

Peterson, Robert W. *Pigskin: The Early Years of Pro Football*. New York: Oxford University Press, 1997.

Pollock, Mabel V. *Our State, Ohio 1823–2003: A Bicentennial History*. Newcomerstown, OH: 1st Books, 2001.

Quinn, Alfred O. *Iron Rails to Alaskan Copper: The Epic Triumph of Erastus Corning Hawkins*. Whiteface, NY: D'Aloquin Publishing Co., 1995.

Rachpwiecki, Rob. *Southwest: Arizona, New Mexico, Utah*. 2nd ed. Oakland, CA: Lonely Planet Publications, 1999.

Rader, Benjamin G. *American Sports: From the Age of Folk Games to the Age of Televised Sports*. 2nd ed. Englewood Cliffs, NJ: Prentice-Hall, 1990.

Riess, Steven A. *Sports in Industrial America, 1850–1920*. Wheeling, IL: Harlan Davidson, Inc., 1995.

Rittenhouse, Jack D. *A Guide Book to Highway 66*. Albuquerque: University of New Mexico Press, a Facsimile of the 1946 Edition, 2000.

Root, Douglas. *Pennsylvania*. New York: Compass American Guides, 2003.

Rossiter, Phyllis. *A Living History of the Ozarks*. Gretna, LA: Pelican Publishing Company, Inc., 2001.

Rudwick, Elliott. *Race Riots at East St. Louis, July 2, 1917*. Chicago: University of Illinois Press, 1964.

Schnedler, Jack. *Chicago*. 3rd ed. Oakland, CA: Compass American Guides, 2001.

Schneider, Jill. *Route 66 Across New Mexico: A Wanderer's Guide*. Albuquerque: University of New Mexico Press, 1991.

Sears, Edward S. *Running through the Ages*. Jefferson, NC: McFarland and Company, Inc., Publishers, 2001.

Starr, Kevin. *Material Dreams: Southern California Through the 1920's*. New York: Oxford University Press, 1990.

Thomas, James H. *The Bunion Derby: Andy Payne and the Transcontinental Footrace*. Oklahoma City: Southwestern Heritage Books, Inc., 1980.

Tulloh, Bruce. *Four Million Steps: Los Angeles to New York—the Famous Runner's Account of His Record-breaking Marathon*. London: Mayflower Books, 1970.

Wallis, Michael. *Route 66: The Mother Road*. New York: St. Martin's Press, 1990.

Watson, Steven. *The Harlem Renaissance: The Hub of African American Culture, 1920–1930*. New York: Pantheon Books, 1995.

Zimmermann, George, and Carol Zimmermann. *Ohio: Off the Beaten Path*. 9th ed. Guilford, CT: Globe Pequot Press, 2000.

Primary Source Material

Government Documents

United States. Department of Commerce. Bureau of the Census. *Fifteenth Census of the United States: 1930 Population Schedule*.

——. *Fourteenth Census of the United States: 1920 Population Schedule*.

———. *Thirteenth Census of the United States: 1910 Population Schedule.*
———. *Twelfth Census of the United States: 1900 Population Schedule.*
———. National Archives and Records Administration. National Personnel Records Center. Military Service Records. Samuel Robinson.
———. Official Personnel Folder. Edward Gardner.
———. Treasury Department. Application for Account Number. Edward Gardner. Dec. 7, 1936.
———. Application for Account Number. Samuel Robinson. March 10, 1937.
Washington. Department of Health. Certified Copy of Death Certificate. Edward Gardner. Num. 6454, Aug. 21, 1966.
———. Certified Copy of Death Certificate. Fossie R. Gardner. Num. 3298, June 7, 1960.
———. Certified Copy of Death Certificate. Minnie Gardner. Num 2216, Nov. 23, 1911.

Letters/E-mail to Author

Eriksen, Kathleen. El Pueblo Historical Museum, Colorado Historical Society. "Re: Black Alabama Steel Workers in Pueblo." Letter. 2 Jan. 2003.
Galbraith, Cathy. The Bosco-Milligan Foundation; Cornerstones of Community: The Building of Portland's African American History. "Re: George and Susan Gardner in Portland." E-mail. 8 Mar. 2002.

Other Primary Sources

Pueblo (Colorado) Library District. *Early Black Residents of Pueblo County in 1900.* 1991.
Official Program: C. C. Pyle's First Annual International-Trans-Continental Foot Race, Los Angeles to New York–1928. 1928.
Official Program: C. C. Pyle's Second Annual International-Trans-Continental Foot Race, New York to Los Angeles–1929. 1929.
Tuskegee Institute. *Annual Catalog Bulletin.* Volume 9, 1914–1915.
———. Volume 10, 1915–1916.
———. Volume 11, 1916–1917.
———. Volume 12, 1917–1918.
Tuskegee University. Office of the Registrar. Transcript. Biography of Student. Edward Gardner.
———. Individual Records of Tuskegee Students. Edward Gardner.
———. Record at Tuskegee. Edward Gardner.
Worksheet A: Individual Time Sheet: Stage Race /Cumulative.
Worksheet B: Individual Sheet Pace per Mile: Stage Race/Cumulative.

Newspapers

Afro-American (Baltimore, Maryland)
Albuquerque Journal (New Mexico)
Amarillo Daily News (Texas)
Amarillo Globe (Texas)

Amsterdam News (African American/New York)
Arizona Gazette (Phoenix, Arizona)
Arizona Republican (Phoenix, Arizona)
Binghamton Press (New York)
Black Dispatch (African American/Oklahoma City)
Bradford Era (Pennsylvania)
California Eagle (African American/Los Angeles)
Carthage Evening Press (Missouri)
Chicago Defender (African American)
Chicago Tribune
Cleveland Plain Dealer
Coconino Sun (Flagstaff, Arizona)
Conway Weekly Record (Missouri)
Custer County Chronicle (Clinton, Oklahoma)
Daily Oklahoman (Oklahoma City)
Daily Silver Belt (Miami, Arizona)
Enterprise (African American/Seattle, Washington)
Erie Daily Times (Pennsylvania)
Erie Dispatch-Herald (Pennsylvania)
Fremont Messenger (Ohio)
Gallup Independent (New Mexico)
Gary American (African American/Indiana)
Globe and Mail (Montreal, Canada)
Goshen Daily Democrat (Indiana)
Hamilton Spectator (Ontario, Canada)
Illinois State Register (Springfield, Illinois)
Indianapolis Recorder (African American/Indiana)
Jamestown Evening Journal (New York)
Jamestown Morning Post (New York)
Joliet Evening Herald News (Illinois)
Joplin Globe (Missouri)
Lebanon Rustic (Missouri)
Liberty Register (New York)
Lincoln Evening Courier (Illinois)
Los Angeles Times
Miami News Record (Oklahoma)
Montreal Gazette (Canada)
New Era (Rolla, Missouri)
New Mexico State Tribune (Albuquerque)
New York Times
New York Post
New York Sun
Oklahoma City Times

Passaic Daily News (New Jersey)
Passaic Daily Herald (New Jersey)
Pittsburgh Courier (African American)
Prescott Evening Courier (Arizona)
Pontiac Daily Leader (Illinois)
Richmond Palladium (Indiana)
Rolla Herald (Missouri)
St. Louis Daily Globe Democrat
St. Louis Post-Dispatch
St. Louis Star
St. Louis Times
San Bernardino Daily Sun (California)
San Francisco Chronicle
San Francisco Examiner
Sayre Headlight (Oklahoma)
Seattle Daily Times (Washington)
Seattle Post Intelligencer (Washington)
Seattle Star (Washington)
South Bend News-Times (Indiana)
South Bend Tribune (Indiana)
Springfield Daily News (Missouri)
Springfield Leader (Missouri)
Sullivan News (Missouri)
Sunday Telegram (Elmira, New York)
Toledo Blade (Ohio)
Tucumcari American (New Mexico)
Virden Recorder (Illinois)
Washington Post

Index